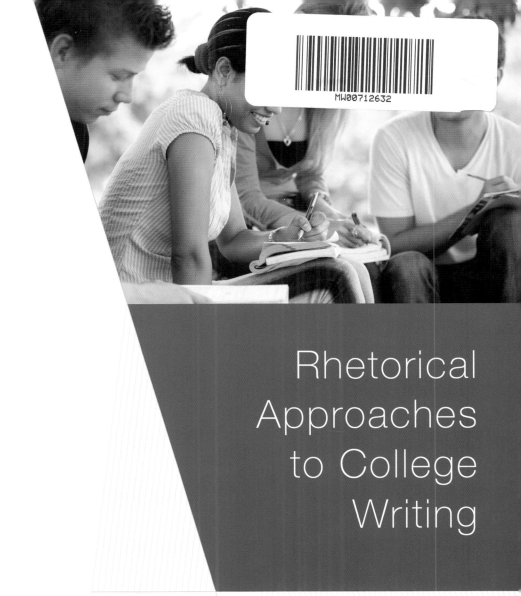

Rhetorical Approaches to College Writing

Meghan H. McGuire

S. Brenta Blevins

Alison M. Johnson

HAYDEN
HM
MᶜNEIL

Hayden-McNeil Sustainability

Hayden-McNeil's standard paper stock uses a minimum of 30% post-consumer waste. We offer higher % options by request, including a 100% recycled stock. Additionally, Hayden-McNeil Custom Digital provides authors with the opportunity to convert print products to a digital format. Hayden-McNeil is part of a larger sustainability initiative through Macmillan Higher Ed. Visit http://sustainability.macmillan.com to learn more.

Printed in the United States of America

10 9 8 7 6 5 4 3 2 1

ISBN 978-0-7380-7732-1

Hayden-McNeil Publishing
14903 Pilot Drive
Plymouth, MI 48170
www.hmpublishing.com

MyersN 7732-1 F15

Table of Contents

Editors

1996–2015

Write Angles: A Journal of Composition

    1996: Bob Haas, Janet Bean, Warren Rochelle

    1997: Diann L. Baecker, Timothy Flood, Jewell Rhodes Mayberry

    1998: Keith Gammons, Beth Howells, Lee Torda

    1999: Judit Szerdahelyi, Katie Ryan, Cynthia Nearman

Writing Matters

    2001: Rebecca Jones, Jackie Grutsch McKinney, Jason Tower

    2003: David Carithers, Heidi Hanrahan, Bethany Perkins

    2004: Rita Jones-Hyde, Chris Porter, Liz Vogel

    2005: Rita Jones-Hyde, Karen C. Summers, Liz Vogel

    2006: Karen C. Summers, Temeka L. Carter, Sara Littlejohn

    2007: Temeka L. Carter, Brandy L. Grabow, Melissa J. Richard

    2008: Melissa J. Richard, Brandy L. Grabow, Laurie Lyda

Technê Rhêtorikê: Techniques of Discourse for Writers and Speakers

    2009: Laurie Lyda, Alan Benson, Will Dodson, Katie Fennell

    2010: Will Dodson, Alan Benson, Jacob Babb

    2011: Jacob Babb, Sally Smits, Courtney Adams Wooten

Rhetorical Approaches to College Writing

    2012: Courtney Adams Wooten, Sally Smits, Lavina Ensor

    2013: Lavina Ensor, Chelsea Skelley, Kathleen T. Leuschen

    2014: Chelsea Skelley, Kathleen T. Leuschen, Meghan H. McGuire

    2015: Meghan H. McGuire, S. Brenta Blevins, Alison M. Johnson

Introduction

Rhetoric, according to Aristotle, is "the art of persuasion." This book focuses on the ways that persuasive language can be used to communicate with others through writing, particularly the writing you will do while at UNCG. Although all writing follows different conventions, the essays in this book are intended to provide you with a critical framework through which to view your own writing and the writing of others. This text is meant to help you acquire a foundational understanding of rhetoric that will help you navigate the various rhetorical situations required in your academic lives, but these principles are also helpful to consider in your professional and personal lives.

The book is divided into four sections, each of which emphasizes a general framework within which to consider rhetoric. *Rhetorical Foundations* seeks to answer two questions: What are we studying, and why does it matter? First, we must understand the fundamental concepts of rhetoric, then the context in which we learn about rhetoric in the academy. *Rhetorical Approaches* examines various considerations we must make each time we communicate, both in informal situations such as with our friends and co-workers and in formal situations such as writing or presenting in the classroom or workplace. *Rhetorical Research* offers strategies and rules of thumb for conducting responsible, effective, and comprehensive research to inform our opinions and support our arguments. Finally, *Rhetorical Situations* examines the rhetorical aspects of academic work. Success in the academy and in life depends in no small part on a mastery of rhetoric, for it is the method we choose for communication in any given situation.

Special Thanks

The Editors of *Rhetorical Approaches to College Writing* would like to acknowledge the continued support of the UNCG English Department, especially Nancy Myers, Scott Romine, Anne Wallace, Elizabeth Chiseri-Strater, Hephzibah Roskelly, Risa Applegarth, Lydia Howard, Alyson Everhart, Anna Tysor, and Sarah Foster. Additionally, we thank our dedicated contributors and the students who inspire us.

1

Rhetorical
Foundations

An Introduction to Rhetoric and the Rhetorical Triangle

Jacob Babb

(handwritten margin note) hen you hare te term Rhetoric," hat do you thinke of?

» A Brief Introduction to Rhetoric

This class may be the first time that you have ever been introduced to rhetoric as an area of academic study. You have probably heard the term rhetoric used in a pejorative sense: "All of his promises were just rhetoric." Such a statement suggests that rhetoric means a collection of empty words as opposed to more decisive action. Statements like this one are often uttered by politicians who benefit from making their opponents look like people who only speak meaningless words. By contrast, the politician accusing his or her opponent of empty talking establishes an implication that he or she takes decisive action rather than wasting time on words. This dichotomy of words versus action implies that the two are somehow isolated from one another, that language and action do not influence one another. Those who study rhetoric, however, believe that language and action are intertwined with one another, that they continuously shape one another. Rhetoric is an ancient field of study, and as such, there are countless definitions for the term. But what most of these definitions have in common is the notion that language has a profound impact on the choices we make in life. In other words, rhetoric induces people to act, even if that action is further engagement with rhetoric.

Let's take a look at three definitions of rhetoric that help provide an understanding of what rhetoric is all about. The ancient Greek philosopher and teacher Aristotle (384 BCE–322 BCE) offers the most famous definition of rhetoric: "Rhetoric is the faculty of discovering in any particular case all of the available means of persuasion." Aristotle's definition places emphasis on the role of language to persuade. For Aristotle, as for many rhetoricians who followed, the study of rhetoric was meant to help people become responsible citizens. Aristotle's view of rhetoric suggests that the best way to reach agreement on contentious issues is to consider multiple arguments and to decide based on the arguments presented what action to take on these issues. In other words, for Aristotle, rhetoric is the basis of democratic engagement in civic life. We must listen to multiple perspectives in order to make decisions about future actions. Aristotle saw clearly the connection between language and action—that the two are inseparable.

Following the Greco-Roman era, the scope of rhetoric slowly widened to include more than just persuasion. For example, the Scottish Enlightenment philosopher George Campbell (1719–1796 CE) defines rhetoric as "that art or talent by which discourse is adapted to its end. The four ends of discourse are to enlighten the understanding, please the imagination, move the passion, and influence the will." The first section of Campbell's definition is not that different from Aristotle's. Both argue that rhetoric is adaptable to different situations. However, Campbell's definition presents the notion that rhetoric is about more than persuasion. Rhetoric is used to educate and to entertain, which can be solely contemplative activities. It is also used to persuade by moving audiences to act. Campbell's definition delineates multiple purposes for rhetoric, broadening its scope beyond persuasion. He makes space for rhetoric to have purposes that are not based in action, but his definition still points to the kind of democratic engagement that Aristotle's definition refers to as well.

"So even though the definitions of rhetoric have broadened in scope since Aristotle's famous words on the matter, persuasion remains one of the central aspects of rhetoric."

The final definition we will look at comes from rhetorician and philosopher Kenneth Burke (1897–1993 CE). Burke specifically points to the interrelation between language and action in his definition: "the basic function of rhetoric [is] the use of words by human agents to form attitudes or to induce actions in other human agents." Burke argues for a *dramatist* theory of rhetoric, which means that he believes that rhetoric springs from a desire to influence human action. Like Aristotle and Campbell, Burke suggests that one of the primary motives of rhetoric is to "induce action," or to persuade. So even though the definitions of rhetoric have broadened in scope since Aristotle's famous words on the matter, persuasion remains one of the central aspects of rhetoric. Each author eventually wrestles with the ethical implications of persuasion. If we can move others to action through language, we must be aware of the danger of such power. To that end, rhetoric is also the study of ethical uses of language.

In this book, you will find that although persuasion remains a key aspect of rhetoric, we define rhetoric more broadly as the study of how human beings communicate with and induce action in one another. Rhetoric depends on the notion that communication does not occur in isolation. We will think of rhetoric in two senses in this course: 1) discursive: rhetoric as the act of inventing texts; and 2) meta-discursive: understanding how texts work. In other words, rhetoric can help you understand how to adapt discourse to certain ends, and it can help you to understand *why* you adapt your discourse in certain ways. It can also help you to read others' texts and to better understand what they meant to accomplish by writing those texts.

» Rhetoric and Writing

Now is the moment to note that the name of this course does not contain the word rhetoric. Instead, the name of this course is College Writing. College writing indicates a specific type of writing, which is sometimes called academic discourse. Most college writing focuses on making claims and providing supporting evidence for those claims. We make claims and work to *persuade* our readers that our claims are valid. That is the kind of writing you will be asked to do in this course.

So what does rhetoric—the study of how human beings communicate with and induce action in one another—have to do with writing? The easy answer is *everything*. But such answers are never satisfactory. Rhetoric and writing are not synonymous, but it is important to think of writing as a rhetorical act. When we write, we ultimately want what we write to be read by someone. In many situations, we want people to respond to our writing. We may write in quiet, isolated spots, but we always write for someone or something. We write letters and emails as direct correspondence with other people. We write essays, term papers, and lab reports in academic settings for others to read, most specifically instructors. Even when we write for ourselves—journals and diaries, for instance—we imagine an audience for those texts. In that sense, writing is always a social act.

It may seem strange at first to think of writing as a social act. Often, writing feels more like a sustained monologue than anything else. Yet that is exactly what this book asks you to do. This book frames writing as a conversation, as a negotiation of your arguments and views with those of others. Academic writing depends on the idea that there is no final word on a subject. No matter how much a writer may know about something or how well she can argue the efficacy of her views, another writer may come along and overthrow her entire argument, or at least take the argument in a slightly different direction. The academic community upholds this dedication to continuously pursuing arguments as a central virtue. Universities exist first and foremost to create new knowledge, and new knowledge only emerges when scholars converse with one another. Since scholars who do similar work do not live next door to one another most of the time, they use writing to communicate ideas and concerns to their colleagues. Scholars invite others into the conversation about their work.

Rhetoricians use a particular tool that reminds us that we are never working in isolation: the rhetorical triangle. The rhetorical triangle illustrates an important concept in rhetoric: communication is not simply the act of a rhetor sending a message to an audience. Communication is far more complex and interactive. The rhetorical triangle illustrates that complexity. We use the rhetorical triangle, which consists of rhetor, text, and audience, as a tool for two key purposes: analyzing texts and composing texts.

Some rhetoricians add an additional element, context, to the rhetorical triangle as an element that surrounds the triangle and influences all acts of communication. The visual below uses a circle around a triangle to illustrate how context envelops the entire communication process.

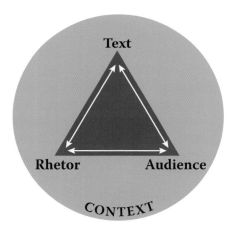

Figure 1. The elements of the rhetorical triangle.

In order to explore how each element of the rhetorical triangle works, we will employ a brief anecdote: in a quiet suburban neighborhood, municipal workers have erected four-way stop signs at an intersection. Drivers from every direction must now stop and yield to each other in an orderly manner. Most people living in the area are happy with the addition of the signs, but one driver decides to write to the city council to oppose the new stop signs.

» Context

Context surrounds the rhetorical triangle. Knowing the context of a rhetorical situation helps us to understand what is happening and why it is happening. Here is some context for our four-way stop intersection anecdote: until recently, there has been no stop sign at the intersection because the neighborhood is quiet enough that there hasn't seemed to be a need for it. But lately, as the area has become more populated there have been a number of accidents. Most of the accidents have been minor, involving only some scratched paint and a few bumps and dents. But recently, one driver speeding through the neighborhood ran into another driver who was crossing the intersection at the same time, resulting in significant damage to the car and an injury that resulted in a hospital visit and several uncomfortable months for one driver inhabiting a full body cast. So the city council, at the urging of citizens living in the neighborhood, decided to post stop signs in hopes that drivers will subsequently be more careful.

For this anecdote, context comes in the form of the story of an accident that resulted in upset citizens asking for legal deterrents to speeding to be added to their neighborhood. By understanding what happened prior to the stop signs being added to the intersection, we can better understand why

> "If we imagine the stop sign as a text…then understanding the context helps to analyze that text."

this rhetorical situation has occurred in the first place. If we imagine the stop sign as a text—a concept we will return to below—then understanding the context helps to analyze that text. We can now read the stop signs as a safety precaution added to the neighborhood because the neighbors asked for the four-way stop. Otherwise, we would not know why the city council chose to put up the stop signs, which would make analyzing the rhetorical situation more difficult.

If we want to think of how understanding context helps to compose a text, then imagine writing a letter to the city council to oppose the new stop signs, arguing that the stop signs are an unwarranted inconvenience. We know why the signs were put up, so we cannot argue that the signs are unnecessary for the safety of drivers and pedestrians who use the street. We can, however, argue that creating a four-way stop is too extreme a response to the problem. Rather than requiring all drivers to stop, stop signs in one direction frees the flow of traffic for one street, stopping fewer drivers passing through the intersection. We could also argue that four-way stops create another problem because they depend on drivers to yield the right-of-way to the first driver to reach the intersection. Since the original problem was that a driver was going through the intersection with little regard for traffic, is a four-way stop going to be a successful deterrent to that driver? The validity of this argument is not especially important for our purposes. Rather, the point here is that understanding context allows us to generate an argument in the first place.

[handwritten margin note: Use a different example that will illustrate this point.]

7

Understanding context is very helpful when you are writing an essay for a class. The instructor provides assignment sheets, learning objectives, and rubrics in order to make the context of your writing as clear as possible. You write knowing that your instructor will read and assess your work, so that forms part of the context of your work. You write knowing that your assignment is meant to help you develop skills and knowledge associated with your course. Your understanding of context helps you to determine many choices you will make when you write an academic essay.

» Rhetor

A rhetor is someone who uses rhetoric in order to communicate with someone else. We use this term because it is broad, covering writers, speakers, and artists. The rhetor is responsible for constructing the text. He or she makes choices when creating the text that affect how the text will be received and interpreted by the audience.

Writers use written language to present their arguments, opinions, and thoughts to readers. They work under the assumption that their writing can be read at different times by different readers. This is one of the chief advantages of writing: we use writing to communicate with people who we cannot talk to face-to-face or people we don't know. Academic discourse depends on writing because it is infeasible for all scholars who have a stake or an interest in a problem to gather in the same place to deliberate. Instead, scholars present their research findings and conclusions in writing so that others can read their work at varying times.

Speakers tend to work under the assumption that their words are more immediate than written words. When a student gives a speech in class, the most important audience for that speech is present in the class at that moment. In most cases, the audience can then respond to the speech, asking for clarification on points or presenting counter arguments that may lead the speaker to refine his or her position on the spot.

It can also be helpful to think of art as rhetoric. The term "artist" covers painters, sculptors, musicians, moviemakers, and others who create texts that we can then classify as art. By thinking of artists as rhetors, we can consider what artists are trying to communicate with their work. Artistic texts are usually thought of only in a framework of aesthetic pleasure. We can enjoy Vincent Van Gogh's *Starry Night* or Pablo Picasso's *Guernica* without worrying about reading these paintings rhetorically. However, artists work to communicate ideas through their texts. Van Gogh's painting challenges notions of representations of reality, which is one of the chief values of his work. Picasso's painting presents a stunning critique of the mass violence associated with modern warfare. Thinking of Picasso as a rhetor enables us as readers to consider the kind of message that Picasso is trying to express in this painting.

Guernica. 1937. Photo Credit: Art Resource, NY. Credit: © 2015. Estate of Pablo Picasso/Artists Rights Society (ARS), New York

When analyzing texts, thinking about the rhetor allows us to consider what the rhetor was trying to accomplish with a text. We can think about what motivated a rhetor to create a text and to make certain choices while doing so. If we think of the city council as the collective rhetor for our four-way stop sign, then we can analyze their choices for putting up four as opposed to two or perhaps think about their choice to go with signs rather than a stoplight. Since the city council represents the legal authority of the city, we can also consider how their authority adds significance to the decision.

When composing texts, you are the rhetor. Being a rhetor means that you are responsible for creating a text that accomplishes the goals you set for your text. If you are the angry driver who writes the letter to city council, your goal is to get some of those restrictive stop signs taken back down. How you approach this affects your ability to persuade your audience. If you write a letter saying that you are really angry about the stop signs because you think they're stupid, the council will probably not take your objections very seriously. Readers tend to react defensively to such statements because they feel like you are attacking them rather than trying to persuade them to change their minds. If you state that you are glad that the council is thinking about neighborhood safety, but you think the four-way stop is the wrong response to the problem, then you will probably find an audience more inclined to listen to you. Carefully considering how you present yourself as a rhetor affects your ethos, and audiences will be more willing to consider your ideas if you represent yourself as someone who is aware of the rhetorical situation. (For more information on ethos, see Christina Romanelli's chapter "Writing with the Rhetorical Appeals.") Being the rhetor means that you have the power to create the text and shape the audience's expectations.

» Text

Although the text is arguably the most important element of the rhetorical triangle because it is the communication act, it is in fact very easy to define. Even when we define text broadly—a stop sign, a letter, a term paper, a song, a painting, and so on—it is easy to determine what the text is. French philosopher Jacques Derrida famously claimed that there is nothing outside the text, suggesting that *everything* is open to interpretation. Derrida's assertion makes all sorts of texts available for interpretation, such as books, articles, paintings, maps, photographs, films, clothing, music, facial expressions, and hand gestures.

When we analyze or compose texts, we have to think about the form a text takes. We make a choice about genre. The essay you are currently reading is not written as a haiku because that poetic form does not lend itself easily to extended discussions. It is an essay because that is the genre a team of editors has deemed appropriate for this textbook. They decided it was the appropriate genre because essays are generally short, expository texts that focus on a single idea. A text presented in a genre that doesn't make sense for the rhetor's purpose can damage our intention to communicate with an audience.

Think about the stop sign. This text is familiar to all of us, one that we hardly even glance at as we comply with its command. The octagonal shape painted red doesn't even require the word "STOP" for us to know what it means. We know how this sign works among other signs, like signs reminding us of the speed limit or forewarning us that we are about to enter a school zone. The genre of street signs works because we have learned through experience reading them to look for the signs and to obey them. Would a sign be as effective if someone went out to the intersection and stapled to a light pole a white piece of paper with "Stop" written on it in magic marker? Probably not.

Now think about the letter opposing the four-way stop. The text is written as a letter from a concerned citizen trying to convince the city council to change their decision. If instead the angry driver had hired an airplane to pull a banner across the sky above City Hall, chances are that the city council wouldn't pay that much attention to the text because it wouldn't be a detailed argument but instead a stunt. Besides, the city council may not even see the banner because the airplane cannot fly over City Hall indefinitely. A letter, however, can be read at any time.

The success of texts largely depends on the choices rhetors make when creating them. In academic essays, for example, a text should present a claim with research and examples to prove the claim. This is why professors often assert the importance of such common elements as introductions and conclusions, thesis statements, quotations, and citations. These formal elements define academic essays. That doesn't mean that academic essays cannot work in different ways within the limits of genre. Some writers like to present epigraphs, which are quotes from other writers added to the beginning of the essay, as a way for the writer to frame a problem. Other writers like to start with brief anecdotes or personal narratives. Some like simply to outline the problem and present the thesis in as straightforward a way as possible. Others like to add visual elements, such as photos or charts, which can be very useful in some circumstances. The rhetor must make choices about the text that best meet the goals the rhetor sets for a text.

» Audience

The last element of the rhetorical triangle is the audience. Without an audience, there is no communication. In fairly simple terms, the audience is the person(s) reading the text. For writers, the audience is the reader. For speakers, the audience is the group of people sitting there listening to the speech. For artists, the audience is made up of those who view or listen to the artwork. When we create texts, we do so with the audience in mind. In her description of the rhetorical triangle, composition scholar Ann Berthoff argues that the line that connects the rhetor and audience is not a solid line because the rhetor cannot always sit with the audience and elaborate on the text. The text must present the argument to the audience on behalf of the rhetor.[1]

What this means is that the audience is not passive. A reader does not simply receive and accept a writer's message. Instead, a reader is able to formulate objections to the text and in many cases, especially in academic discourse, to create a new text as a response to the prior text. The audience inhabits at least as powerful a position as that of the rhetor because they get to decide how to interpret a text and what to do with its arguments.

Returning to our four-way stop one final time, think about who the audience is for these signs. The city council has responded to requests from citizens, so the audience is actually those citizens. The signs essentially inform the citizens that the city council is responsive to their needs and desires. The audience is also, of course, anyone who drives up to the intersection. Any driver who approaches the signs is expected to see the signs and to stop. This example is

---

1. Ann E. Berthoff, *The Making of Meaning* (Portsmouth, NH: Boynton/Cook, 1981).

excellent for illustrating the idea that the rhetor has no real control over how a text will be interpreted by the audience. While the city council can reasonably expect most drivers to do as the signs require, they cannot control all drivers. Some drivers will go right through the intersection regardless of the signs. Others may comply with traffic laws, but they may not be happy about them, leading to letters being sent to City Hall to oppose the new signs. As rhetors, the city council can only do so much. They elected to put the signs in place, but it is then up to the audience to decide what to do with the text: the signs.

Likewise, the angry driver who writes a letter to City Hall cannot control how the council will react to the letter. Possible reactions vary from a form letter thanking the citizen for his or her concerns without any further response, to the city council taking down some of the stop signs in order to create a different flow of traffic as suggested in the letter. Members of the city council could read the letter and be upset because they have already done what concerned citizens asked them to do, but now they are being asked to undo that decision. The point is this: a rhetor can only present a text to an audience. The rhetor must do his or her best to present a text designed to persuade the intended audience, but ultimately the audience will interpret the text.

» The Rhetorical Triangle as Relational

This chapter has looked at the elements of the rhetorical triangle separately from one another as a means of explaining how each works. However, it is useful to remember that the elements always work in relation to one another. We can think of how each individual element works with all the others. The rhetor writes the text attempting to anticipate the needs and possible responses of the audience and considering the context of the situation while composing the text. This is a vital point to remember when using the rhetorical triangle either as a tool for analyzing a text or for composing a text. Every element of the rhetorical triangle affects all of the other elements. The relational aspect of the triangle is what makes it so useful for understanding rhetorical situations. The rhetorical triangle simultaneously reminds us of the complexities of communication while helping us to unravel and better understand those complexities.

Rhetorical Context Is (Almost) Everything

Amy Berrier

When you write a job resume or text a friend, you may not be thinking in the rhetorical terms of "context" and "audience," but your ability to successfully communicate to specific audiences demonstrates your understanding that different contexts require different types of writing strategies. Rhetorical context shapes your audience's expectations. Being successful in a specific context means that you can communicate your message in an effective way to that specific audience's expectations based on the rhetorical situation. The ability to identify the context and adjust your communication strategies accordingly will facilitate your success in academic and professional writing, not to mention other types of composition. The tricky part is slowing down and being consciously mindful of how each new context alters your audience's expectations and how you communicate. That is, if you are speaking to an audience of parents about video game violence at a school sponsored event versus a private meeting at home, you will slightly tweak the audience's (parents) expectations about what you might say as a rhetor and how to approach this audience based on the circumstance. To help us understand how context and audience shape each other, we will first look at a few familiar examples and then move on to an example that closely models an assignment you might have in your College Writing class.

In writing, context influences all other aspects. The chapter "An Introduction to Rhetoric and the Rhetorical Triangle" in this book looks at how the rhetorical triangle (a device used to understand the complexity of communicating), can assist us in positioning our thoughts about *what* we want to communicate and *how* we might best achieve our goal. In the diagram of the rhetorical triangle, we note that context surrounds all the other elements of the communication process. This does not mean that understanding context is more important than understanding the rest of the triangle, but it does mean that context directly influences all other elements. Context determines genre, tone, choice of vocabulary, use and amount of evidence, and even use or lack of punctuation.

The rhetorical context of a situation includes the concepts of timing and stance. For context, consider the circumstances under which you are perceiving an idea. Depending on your circumstances, a police officer could be protecting you or harming you (if you are unjustly arrested). Everything occurs in relationship to surrounding circumstances. When considering stance, ask yourself, "What is my motivation for communicating?" If you are researching automobiles, are you thinking from the point of view of an environmentalist wanting to protect the earth or the CEO of a car company wanting to make more profit? The stance that people come to certain situations with shapes how they interpret different texts and make meaning. Context also relies on timing. When are you perceiving something? Are you understanding ocean waves on a sunny day or as a hurricane approaches? When we think about how audience and context shape one another, it is useful to consider not only context, but subsets of context: timing and stance.

It can be confusing to separate these various elements from each other. To help our understanding, let's look at some examples of how audience affects context and vice versa. Audience shapes context in various ways, but let's look at a familiar example in which you need to communicate to your audience that you will have to miss a prior engagement: you committed to attending the event, but you are unable to go. If you needed to communicate to a friend that you were going to miss their party, you might text something that looks like this: "missing party—sorry—have fun!" This brief, informal tone is perfectly appropriate communication to a friend. However, if you need to email a professor that you are going to miss class you would use the formal aspects of emailing such as a salutation, a body with complete sentences, a closing, and a signature. The email might look something more like this:

> *Dear Professor Jones,*
>
> *I will not be in class this Wednesday because I have the flu. I am continuing to follow the syllabus in regards to class reading and assignments and I am also happy to make-up any assignments that I might miss. I hope to be feeling better by Friday's class, if not, I will email you my paper assignment that is due that day.*
>
> *Sincerely,*
>
> *Elizabeth Smith*

While this email might seem overly formal to you, it is appropriate for the audience because you are presenting yourself as sincere and professional. If you emailed a professor (or employer) in the same way you might email a friend, you would be misreading the expectations of your audience, which can cause a negative representation of your ethos. A professor might assume that you are careless and sloppy in your thinking and writing, thus not a serious and committed student. Being aware of how your audience shapes the context of your writing increases your control in the rhetorical situation in which you are writing.

Let's move on to another example. Your professor asks you to turn in an informal writing assignment entitled "What is College Writing?" Since for this assignment your professor is requesting an informal piece of writing, you can probably quickly type out your personal thoughts and not have to worry about using evidence or be as vigilant about correctness in punctuation and vocabulary. However, if a professor assigns a formal writing assignment, you will need to think more carefully about your composition process. Because it's a formal assignment, you know that your professor's expectations are likely more specific with regard to the correctness of form, tone, vocabulary, use of evidence, citation, and punctuation. For both these assignments your audience is the same, but because of the context (formal or informal) your writing will change to meet the professor's expectations.

In your College Writing class your professor tells you to read Martin Luther King, Jr.'s "Letter from the Birmingham Jail" and analyze the audience and context of the piece. To begin this assignment you might research the historical context of Dr. King's letter; you discover that he wrote the letter while in jail for his part in the Birmingham Campaign, a non-violent civil rights protest whose aim was to challenge the segregation system of Birmingham, Alabama. In an even broader historical context, you discover that in 1963 Birmingham's segregation laws were not unique, they were a part of the widespread laws regarding segregation, commonly referred to as "Jim Crow" laws. The "Jim Crow" laws, implemented in numerous states, required separate schools, hospitals, and even separate dining areas for white and black citizens. Thus, you discover that Dr. King's protest, while specifically taking place in Birmingham, was part of a wider movement for civil rights for black Americans. You now understand the broader historical context in which Dr. King wrote his letter, but what about the specific context? The letter was in direct response to an open publication written by white ministers criticizing Dr. King's actions. These ministers denounced Dr. King's non-violent protests and stated that concerns about racial segregation should be addressed in the court system, not in the streets.

As such, Dr. King chose to construct a formal letter directed to the specific audience who criticized his methods of protest. Also, Dr. King thought about his audience and what their expectations would be; because his audience (white ministers) was antagonistic to his methods, he chose to use many Biblical references to support his assertion that his actions were just. For example, Dr. King created a parallel between his role in the Civil Rights movement and the Biblical story of the Apostle Paul who conveyed the gospels of Jesus Christ to a wide audience. Since Dr. King's specific audience were ministers, he strengthened his message by using their shared Christian commonality to give his message a weightier significance. Also, since his audience was concerned about the possibility of violence, Dr. King appeased his audience's fears directly by using formal and calm language to explain his actions. In these ways Dr. King utilized the full power of rhetoric to discern how his audience shaped the context in which he was writing.

In this chapter we have looked at several examples of how context and audience shape each other. In order to succeed in college and professional writing, you need to remain conscious of your rhetorical choices. Paying special attention to rhetorical context helps us slow down and be more mindful of the choices that we make.

Writing with the Rhetorical Appeals

Christina Romanelli

Even a basic knowledge of rhetoric can be very empowering. Consider a situation in which most students feel disenfranchised, such as when a student receives a grade that is lower than he or she thinks is deserved. Recasting this as the beginning of a new rhetorical situation rather than viewing the grade as the end of the writing process can be very productive. Receiving the grade then becomes the motivation for a new text and a new rhetorical triangle, in which the student is the rhetor, the instructor is the audience, and the text is the email the student sends to express her concern about the grade. (For more information on the rhetorical triangle, please see Jacob Babb's chapter "An Introduction to Rhetoric and the Rhetorical Triangle.") The student (let's call her Alice) uses her knowledge of the rhetorical appeals to compose an effective email.

The rhetorical appeals are the methods by which a rhetor persuades his or her audience as discussed by Aristotle, a Classical philosopher and rhetorician, in his treatise *Rhetoric*. Aristotle outlined three appeals: *ethos*, the appeal of the credibility of the rhetor; *pathos*, the appeal to the emotions of the audience; and *logos*, the appeal of the logic of the message. Like all aspects of rhetoric, the appeals exist and influence our communication whether or not we understand or even acknowledge them; however, a conscious use of the appeals can help us produce better writing in which our credibility, the audience's emotional reactions, and the sound logic of our ideas work together to accomplish our purpose.

» Ethos

Ethos, or the "ethical appeal," is the way in which the writer builds his credibility with the audience. Quintilian, another famous Classical rhetorician, defined the rhetor as "a good man speaking well," which makes it seem that writing requires a certain moral quality and that a "true" rhetor would not need to argue for his own goodness. Actually, all rhetors must cultivate their credibility with the audience in a variety of ways. Credibility can be garnered through credentials, character, personality, intelligence, morals, and attitude. For most course assignments, students craft their ethos by completing the requirements of the assignment, dealing with source material fairly, and fashioning sound arguments. In Alice's case, she has a rather automatic ethos in the classroom because she has a very clear role as a student to fulfill that has a long history in our society.

At first, Alice might be confused by how she can develop ethos in her message to her instructor. She knows that ethos is the cultivation and communication of her credibility as a rhetor, so she can safely assume that everything her professor knows about her is already affecting her ethos. Some of this information is working to her advantage. For example, Alice always participates in class, responding to questions and completing classwork neatly and on time. Other aspects of her ethos are not so positive: Alice has a hard time getting up in the morning and has been late for class twice. Once she overslept and missed her class altogether. There is very little that Alice can do to change what has already occurred between her and her professor; however, she can make things better or worse based on how she communicates to the instructor in regard to this issue. She has many opportunities to increase her credibility as a student who can write well.

The very first thing she can do to increase her credibility is to be honest and forthright about the situation. The last thing Alice wants is to upset her instructor because that would decrease the likelihood of her successful communication, so she wants to present herself as humble and appreciative of her instructor's efforts. She may want to start by thanking her professor for the helpful comments on her project, giving specific examples to show that she is the kind of student who cares enough to read the comments thoroughly. She will want to ask her question in a non-confrontational way, requesting more information about her grade rather than insisting that it is wrong, thus showing that she is genuinely interested in her own improvement rather than simply wanting a different letter assigned to her efforts. If Alice's instructor believes she is only concerned with the letter grade rather than the learning, she may see Alice as someone who misunderstands the purpose of education.

Rereading the email she has written to be sure she has spelled everything correctly and that she has punctuated every sentence will also cultivate a sense of responsibility. Finally, Alice will need to pay attention to formatting guidelines and conventions. In an email, this requires a greeting, the more formal the better in the case of written communication because anything less than formal could be perceived as disrespectful or even confrontational. She should probably start with "Dear Professor Jones," for this greeting indicates that Alice is aware of her professor's title and finds conventions like salutations to be polite and worthy of her attention. She should make a visible separation between the body of the email and the greeting by leaving a blank line or two. She should also close her email with "Sincerely," and she should write her full name and the course and section number. All of these things will help Alice create credibility in her email to her instructor because they show that she is aware of the conventions of professional discourse and wants to be seen as someone who is participating in the professional relationships of academia.

We may consider emails to be a chatty and informal method of communication because they are so quick, and, indeed, they can be used that way with individuals with whom you would speak that way normally. It is important to remember that emails are still written forms of communication, however, and that while they are appropriate for a formal request like a grade change, the style of writing in the email must match the content rather than the "quick" and "easy" associations with the medium. Not using the appropriate formatting, diction, and tone in the email could do irreparable damage to Alice's ethos. If she does not use a greeting, types in all caps, uses slang, or fails to edit, Alice's instructor may believe that she is being rude, confrontational, or unprofessional.

» Pathos

Pathos, or the "emotional appeal," is the least valorized of the rhetorical appeals. In fact, pathos is often demonized as manipulative or unfair in an argument; however, a well-wrought appeal to the audience's emotion is often more effective than a dozen logical reasons for believing something. Our culture places a great deal of emphasis on "following your heart," so it is important to take pathos into account as part of any good argument because no audience is persuaded by logic alone. The elements that make up pathos are often stylistic. How we write our opinions is as important to emotional response as what the opinions are. Most individuals will cringe and recoil when being yelled at, even if what is being yelled is praise. In the same way, style conveys tone and can either ensnare or repulse the audience. Additionally, which examples a writer chooses to prove his or her point often determine the emotional response the writing will receive. Description, figurative language, and diction all help to evoke emotion in the reader, but so do the overall tone and voice of the writing.

Despite the fact that pathos is an appeal to emotion, successfully utilizing the appeal in any situation requires significant critical thought. If an appeal to emotion becomes obvious, it can look like pandering, or worse, manipulation.

19

Thus, it is of the utmost importance that Alice carefully considers how she wants her professor to feel when she reads her email. Pity is perhaps the most commonly appealed to emotion when working with professors, but partially because instructors read so many excuses from students, only the most believable and extreme tend to have the desired effect. It is important for Alice to be honest about what has caused her problems with her assignment, but it is equally important to avoid any attempt to abdicate responsibility for her grade. Thus, if Alice's younger brother was hospitalized, requiring two consecutive weekend trips home to Virginia, it is acceptable to mention it in the email; however, it is equally important for Alice to mention that she understands that she should have written to her professor when the accident occurred to discuss her options rather than waiting until the project was already graded. This will appeal to both the emotion of the instructor and Alice's ethos as a new student learning her way around the college environment.

Since pathos is cultivated through specific choices of words and examples, it is important to keep the style appropriate to the genre. Alice should avoid using overly charged language or absolutes that could irritate her reader. A simple and direct style will be much more effective than anything overly stylistic in this rhetorical situation. Overall, it will be more effective for Alice to appeal to the common values that she and her professor share. These may include excitement about the subject matter under examination, pride in intellectual achievements earned, or dedication to correctness and detail. Alice can appeal to these emotions by referencing specific pieces of knowledge she has gained in the class and perhaps mentioning how her project helped her understand something differently. Again, pathos and ethos are closely connected here. Alice's professor may feel a sense of pride reading about what Alice has learned in her class, but she will also take Alice more seriously as a student if she believes Alice is interested in seeing how her assignments are relevant to real world situations.

Pathos, even when carefully considered, may have an undesired effect on an audience. One of the constraints on any successful communication is that the writer cannot know exactly how the audience is feeling at any given moment in time. This is perhaps even more true of email since it can be accessed at any time from any place. If Alice's instructor has received several requests for grade changes, she may be less disposed to receive Alice's well, especially if many students are appealing to her sense of pity or compassion at one time. Pathos may not always work in the way we intend, and for this reason, when it is possible, it is a good idea to have a member of your intended audience read through your work before you submit it.

» Logos

Aristotle considered *logos* the most important of the appeals, and it is easy to see why he thought so. Logos is the appeal to reason, also known as "the rational appeal." The best appeal to logos in any communication is a solid argument with convincing reasons and lucid analysis. In an essay, your logos consists of your thesis, reasons, evidence, examples, and analysis. It also consists of your organization of ideas and the transitions you put between those ideas. Though you may hear people describe logos in terms of systems of logic, using terms like claim, warrant, backing, etc., take comfort in the idea that these concepts are not drastically different from the thesis, reasons, evidence, and analysis with which you have already become familiar in your previous English classes.

Above all else, what is most likely to convince Alice's instructor to either change her grade or offer her an opportunity to increase her grade is the appeal to reason: logos. Just as with an essay, the best appeal to logos is a clear argument supported by logical reasons and evidence. Alice will be well served to spend some time reviewing the criteria of the assignment, the rubric (if she has one), and her performance so that she can explain clearly and succinctly why she believes she deserves a higher grade or another opportunity to prove she can meet the requirements.

One effective appeal to logos might consist of evaluating her own work against a standard that she feels her instructor has set either in class or with a rubric. For example, if Alice received a 'D' on her project and the rubric states that a 'D' project "attempts but fails to meet the requirements of Course Goal #1," Alice should be looking for concrete evidence that her project meets the requirements set out in that particular course goal. If Alice can show that she met the course goal *and* she carefully cultivates her ethos and pathos, she may have an opportunity to show this to her instructor. Another effective appeal to logos might involve detailing the causes of her low grade in the hopes that her instructor will allow her to complete the work again. While this is directly tied up with pathos and may depend on what emotion she is able to evoke from her reader, this is a much more effective logical appeal than explaining the effects of her low grade and expecting her instructor to feel those are the instructor's responsibility because this may make her instructor feel defensive.

Logos, though often considered the most important of the appeals because we want to believe that reason is the best of human qualities, cannot be used in isolation from either ethos or pathos because all of them occur simultaneously whether they are used effectively or not, and focusing on logos alone will fail to be convincing almost all of the time. An arguable thesis and logical reasons are important, but they are not more important than Alice's ability to present herself as a conscientious student who wants to learn as much as she can from her sympathetic and supportive instructor. Consider these two drafts of Alice's email to see which you think is more effective:

> *Professor Jones,*
>
> *I do not deserve the 'D' you gave me on my project. According to the rubric, a 'D' is awarded to projects that "fail to meet the requirements of Course Goal #1." I met the requirements of that course goal when I explained that the organization used behavior theory as the basis for their rehabilitation techniques. If I get a 'D' on this assignment, I cannot get higher than a 'C' in the course and that will mess up my GPA. I might lose my scholarship.*
>
> *Please change my grade.*
>
> *Sincerely,*
>
> *Alice Smith*
>
> *PSYC 150*

In this email, Alice uses logos when she explains why her project met the requirements and the effects of having received a D, but she does not carefully cultivate her ethos as a student. She presents herself as someone who refuses to take responsibility for her actions, is overly concerned with grades, and sees her instructor as an adversary. She shows her inexperience in communicating professionally by demanding a grade change rather than the opportunity to learn more from her instructor. She mentions that she is a scholarship recipient, but that is unlikely to sway her instructor given the overall tone of the piece. The tone contributes to the pathos, which seems overly aggressive and designed to evoke fear or guilt. An appeal to fear or guilt is very likely to backfire and evoke hostility and resentment from her instructor. In actuality, it is likely that Alice didn't intentionally craft her email this way, and this is exactly why it is important to be aware of how the appeals affect writing and to use them consciously. If Alice does so, she might end up with an email more like this one:

> *Dear Professor Jones,*
>
> *Thank you for the comments on my Local Organization project. I am very interested in finding out more about the possibilities for other theories in helping individuals with autism, and I plan to research this further for my final paper. I'm sure I will find the books you suggested useful.*

> I do have a concern about my grade on the project. I understand that I did not explain the connection between the research and the methods of the organization explicitly enough, but I do think that I met the requirement on the rubric that I "state the theoretical underpinnings of the organization's practice" in my paper. On the third page of my project, I wrote, "Horses Helping with Autism uses a behaviorist approach in their classes for individuals with autism." I'm confused about how this does not meet the requirements for at least a 'C.' Would you please explain this to me at your convenience? If there is any opportunity for me to provide further evidence that I have mastered this course goal, I would be happy to complete additional work.
>
> I understand that you are very busy, and I do not wish to burden you with my questions, but it's very important to me to keep up my grades and gain as much as I can from this psychology course since it is closely related to my education major.
>
> I appreciate your time.
>
> Sincerely,
>
> Alice Smith
>
> PSYC 150

Which email is more likely to receive a courteous reply from Alice's instructor? In the second email, Alice paid close attention to all three appeals, and this resulted in a much more polite and effective communication of her concerns. She presents herself as a student who cares about learning more than grades, and she envisions her instructor as someone who is willing to work with her, evoking a cooperative spirit. Alice provides examples and reasons for why she and her instructor should continue to communicate about this grade and reach some understanding together. We can see that the appeals work best in concert with each other, and that no matter how logical our argument is, it is unlikely to be received favorably without attention to our ethos and the emotions we want our audience to feel as they read. This is equally true of any essay written for College Writing or for other courses.

The most significant difference between an email to your instructor and an essay you compose is the rhetorical situation. The rhetorical triangle in Alice's case is clear and simple, but when you compose an essay for your class, you may be required to invent some or all the aspects of the rhetorical triangle. You will need to imagine an audience separate from your instructor or at least wider than your instructor in order to tailor your appeals to them. You will still have some automatic ethos as a student, but you will augment your appeal to authority by correctly referencing and citing the arguments of others who have been published. Your appeals to pathos will be muted and understated as is appropriate for an academic subject and a scholarly audience, but you will still craft your style and your tone carefully. You will need to craft a thesis and reasons for that thesis that are appropriate to the amount of research you can do and the conversation which you are entering.

Planning and executing effective persuasive communication is difficult and requires practice, but the process begins with a consideration of your credibility as a writer, the emotions you want to evoke in your audience, and the logic of the message you want to convey. The writer who carefully considers the rhetorical triangle and how to use the appeals in relation to that triangle will have an easier time composing an initial draft and will get closer to the artful interweaving of the appeals than a writer who opts not to consider the situation or the questions brought forward by the appeals.

Reading for the Rhetorical Appeals

Lauren Shook

» Ethos

Ethos (ethical appeal) establishes the base of any text, so a rhetorical analysis should start with analyzing ethos. Essentially, you are looking for two components: 1) the rhetorical triangle—rhetor, audience, and text—and 2) the context of the text and how it establishes ethical standards and/or readers' expectations. These two components are intricately linked together. Ethos is rooted in the situation of the text (context) and in readers' ethical standards as based upon past experiences. Thus, a writer must define the context in order to gauge his or her readers' expectations and reception of his or her message. Let's use Sojourner Truth's speech "Ain't I a Woman?" to see how to identify and analyze ethos. Truth delivered "Ain't I a Woman?" at a women's rights convention in Akron, Ohio, in 1851 (the context). In her speech, she demands rights for African-American women.

First, when identifying the rhetorical triangle and its components, imagine that the message resides between the writer and audience and that the writer's goal is to communicate effectively his or her message to the reader. Once you identify the message of a text, ask yourself, "How is the writer relaying the message to the reader?" To answer that question, you need to pinpoint the writer—the person sending the message, and his or her purpose or motivations for doing so—and the intended audience—the person or group of people receiving the writer's message and their expectations, beliefs, etc. Since a writer always considers his or her audience, let's begin with looking closely at what comprises an audience. Various factors influence an audience's reception of the writer's message, such as gender, ethnicity, class, education, etc. While these factors can be separated, writers usually combine them. Thus, a writer may address only women but he or she probably also considers the age range or class of women. Sometimes writers make their intended audiences easily identifiable, but oftentimes we must determine the audience from the textual clues provided by the writer, such as the writer's subject matter and use of language. We can also identify audience by considering the text's source—the place where the text originates (magazine, newspaper, academic journal, website blog). For instance, noting whether a magazine column on relationship advice comes from a men's or women's magazine will help determine the intended audience.

> "Once you identify the message of a text, ask yourself, 'How is the writer relaying the message to the reader?'"

Let's see how Truth treats the concept of audience in "Ain't I a Woman?" In her speech, she immediately addresses her audience, moving from a general audience to a more specific one. "Well, children," she begins, "…I think that 'twixt the negroes of the South and the women at the North, all talking about rights, the white men will be in a fix pretty soon." That she calls her audience "children" indicates that she considers herself a mother or a teacher who has a lesson for her audience, children who have something to learn. Also, Truth names three groups of people with an eye to racial and geographical difference—African-American Southerners, Northern women who are presumably white, and white males from the South and the North. Here, Truth identifies the audiences that her argument for African-American women's rights will affect, and her inclusion of such a wide array of people demonstrates that she considers her message invaluable for all to hear, which creates an atmosphere of importance. Truth also directly addresses the people present at the convention: "That man over there says that women need to be helped into carriages," and "Then that little man in black there, he says women can't have as much as men, 'cause Christ wasn't a woman!" While we may not know at first exactly who she means by "that little man in black," we can deduce that he is a preacher because of her reference to his opinions about Christ and women.

Let's suppose momentarily that Truth does not directly name her audience. We could just as easily determine the audience from the context of the speech (1851—about ten years prior to the Civil War and in the midst of a women's movement promoting rights for women, particularly suffrage). We know that she delivers her speech at a women's convention; thereby, we know that the audience will mostly consist of women. Furthermore, we should anticipate that people who are against women's and African-Americans' rights will also be a part of the audience. In addition to Truth's identification of particular audiences, she also speaks to her audience's expectations about her as not only a woman but also as an African-American. Her use of informal language and her admittance that she does not know what intellect is—"Then they talk about this thing in the head; what's this they call it? [Intellect, someone whispers]"—plays to the contemporary conception in the 1800s of African-Americans and women as mental inferiors, a thought forwarded by some white men (and some white women as well). Yet while she meets these expectations of her audience, she also shatters the stereotypes simply by delivering such a pithy, rational speech.

The other crucial component of analyzing ethos is identifying the writer of the text and examining his or her credibility. Ask yourself, "Why do I trust the writer as the authority figure on the subject?" Perhaps the writer is well-known, or the writer's credentials or a short biography accompanies the text. If not, we must consult the text itself. Within the text, we should look closely at the writer's command of language, his or her appeal to higher authorities, and supporting evidence. These elements of a text will highlight the writer's credibility, proving that he or she knows enough about the subject in order to relay trustworthy information to the reader. Why do we accept Truth's authority as an advocate for African-American women's rights? First, we know she is credible because she is an African-American woman who was once a slave, as she tells us: "I have borne thirteen children, and seen them most all sold off to slavery, and when I cried out with my mother's grief, none but Jesus heard me! And ain't I a woman?" In addition to the emotional aspect (pathos) of this statement, she makes an ethical appeal to mothers and subtly identifies three more audiences—mothers, Christians, and Christian mothers—via her reference to "mother's grief" and to Christ. Furthermore, this statement most effectively proves her authority on the subject because she has firsthand experience as a suffering African-American woman, and we tend to value firsthand experience.

Of the three rhetorical appeals, ethos is relatively easy to detect and analyze in a text. You must always be aware of the rhetorical triangle—rhetor, text, and audience—and how these three components interact with each other. Finally, always consider the context of the piece of writing. The rhetorical triangle and its context are two crucial components of ethos, so keeping them in mind will ensure that you are thinking correctly about ethos.

» Pathos

Pathos (emotional appeal) refers to the emotions or moods that the writer hopes to incite from his or her audience. Because writers employ pathos as a way to get an emotional response from readers, pathos is easily linked to ethos; remember that part of a writer's ethos resides in his or her successful prediction of the audience's reaction to his or her message.

You may be wondering how one can identify emotion in a text. First, as with any analysis of a text, you must be able to name the message and audience. Imagine for a moment an army recruiter who is attempting to convince a group of male, high-school seniors (audience) to enlist in the army (message). He might use various references to well-known, respected patriotic men who have answered their call of duty to serve their country. Maybe he will also employ strong word choices such as "heroic," "bold," or "daring." Though it may not be obvious at first, a close analysis of the army recruiter's wording reveals that he purposefully uses pathos in order to spark an overwhelming sense of national pride in his male audience, prompting them to join the military. From this example, you should see that we identify a writer's pathos through his or her diction (one's wording according to the context).

As with the above example, employing pathos involves a conscious selection of specific word choices and emotionally charged language. Because words not only have denotations (the actual definition of a word) but also connotations (the negative or positive associations that accompany words), a crafty wordsmith knows which specific words will best elicit responses from readers. Another element of pathos is tone, the way a writer sounds on paper, which can be found by noting the connotations and emotionally charged language that the writer uses. Consider the difference between these two sentences:

1. You should vote because voting is a right given to all Americans.

2. You absolutely must vote; otherwise, you are unappreciative of your rights as an American citizen and are being unpatriotic.

In addition to the use of ethos that calls attention to American ethics regarding voting, these two sentences greatly depend on pathos—specific word choices, connotations, and emotionally charged language, all of which result in differing tones. The first encourages Americans to vote by implying that by not voting, one disregards his or her rights as an American citizen. The second sentence, however, forcefully accuses the reader of being "unappreciative" if he or she does not vote and goes so far as to label the reader "unpatriotic." The first sentence achieves its encouraging tone through the word "should," whereas the second sentence contains the word "must." Although the words are synonyms, the connotations of the words suggest a vast difference in how we respond to each word. We associate "should" with morals; one might vote because it is the proper thing to do. "Must," however, implies that one needs to vote because American citizenship requires and even demands it. The difference between "should" and "must" is an example of how specific word choices affect tone.

While specific word choices and emotionally charged language are perhaps the easiest ways to identify pathos in a text, another important tool of pathos is the use of references or allusions. When a writer references a particular person, place, or event, the purpose is to connect his or her audience's emotional reaction to that reference. To return to our previous example, if a writer wants to persuade an audience of college-aged women (18–22) to vote, she might reference the Suffragist movement and individual women who dedicated their lives to achieving suffrage for women. Similarly, if the writer is addressing an audience of young African-Americans for the same reason, he or she might allude to figures like Sojourner Truth, who, as we've seen, advocates African-American women's equality and thus takes a step in realizing women's vital role in voting. Martin Luther King, Jr., the influential Civil Rights leader, would also be an excellent historical person to use as an example of someone who worked to achieve African-Americans' right to vote. In either case, the writer alludes to either the Suffragist movement or the Civil Rights movement (or both) in order to motivate people to vote, illustrating that others have secured the freedom for them to do so while enduring hardship and persecution in the process.

To locate specific moments where one employs pathos, let's analyze Truth's "Ain't I a Woman?" to recognize Truth's manipulation of language and references and/or allusions to persuade her audience of the necessity of African-American women's rights. First, as Truth opens her speech, she calls attention to the "racket" or the noise surrounding the debate for women's and African-American men's rights that makes "something out of kilter." The use of "racket" and "kilter" connote a chaotic world that bars some humans their rights, which she intends to correct. In addition to specific word choices, Truth uses emotionally charged language to affect her audience when she laments, "I have borne thirteen children, and seen them most all sold to slavery, and when I cried out with my mother's grief, none but Jesus heard me! And ain't I a woman?" Truth wants her audience, especially her female audience, to recognize that she is not only a woman but a mother who has experienced heartache (a moment of building her ethos as well). The use of "cried" and "grief" emphasize the tone of heartache. Finally, Truth also makes allusions easily recognizable to her audience when she counters the erroneous claim that "women can't have as much rights as men, 'cause Christ wasn't a woman!" She asserts that Christ came "From God and a woman!" Thus, not only does she refer directly to Christ, a form of authority for the preachers in her audience, but Truth alludes to Christ's mother, Mary. She reminds preachers that if one is to believe the Bible, then Christ does indeed come only "from God and a woman," Mary. Moreover, Truth's choice to refer to Mary emphasizes her previous remark about a "mother's grief" because Mary, too, experiences a "mother's grief" when she watches Christ's crucifixion. We can see that Truth's meticulous word choice, emotional language, and allusions all reinforce the idea that she is a woman and should receive equal rights.

Truth's speech is full of pathos, so it becomes easy to analyze for pathos. Other texts may not contain such an easily identifiable use of pathos. If this is the case, just remember to look closely at word choices and emotionally charged language (and/or tone) and to keep an eye open for references and allusions.

» Logos

Logos (rational appeal) refers to the logical underpinning of an argument. By identifying an argument's logos, we can determine the argument's rationale and the validity of the argument. Just as with ethos and pathos, in order to identify logos in a text, you need to locate the message. Yet unlike ethos and pathos, logos involves checking if the argument's supporting claims and evidence affirm the thesis. For instance, if you read a movie review of the newest summer blockbuster in which the reviewer asserts that this comic book-turned-movie has a gripping plot line along with amazing visual graphics, then she would need to support such a claim by clarifying what constitutes a gripping plot line and by providing evidence of the movie's stunning graphics. If you still need proof that her opinion of the movie is valid or if you are convinced that this is the movie for you, then you might actually venture out to see the movie. In either scenario, the writer has completed her job of persuading you to consider watching the movie.

Logos, however, involves much more than just verifying the validity of a writer's claims. Indeed, logos is associated with somewhat convoluted terminology, such as burden of proof (the obligation of the writer to prove his or her claims), fallacies (illogical or faulty reasoning), claims, grounds, warrants, and counterarguments. While the task of analyzing logos in a text could seem daunting given the surrounding terminology, you should remember that logos is simply the sound construction of an argument, meaning that a writer clearly states his argument and leads the audience through it step by step. Along the way, he provides reliable and clear evidence for each step, demonstrating how each step leads to the next in a logical fashion. Sometimes a writer's evidence takes the form of statistics. In this section, for sake of brevity and clarity, we will not consider all of the above components in detail. Instead, we will return once again to Truth's "Ain't I a Woman?" as a concrete example of how logos functions in a text.

> "Logos (rational appeal) refers to the logical underpinning of an argument. By identifying an argument's logos, we can determine the argument's rationale and the validity of the argument."

Logos, similar to pathos, is inextricably influenced by ethos and context, so we should first examine how Truth uses logos in order to construct a good ethos for herself. Truth, remember, is arguing for African-American women's rights in the midst of advocates and opponents of equal rights for women and African-American men. In her first point, Truth remarks,

> *That man over there says that women need to be helped into carriages, and lifted over ditches, and to have the best place everywhere. Nobody ever helps me into carriages, or over mud-puddles, or gives me any best place! And ain't I a woman? Look at me! Look at my arm! I have ploughed and planted, and gathered into barns, and no man could head me! And ain't I a woman? I could work as much and eat as much as a man—when I could get it—and bear the lash as well! And ain't I a woman? I have borne thirteen children, and seen them most all sold off to slavery, and when I cried out with my mother's grief, none but Jesus heard me! And ain't I a woman?*

Here, Truth carefully and logically draws attention to her role in society. She first identifies how society treats women with respect by placing them onto a pedestal, yet no one treats her as such. She then powerfully questions, "Ain't I a woman? Look at me!" Truth uses her physical body as proof (evidence) to persuade her audience that she is, indeed, a woman. After asserting her womanhood, she then juxtaposes herself and her abilities to those of a man, demonstrating that she is not a man but a woman who can outdo a man. Again she demands, "And ain't I a woman?" If her audience is still skeptical, she refers to her ability to give birth—something only women can do. The reference to motherhood serves as further proof of her womanhood as does the "mother's grief" that she feels at the loss of her children. Within the cited portion of her speech, Truth builds her ethos as a woman through three facts (evidence): she is a woman; she is not just a woman, but a black woman; and she is a mother. She thus uses logic to present herself as someone we can trust as an authority on the subject. As readers we can analyze her facts (the logic of an argument) to determine if she has provided enough evidence to prove her expertise on the subject for African-American women's rights. Here, logos helps construct ethos. As readers distanced in time from Truth's argument, we might turn to articles and/or books on female slavery to test Truth's logos and ethos. In such academic texts, we would find statistics and historical proof for Truth's claims, which come from her own experience.[1]

After identifying how logos and ethos work together, we should then decide on the validity of Truth's argument by noting her steps of logic. As we've seen above, Truth first employs logos to establish her ethos as an African-American woman. She then addresses a counterargument that women do not possess intellect and therefore should not be allowed equal rights: "Then they talk about this thing in the head; what's this they call it? [Intellect, someone whispers]. That's it, honey. What's that got to do with women's or negro's rights?" Truth's ironic, modest claim not to comprehend intellect, or to even know what it is called, belies her very use of intellect to construct her argument. Furthermore, Truth subtly connects her point about intellect to her previous point that she is a woman through her word choice. In her previous point (the above block quote), Truth declares that "no man could head me," and now she playfully refers to intellect as "this thing in the head." In the first instance, "head" means that no man could lead or control Truth, but this declaration reinforces the idea that she has intelligence—no man can outsmart ("out-head") Truth. She must overturn the belief that women are mentally inferior to men, and she covertly does so through her use of crafted logos.

Next, Truth addresses a religious counterargument that women should be barred from rights because "Christ wasn't a woman!"—a claim that Truth refutes by simply reminding her audience that Christ was "From God and a woman!" and that man was not involved. Her reference to Christ also connects to her earlier statement that in her "mother's grief, none but Jesus heard"

---

1. See Deborah Gray White's *Ain't I a Woman?: Female Slaves in the Plantation South*, and specifically her chapter called "The Nature of Female Slavery." (New York and London: W.W. Norton and Company, 1985).

her. Finally, Truth ends her speech with a reference to Eve, who "was strong enough to turn the world upside down," and Truth insists that the women attending the convention should be able to "get it right side up again!" Thus, the women advocating for women's rights should succeed in restoring the world to a state of equality. In ending her speech, Truth effectively brings us back to her opening statement that "there must be something out of kilter," indicating a sense of chaos over the debate of women's and African-Americans' rights. What begins "out of kilter" at the start of her speech transforms into "right side up" at the end, and reaching this achievement, Truth casually concludes with "ain't got nothing more to say." In short, Truth carefully connects each of her arguments together through key words and repeated phrases (even the refrain, "ain't I a woman"). The steps of her argument follow one another logically in order to emphasize her belief in women's rights, specifically African-American women's rights.

While logos can seem daunting, remember that analyzing a text for logos simply involves first identifying the argument and then the particular evidence or support for that argument. Consider the writer's use of key words and repeated phrases. Finally, with logos, remember to examine the construction and structure of the argument.

The Canons of Rhetoric as Phases of Composition

Will Dodson and Chelsea Skelley

While the appeals help us understand how we communicate and interpret, the canons of rhetoric help us understand the ways we can craft our communication. The word "canon" means "set of principles," so canons of rhetoric mean techniques, ideas, and rules of thumb for different aspects of communication. The canons of rhetoric are five categories of principles about how we compose our communication: invention, arrangement, style, memory, and delivery. They are phases of composition, rather than separate stages, because in practice the canons are interrelated and inseparable. We can, however, think about them separately to focus on our specific processes of composing, which is useful both for study and for strengthening our own rhetoric.

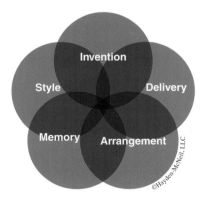

Figure 1. The canons of rhetoric have a recursive relationship, and each canon involves utilizing all the others.

We do not know for certain when the canons were first defined as five components or who put them in their traditional order—invention, arrangement, style, memory, delivery. Roman rhetoricians organized and updated rhetorical actions identified by the Greeks and explored in detail by Aristotle, but their exact origins are unknown. In practice, the canons are complex because in composing there is no linear order by which we move from canon to canon.

The "order" is more recursive, or circular, and we tend to use all the canons at once but emphasize one or another at different times. Look at Figure 1 (on previous page) and notice how all the canons can enter the foreground at one point and then recede while another enters the foreground, and so on. Whichever canon is emphasized at any one time, it still includes the other canons within it.

This chapter offers a brief introduction of each canon to provide a clearer picture of the scope of composing. First, we will briefly define each of the canons. Then, we will consider how the canons work together as phases of composing.

>> Memory

Rhetorical *memory* is a particularly complicated and often misunderstood canon. However, memory holds the canons together in their recursive relationship. Frequently memory is often thought to denote mnemonics, or methods for memorizing, which we use all the time. For example, in elementary school you may have learned the color spectrum by the mnemonic "Roy G. Biv." The name reminds us that the spectrum includes red, orange, yellow, green, blue, indigo, and violet. Another mnemonic is the tune of the ABC song, which helps us remember the letters with its rhythm and melody.

Rhetorical memory does include mnemonics, but there is more to it. The Roman rhetorician Cicero called memory the treasure house of invention because as we research topics, our memories help us synthesize ideas in new and interesting ways. We use our memories to "invent" new ideas. In fact, this use of memory reveals that words themselves are mnemonics. Every word is a symbol that denotes a standardized definition, and in connection to other words in a sentence, connotes some personal cultural significance. For example, read the word "education" and think about what comes to mind. In addition to the dictionary definition, you'll think of your own feelings about education, your experiences in school, subjects you like or dislike, what you think is important about education, debates, controversies, cultural differences, and so on. Rhetorical memory involves making connections—sometimes connections that do not seem obvious—and arranging them so that they make sense to an audience. Further, in a networked society with library databases and the Internet, you have access to almost unlimited information. So, your memory also serves as a kind of compass to help you establish a direction to search through information systematically, which again, helps you establish ethos.

Think of "education" again, and complete the brainstorm exercise mentioned above: as quickly as you can, write all the words or phrases that pop into your head. Ask yourself why those particular words or phrases popped into your mind. You will begin to identify your own stance toward the topic—beliefs, feelings, biases, what you know, what you don't know. Once you take stock of your preexisting stance, you can identify what might be common knowledge for your particular audience and what it would take to be a credible writer about the subject. This brainstorming exercise uses memory to reveal what you and your audience will *need* to know; understanding these needs, in turn, guides your research.

Rhetorical memory grounds the other canons in a specific rhetorical context. We use our memory to determine our ethos toward a topic, which starts us on the process of invention. What is your subject? What are you going to say about it? What preexisting beliefs and ideas do you and your audience have that must be acknowledged? In conjunction with arrangement, memory involves thinking about the order in which your audience will retain your material most easily. What does your audience need to know at the beginning of your paper, presentation, video, etc., in order to understand what comes next? What order of things would make sense or would be easiest to remember? Memory also informs style by helping decide what sort of language would be appropriate to a given audience, and what sort of examples and phrases would be most memorable. Finally, memory contextualizes delivery by considering the social and/or professional conventions of how you will communicate. What is your medium? Is this a research paper, a personal email, a professional communication, formal speech, or informal conversation? Each medium has its own conventions. As we look at each of the other canons in more depth, notice how without rhetorical memory to put writing, speech, or other texts into a specific context, the other canons cannot work effectively.

» Invention

Invention, simply put, involves deciding what to say. When we prepare to write or speak, we plan our material. We decide on a subject, research materials about the subject and its related subjects, and brainstorm how we will approach the subject for particular audiences in specific contexts. This approach helps you offer a fresh take on a subject to ensure that people will care about what you have to say. You want to establish an ethos of credibility and innovation.

Invention also helps us decide on the form of our speech and writing. This is nearly as important as determining what we will say because *how* we frame a subject has a huge impact on how the audience interprets it. Invention helps us determine questions of arrangement and style. In classical rhetoric, *topics* are categories of relationships; they are the ways in which the subject is framed. We might make comparisons and say one thing is better than another or two things are similar or different. Or we might try to define what something really is or explain how something works by looking at it closely. We use topics that our audiences can recognize in order to offer them new ways of thinking about our subject. In this way, invention, with the help of memory, involves thinking about our subject.

For instance, imagine a common situation: you are preparing to write about the education system in the United States, and you simply write, "American education has a long and complex history." That sentence tells your audience nothing they don't already know. You need to put forth a particular point of view. Part of your invention process could include brainstorming sessions that develop from the word-association exercise discussed earlier in the *Memory* section. Look at all the words and phrases you wrote down, select a few that seem compelling, and repeat the exercise. Start trying to get more precise phrases and even sentences to help you form a hypothesis. Then, ask yourself why certain words and phrases seem more compelling. Asking questions is particularly important because it helps shape your perspective. (For more about invention and inquiry, see Kathleen T. Leuschen's "Invention, Asking Questions to Find a Starting Point.") After conducting a little research, you might develop the hypothesis into a strong thesis, which can then form the direction for your paper.

» Arrangement

As we decide what we're going to say, we decide the order with which we'll say it. Arrangement is a question of intelligibility. What does the reader or listener need to know first in order to make sense of what comes after? Arrangement involves the most logical progression of material designed to achieve the desired reaction from an audience.

To decide on the best arrangement, as you research and invent your subject you might produce formal or informal outlines. Using that outline, you can conduct more research, brainstorm more ideas, and identify key phrases and examples you will use to establish your style. As you do all these things, you'll find yourself rearranging the outline even as you start preparing or revising the paper. This process is important. You start with a plan—the outline—of arrangement, and then as you develop your ideas through invention and research, you rearrange and clarify your plan, deciding which of the various types of arrangements will best suit the specific situation.

Regardless of what type of arrangement you choose, successful arrangement builds from sentence to sentence—orienting readers to your subject, and finally convincing them of your point of view. For instance, for your paper on education, you decide to write about the problems of standardized testing and offer an alternative. Logically, you wouldn't start your paper by immediately explaining your new way of testing student learning outcomes. Your audience might understand what you're saying, but what would they do with the information? For the audience to know why your alternative is necessary and appropriate, you first need to explain the context of standardized testing, its shortcomings, and support those claims. You orient your reader to the history of standardized testing and the relevant educational, social, and political issues before making your argument and introducing new information. Through a careful, logical arrangement, you guide your audience, helping them understand the systemic problems with standardized testing, then offer up a viable solution.

Logic depends on arrangement, but do not think this means arrangement is not a creative part of writing. There are numerous ways to arrange your ideas for various genres and contexts. (For a detailed discussion of arrangement styles, see Chelsea Skelley's "Arrangement as Rhetorical Composing.")

» Style

Whereas invention focuses on *what* you want to say and arrangement focuses on the *order* you make your points, style focuses on *how* you say it. This canon includes consideration of syntax, diction, word choice, grammar, and ambiguous terms like "tone," "flow," "rhythm," and "voice." Compare the sentences:

1. "American education is in trouble, and reforms are necessary."

2. "American education faces a crisis, and without immediate reforms our young people will be robbed of the tools they need to succeed in the world."

Can you see how important word choice is to excite emotional inclination toward a subject? Compare "trouble" to "crisis," for example. Furthermore, note the specific detail in the second sentence that contributes to your interpretation of "crisis." Similarly, the length and syntax of your sentences—for example, the passive verbs in the first sentence versus active verb construction in the second—affect the way your readers react to your subject. The second sentence is more emotionally charged, while the first sentence is calmer and more measured in tone. Your style depends on your intentions. How do you want your audience to react?

Style also refers to aesthetics, which also depends on the audience. For example, when talking to friends, your style might be very informal, possibly include slang (even vulgarities), or inside jokes that are specific to your circle of friends. If speaking for a class, you probably will adopt formal conventions—the "standard English"—and use more precise language. Using words in striking ways, perhaps through clever turns of phrase or an elegance of rhythm, can make your writing and speaking much more effective than unimaginative phrasing and monotonous sentence structures.

Additionally, punctuation is a subtle but important aspect of style. Punctuation gives cues to the reader about the speed and rhythm with which she or he should read, and it also shades the writing with nuanced aspects of pathos. Occasional question marks and rare exclamation points send definite emotional cues; commas, hyphens, and periods signal rhythmic pauses and syntactic connections; parentheses and dashes set off important digressions; quotation marks indicate the inclusion of research; and semicolons separate long lists or join independent clauses that are closely related. Punctuation ultimately works with diction and syntax to give readers clues about the writer's intended tone.

Style is fluid, and it informs many aspects of your writing. (For further discussion of the canon of style and its creativity and play, see Ann-Marie Blanchard's chapter "The Play of Style.")

» Delivery

Widely defined, delivery applies to all forms of communication. It is our performance of our subject; it is the medium we use to communicate, be it speech, writing, video, photograph, painting, dance, etc. Delivery in oral communication refers to how we speak: our tone, pitch, volume, gesture, facial expression, and so on. Delivery applies to writing in terms of how it is presented. The format of academic papers, for example, involves proper observation of the conventions of MLA, APA, Turabian, or other citation styles. Delivery involves the conventions, or genres, of communication: letter, essay, dialogue, novel, etc. Delivery also includes stylistic and memory considerations, such as paragraph and sentence length. You must consider how easily your audience will be able to read your writing. Though delivery is listed last of the canons, it's often considered first. We decide—or we are assigned—the form in which we're going to write or speak, to what audience, in what context, and about what subject.

The key questions of delivery are: (a) to what audience and (b) in what medium? As you answer those questions, you continue to invent your perspective on the subject and develop ideas about how to arrange and stylize your speech and writing in order to deliver it effectively. (For more discussion of delivery, see Brenta Blevins's chapter "It's All—Well, a Lot—in the Delivery.")

» Recursive Phases

The canons apply to all our rhetorical choices. We use rhetoric whenever we have to make a choice about how to communicate with another person or group of people. Consciously or not, you make choices about the language to use, the format and genre to best communicate what you want to say, and many other decisions. This often includes everyday situations like performing a task (e.g., being a student or an employee), reading an advertisement, or discussing an important issue with your friends, family, or instructor. Each of these scenarios likely occurs fairly frequently in daily life, and the canons can help you compose effective communication within them. For college writing, the canons will help you to shape your communication across multiple contexts and genres. Whether writing a paper, giving a presentation, working in a collaborative group, or other situations, the canons' interconnectivity can help you make rhetorical choices to best communicate your point of view.

Your hypothetical research paper on education demonstrates this interconnectivity in the decisions and processes of composing. Your instructor has already established the required format: research paper (delivery). So, you think about what feelings, biases, questions, and ideas you have about the subject and what research you need to conduct to more comprehensively understand it (memory). As you research, you decide what position you will argue through brainstorming, asking questions, and other activities (invention). You think about how you will arrange your research to support that position, and you draft an initial outline (arrangement). As you conduct more research (memory), you revise your position, clarifying your ideas (invention) and re-ordering your paper's structure (arrangement). You jot down words, examples, analogies, and other devices to help your audience see the subject the way you see it (style). To be most effective to your audience, you consider what information your readers need to follow your argument (arrangement), what word choices will have the most impact (style), and what aspects of the topic readers will recognize immediately or will need more explanation to understand (memory). As you draft the paper, you prepare it in the proper format, citing your research, and creating a bibliography (delivery). Further, you choose the format to submit your work (based on the instructor's preference), opting for a hard copy or electronic copy (delivery).

Though we can think of each canon separately for the purpose of discussion, each should be considered a phase of an overall act of communication. That is, consideration of invention also involves arrangement, style, memory, and delivery; consideration of arrangement involves invention, style, memory, and delivery; and so on. We do not think and write linearly. We engage these creative phases recursively, constantly rethinking and reworking our rhetoric so that we can communicate most effectively. The purpose of thinking deliberately about each canon is to improve the precision of our communication, but to think of the canons as isolated from one another fractures your point of view and may cause you to lose sight of the point of your writing in favor of its individual elements. These concepts, once you've thought through them and put them into practice, can help you develop stronger communication skills.

Academic Integrity

Charles Tedder

There are many ways to understand the concept of academic integrity. Students, instructors, and administrators often think of academic integrity in terms of failure: students "violate" academic integrity when they cheat on a test, lie about the work they've done, or plagiarize in their writing. For obvious reasons, this last transgression, plagiarism, is the focus of academic integrity in the classroom. In this context, academic integrity is often reduced to the demand that students correctly follow citation guidelines, the Modern Language Association (MLA) style, for example, and thus avoid plagiarism. Another way to think about academic integrity is giving credit to one's sources: this model is grounded in intellectual property or copyright law, which in turn is based in the principles of capitalism. While neither of these models—failure or giving credit—is wrong *per se*, this chapter imagines academic integrity differently. Academic integrity, for our purpose, is not a question of "correct" adherence to the law but rather the cultivation of certain *values*, or habits of good behavior, that accomplish something good in the world.

Simply stated, mere *correctness* is not the same as *integrity*. There are more substantive concerns to wrestle with, and they take longer to master than citation mechanics or the vagaries of copyright law. To understand academic integrity, we have to understand the academy itself because the values of academic integrity are grounded in the rhetorical situation of academic writing. And since the academy itself is historically linked to the emergence of democracy in Western civilization, the ethics of its discourse are precisely the values of a free and egalitarian society, including values such as *honesty, trust, fairness, respect*, and *responsibility*.

» The Rhetorical Situation of Academic Writing

Around 400 BCE, the philosopher Plato founded a school that would become known as his "Academy." Since then, *academy* has meant a place where people congregate to share ideas and develop knowledge. When phrased "*the* academy," the term usually refers to the institutionalized practices of scholarship and teaching that comprise higher education. Thus, any college subject can be thought of as a gathering of like-minded or similarly employed people. For example, *biology* is the gathering of people interested in living systems, *history* is the gathering of people interested in understand humanity's past, and *nursing* is the gathering of people interested in practicing health care. The purpose of such gatherings is generally described as *the production and distribution of knowledge* or, respectively, scholarship and teaching.

The academy's collective scholarly knowledge and professional expertise develop over time as its individual members share discoveries, ideas, or techniques. Sometimes this means a scientist discovering something "out there" in the natural world. Sometimes it means an artist or critic refining aesthetic technique and appreciation in the fine arts. Sometimes it means a philosopher or sociologist sharpening, through critical discussion or debate, the ideas and policies that shape society. Sometimes it means the practitioners of a given profession refining their methods and instructing new apprentices.

"Simply stated, mere *correctness* is not the same as *integrity*."

Students can be considered new members of the academy, arriving at the latest moments in multiple, interconnected conversations that have been going on for a few decades or a few centuries. With the help of their instructors, students can "catch up" with the conversation and make their own contributions.

Although students will still engage in actual academic conversations in their classroom discussion, the larger "conversation" or *discourse* of the academy is metaphorical. In practice, scholars carry on their academic discourses through a series of publications in which they report their research and respond to each other, and doing so through print publication has the great advantage of allowing the conversation to spread out in time and space and include more people: scholars can read the writings of people on the other side of the world or from hundreds of years ago, and they can hear from more people than can be seated around a seminar table.

On the other hand, it also becomes difficult for any one person to "hear" the entire conversation since the conversation is spread among more books and articles than one person can read. For this reason, each time someone makes a contribution, she spends some time restating the earlier contributions that she is responding to. Since readers may or may not be familiar with the preceding parts of the conversation, it is necessary to recapitulate those parts that are relevant to the current contribution.

All academic writers, then, write explicitly about the books and articles to which their own work responds. Over time, the academy has created fairly specific and detailed rules for doing this kind of thing. Scrupulously adhering to these rules, usually referred to as "citation guidelines," will always be one meaning of *academic integrity*. Various disciplines and professions have independently developed citation systems to suit the needs of their members. For example, the MLA style uses names and page numbers to draw fine details from literary texts, while the American Psychological Association (APA) style uses names and publication dates to foreground the most current research in the field. (See Ben Compton's chapter "Rhetorical Elements of Academic Citation" for further discussion of citation styles.)

MLA, APA, and Chicago/Turabian are the most common citation styles for academic professions. Citation styles dictate a standard format for writing research papers and referencing sources.

Common styles:

- MLA (Modern Language Association)—for English and the Humanities

- APA (American Psychological Association)—for Psychology and Social Sciences

- CMS (Chicago Manual of Style)—for History and some Humanities

- CSE (Council of Science Editors)—for the Sciences

Each format emphasizes the information most important to the discipline. For example, APA and CSE formats list dates of publication next to author names because up-to-date studies are important for researchers. MLA lists dates of publication last because often humanities researchers focus on very old texts, and the publisher information is more important for determining authentic works.

Academic writing, then, is a cooperative endeavor among like-minded individuals, even though it sometimes takes on an overly vicious, "argumentative" tone. Ideally, the grace and professionalism to avoid petty squabbling or mean-spirited disagreement in favor of productive dialogue should be among the key values that mark academic integrity. The paradox of a discourse that can be sometimes divisive and at other times cooperative arises from two competing ways of understanding the purpose of an academic "argument": the divisive and cooperative models. Each understanding produces a different model of the rhetorical situation in which academic writing is performed.

In the divisive model, two intellectuals square off against each other in a kind of shouting match, each trying to "win" the argument at the loss of the other. In the cooperative model, the intellectuals stand shoulder-to-shoulder, turned towards a third element, the object of their shared inquiry. In this model, instead of trying to best each other, individuals work together to produce and distribute new knowledge or expertise about some part of the world we all live in. They do so by *making a claim and arguing its merits*, modifying their claims as they communicate with each other. In this way, the academy and academic rhetoric are not defined by persuading others to adopt one's own answers to questions of belief or policy. Rather, the academy is something that people create together: *It is a process of shared inquiry*. And they can only do it well in a rhetorical community founded on honesty, trust, respect, and responsibility. John Gage, a scholar of rhetoric, considers how these values should—even *must*—shape academic writing. His ideas inform the rest of this essay.[1]

» The Values of Academic Integrity

Up to now, this chapter has explained how ethical behaviors, or values, characteristic of academic integrity are grounded in a particular understanding of the rhetorical situation of academic writing. We can briefly state how the purpose of academic writing shapes the values we call "integrity" in this context: because the purpose of academic writing is to produce and distribute knowledge, an academic writer with integrity cannot intend to win an argument at any cost. Said another way, if a writer's only intention is to prove other people wrong, then the purpose of academic inquiry—knowledge—will be lost along the way. Academic inquiry entails an understanding of knowledge (an *epistemology*) that holds all knowledge to be local and communal (shared) and treats the creation of knowledge as a process of reciprocal, mutual, generous engagement with other people. In order to function properly, this process must be based on trust.

Academic integrity means not only earning the trust of others and being responsible in using other people's work as part of our own (we will consider this next), but also trusting in the basic honesty and responsibility of our colleagues, at least until there is good reason not to do so. In other words, academic discourses take as their starting point any claim (statement, belief, or fact) that can be argued over by people with *good information* and *good intentions*. Any academic writing will fail, rhetorically and ethically, if it addresses others as though they are anything other than well-informed and well-intentioned.

Before we can engage other people in academic discourse, we must assume the good intentions of others, at least as a starting premise. In other words, when

---

1. John Gage, *The Shape of Reason*, 4th ed. (New York: Pearson Longman, 2006).

writers address readers through academic writing, they make an implicit pledge that the reader is someone worth writing for, someone who might receive the writing in good faith.

Therefore, when writers choose to engage other people in academic discourse, they should adopt a "principle of generosity." Students who are asked to begin interacting with others in an academic setting have to learn to make their own points without doing so at the expense of others. This means taking others at their word and responding to the quality of their arguments. Moreover, students as academic writers should be open to the possibility that the other person may "win" the argument, may teach us or convince us of something. No one should practice academic writing without being willing to have her mind changed by other people.

"Because the purpose of academic writing is to produce and distribute knowledge, an academic writer with integrity cannot intend to win an argument at any cost."

The principle of generosity includes the values of fairness and respect as well. When a writer incorporates other people's contributions into her work, this incorporation usually takes the form of something that is agreed with and built from or something disagreed with and argued against. Often it's a little of each. Rewriting another person's words takes some care, since meanings can be easily twisted through careless paraphrase or a quotation taken out of context. One of the most common distortions is to reduce someone's position to an approximate cliché. For example, someone who argues that citizenship in America is a complex status that changes over time and means different things to different people may find himself caricatured as simply "pro-immigration." Academic writers with integrity know it is important to represent another person's claims fairly, in good faith, without distorting their language to serve selfish ends.

Over time, people who think about writing and speechmaking have named several mistakes or *fallacies* that can undermine ethically responsible rhetoric. Two mistakes in particular can be thought of as failures of *ethos* (the writer's character or credibility) or *ethical fallacies*. One is called the *ad hominem* (to-the-person) fallacy. This fallacy occurs when a writer attacks the person she disagrees with rather than offering counterpoints to the other person's arguments. Since the goal of the academy is to develop knowledge together, good academic writing should always address the guiding topic at hand rather than the person with whom the writer might disagree. For example, instead of protesting that heightened security at airports is the work of "authoritarian" government officials, we could question the merits of such a practice by asking if it actually makes us safer. While much academic writing is *agonistic*—made up of arguments that include "attacking" and "defending" claims—writers maintain their integrity when they argue positions and claims.

Another ethical fallacy is called the *straw man* fallacy. This is when a writer incorporates the weakest or least relevant part of what someone has written so that the offending writer has an easier time making her points sound better. For example, in the abortion debate, pro-choice advocates often characterize their opposition's position only as setting aside the concerns of the mother, without addressing what pro-life advocates consider to be the core of their position: the life of the child. On the other hand, pro-life advocates often characterize abortion as a method of birth control, without acknowledging the pro-choice position's core: providing safe and accessible care without making value judgments. In a true spirit of generosity, academic writers should always respond to the strongest arguments made against their position, even when doing so makes those positions more difficult to hold. By addressing the ideas or evidence that offer the greatest challenge to a given part of the conversation, knowledge and understanding are advanced rather than an individual writer's career or self-esteem.

> "More than anything else, academic integrity means an ethical engagement among the many people who are placed in contact through writing."

More than anything else, academic integrity means an ethical engagement among the many people who are placed in contact through writing. This includes both the writers drawn from and the readers written to. A guiding principle for writing with academic integrity is simply keeping in mind these different people and making a commitment to work with them ethically and respectfully.

» Why We Should Cultivate These Values

Having considered the rhetorical situation of academic writing and what it means to act in this situation with integrity, we can conclude this chapter with two value-based arguments in favor of acting this way. In other words, the preceding paragraphs have described *how* we write with academic integrity, while the following argue why we *should*—that is, why academic integrity is *good*.

First, cultivating academic integrity produces better rhetoric. Writing with academic integrity establishes and maintains *ethos*, the rhetorical appeal to readers based on their perception that the writer is someone worth listening to. A writer appeals to *logos* by avoiding logical gaffes such as *ad hoc* fallacies (false conclusions of cause and effect). Appeals to *pathos* must avoid emotional pandering such as *ad populum* fallacies (the claim that everyone-else-is-doing-it-and-so-should-you). In the same way, *ethos* is maintained partly by avoiding failures of academic integrity, what we called ethical fallacies above. Only when a writer engages her work and audience with integrity will readers trust in her enough to give the text a fair hearing.

The second reason to write with academic integrity comes from its historical precedence in Plato's Greece. This period in history gave us the academy, the study of rhetoric as a topic of inquiry, and the democratic political system. Why did rhetoric teachers appear about the same time as democracy itself? It only became important to know how to speak (and write) well after speaking (and writing) became part of the political process, part of how power gets used in a community. A commitment to academic integrity is a commitment to a certain kind of power structure, one that we hope contributes to human freedom and dignity.

"Academic integrity goes to the heart of why we are writing at all. It is a commitment to other people and to the value of human conversation."

The values of academic integrity are the basic values of democracy, a free and open exchange of ideas founded on a simple egalitarianism in which we all can make our contribution to decisions of belief or policy. Writing with academic integrity, then, does not mean a documentation style, facility with three dozen useful signal phrases, comprehension of "fair use" standards, or the correct formatting of footnotes in Microsoft Word. Academic integrity goes to the heart of why we are writing at all. It is a commitment to other people and to the value of human conversation.

The Portfolio Process

Brian Ray

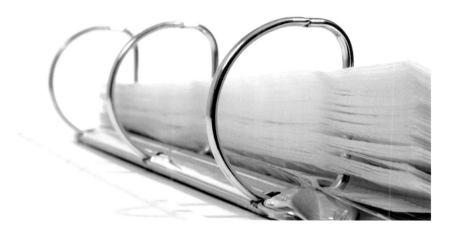

Students sometimes compare writing to the experience of having teeth pulled, going to church too early on a Sunday morning, or desperately running into a house with a spilling bag of groceries. Writing might even feel like watching a horror movie. These comparisons all implicitly perceive writing the same way—painful and objectifying. Writers using these analogies see themselves as the passengers of their writing, not the pilots. On the other hand, experienced and professional writers describe writing as backpacking, conducting a train, herding sheep, sailing a ship, or building a house. Big difference! But these pros started as novices. They arrived at more positive and active views of writing somehow. And their method is not a secret.

The pros might have gotten where they are any number of ways, but one method recreates their experiences. It's called the portfolio-based course. Not the most dazzling name, but the idea is what's important.

The first day of class, College Writing instructors will probably introduce the writing portfolio, a simple idea that's easy to dismiss at first. On the surface it sounds mainly like a second chance. People who make mistakes on their drafts the first time get a do-over. Meanwhile the good writers who nail their assignments the first time can correct a few typos, sit back, and enjoy life. But that's not how the portfolio works. Instead, college writers will use revision and feedback to take charge of their essays like never before. Portfolios help writers learn to pay more attention to their growth as writers, with less anxiety about each individual paper.

Portfolios come in all shapes and sizes. Sometimes instructors have already made up their minds about what they want to see at the end of the semester: two revised research papers and a personal essay, for example. Other times they leave it up to the members of the class to decide what exactly goes into the mix and how to organize it. In any case, the portfolio enables students to perform a number of rhetorical acts. By choosing which papers or projects to include, students communicate to their instructor how they see the course as valuable to them, which lessons they found the most enriching, and how they have developed as both writers and individual intellects.

If the instructor has already determined most of the content beforehand, however, then students can still use organization and presentation (delivery) as a way to comment on the course. For instance, how do you want your instructor to read your portfolio? Should your instructor read all final drafts, crisp and new, and then read all revisions? Reading this way would emphasize the papers themselves, almost hiding the work that went into producing them. Or would it be better to read each paper from first to final draft? Organizing the portfolio this way would encourage more attention to the changes that occur between drafts. Consider also how many drafts should be included. Many instructors might ask only for a first and final draft. Nonetheless, students might actually decide to submit every single draft of a particular paper, including those used in peer review sessions and those that neither students nor peers evaluated. In that case, students send a message that they worked hard on the paper and developed their ideas over a long period of time. Doing this, all students reconstruct the course through their own interpretive lenses.

But college writers have more explicit ways of advising their instructors how they wish their work to be read and judged. Most portfolios require a reflective statement or critical rationale essay to articulate, identify, and justify the choices they have made in their writing. The rationale essay serves as an important rhetorical opportunity. It provides each student a voice to discuss how the course has or has not improved their writing or critical outlook. This essay also gives everyone the authority to judge and interpret their own progress, speaking back to the grade book. Instructors may not require their students to make every single revision they suggest in order to attain full credit. Rather, they might look to the rationale essays to gauge how students have incorporated feedback and to evaluate to what extent students have developed a critical perspective toward their own work. For example, a student could discuss in his rationale essay how he decided to focus efforts on the research and content of a piece, meanwhile acknowledging possible weakness in structure and organization. The rationale essay can explicitly state what further revisions could be done with more time. An essay that engages in such critical reflection has the potential to convince or persuade an instructor to respond more positively—even to slightly alter the criteria used to evaluate such a paper. Hence, the critical rationale essay constitutes an extremely important rhetorical dimension of the portfolio.

College Writing instructors look for self-awareness, voice, and confidence in these final words, which are not always "graded" themselves so much as they are listened to, searching for evidence that their students have matured as writers and critical thinkers. In this light, students should spend some time deciding what they want to communicate through their portfolios, how to communicate this, and why. A student who has included five drafts of a personal essay and two drafts of a rhetorical analysis might spend some time explaining why their process became more involved for some assignments than others. The difference might allude to a greater degree of investment in the personal writing compared to the analytical. Conversely, it might owe to increased difficulty of finding voice in a narrative versus the relative anonymity of academic discourse. Instructors really are interested in hearing their students weigh these issues at the end of the semester. Someone who dismisses the rationale essay as just another assignment is throwing away a chance to have some say in how his work is read, to engage in some final dialogue with his instructor. It's likely that many inexperienced writers have never been asked to talk at length about themselves *as* writers. Take advantage of this novel opportunity.

Revision, at first, does not sound like fun. Before college, the very word "revision" means that something has gone wrong and needs to be fixed. But college writing takes a very different spin on this process. Revision entails looking again, not just at the paper itself, but at the very ideas and experiences behind the writing. Revision gives all writers more control over what they think about the world. A writer might remember hating a trip to visit grandparents when constructing the first draft of a personal essay. But rewriting that experience can lead to a metamorphosis of consciousness and identity. Revising an essay about abortion rights or skydiving may lead to new thoughts on ostensibly familiar subjects. Ideally, then, a writing instructor doesn't just point out things to "fix" in a paper but asks questions in order to facilitate these intellectual shifts. The goal, of course, is not to change those views but to strengthen them by understanding them better. An essay might go through five drafts, but one more draft after that might change everything about one's perspective on that topic. That's not just fixing problems. That's exercising power over the world.

Nobody can ever perfectly and completely put down his or her thoughts about any issue the first time around. People who believe they can have probably never revised any of their work, so they don't know what they're missing. In fact, most people sit down a dozen times or more to produce a polished piece of prose. The great thing about most writing courses is that instructors *want* to read lots of drafts of papers. They're happier to see an essay grow from a seed to a tree than they are to see only the tree.

"Revision gives all writers more control over what they think about the world."

Revision also translates into agency. If there is one thing a portfolio course helps to alleviate, it is the procrastination at the root of binge writing, otherwise known as eleventh-hour writing. Binge writing, more than anything, leads to the sensation of objectivity. Those novice writers from the beginning of this essay, who view writing as severe torture, only think about what writing does to them. They do not think about what writing can do for them, or how they can use writing to address the world and change reality.

Too often, students will let their anxiety about a paper build until a day or two before the deadline. The night before, they crank out the minimum number of pages after much suffering, and in their haste either rush through or skip altogether vital steps such as brainstorming, planning, outlining, incubation, revision and editing, and proofreading. New writers eliminate these steps not always out of laziness but because they begin each paper in a state of dread, already exhausted by worrying about a big fat "F" that symbolizes and confirms their failures. That's not power from writing. That's a nightmare, and it's easy to avoid. Writers are not consciously committing a sin when they binge write. They simply have not learned healthier ways. Taking a revision-based approach to writing gives a student control over his or her work and subsequently gives him or her greater capacity to communicate ideas effectively. The difference between "F" and "A" is no longer a complete jungle. This does not completely prevent binge writing, of course. But if implemented wisely and followed through, the portfolio system acts preemptively against such problems.

Beginning writers have often heard it's good to start papers "early," but they are told the wrong reasons for doing so. In fact, there is no such thing as starting a paper "early." Inexperienced writers may not notice it, but their brains start interrogating an assignment the day they get it. Using these brainstorms and writing a little each day makes for more confident and independent writers who can figure out themselves and the world, solving complex problems with their pens and brains. Ideally, the portfolio-based course reinforces these good habits.

Portfolios, simply put, give everyone the benefit of learning from their writing rather than simply from their supposed mistakes. The idea of learning to write as learning to avoid mistakes goes out the window. Mistakes become natural aspects of writing, although the process-focused instructor still cares about final drafts. Even if instructors do not place excessive emphasis on grammar and style, these technical aspects are also critical aspects of writing, and they serve an important role in communication with others. Errors decrease a writer's agency because they send a variety of negative messages to readers. Other conventions like thesis statements and the use of quotations and punctuation have the same impact on agency. The portfolio course does away with some of the pain novice writers have suffered from the imposition of these conventions, but the ultimate point of portfolios is to help writers achieve those tough goals. Taking this philosophy seriously leads to a better writing life—one that turns writing from a dentist appointment into a journey.

2

Rhetorical
Approaches

Reading Critically

Sonya Blades

In his essay "The American Scholar," Ralph Waldo Emerson challenges the common idea that reading is the passive absorption of others' words and ideas. He states, "One must be an inventor to read well…. There is, then, creative reading as well as creative writing."[1] We often think of writing as active and the writer as the creator of meaning, but reading *critically* is also a way to create meaning; hence it is also referred to as *creative* reading. Reading is itself a kind of composition. Reading and writing go hand-in-hand, and in order to read critically or creatively, one must go beyond simply reading over words on a page to form one's own conclusions.

An active reader must work to understand, interpret, and analyze a text. The key to fully understanding what we read is to ask questions and to try to supply answers to those questions. What is the author saying? How do you know? What exactly is being argued? What supporting points, or evidence, are at work? This process of questioning involves the reader's decoding of the text, or identifying the text's meaning. Interpretation and analysis take this process a step further by asking *how* the writer says what is being said as well as how the reader understands what is being said. A reader analyzes a text by reading it closely, looking for meanings or implications, and placing the text within a broader context such as the author's life, the cultural surroundings, and the historical background. Interpretation includes the assumptions and previous knowledge of the reader. For example, one person might find the sarcastic humor in a particular text offensive, depending on the seriousness of the subject matter and how his or her understanding of the text is affected by previous knowledge and experience. Someone who has grown up in the South and has faced some form of discrimination for having a strong Southern accent could find David Sedaris' caricatures of Southerners in *Me Talk Pretty One Day* demeaning and offensive, but someone else with different experiences or who has knowledge of Sedaris' biography (while born in New York, he was

---

1.   Ralph Waldo Emerson, *The American Scholar* (New York: American Book Company, 1893), 29.

actually raised in Raleigh, North Carolina) might better understand the playful satire of his work. Reading critically involves actively trying to understand what is being said while applying one's previous knowledge and experiences. In other words, it means that a reader must balance what is being said with both how it is being said *and* what assumptions the reader brings to the table. As active, critical readers, we all have the job of simultaneously understanding, interpreting, and analyzing a text.

When thinking of how to critically approach a text, it is helpful to think of the act of reading as a conversation between readers and writers. As both scholar and reader, your job is to wedge yourself into that academic conversation. We communicate by responding to others, which Kenneth Burke describes as a "parlor" of academic conversation where scholars come and go, adding to an on-going conversation where they see fit. Joining the academic conversation begins with reading critically. The reader 'listens' for moments to respond. When a sentence strikes you as in line with your own understanding, or when it resonates with another author's idea, you might 'respond' to that sentence both in your head and by writing in the margin something to the effect of "This reminds me of…,""I agree because…," or perhaps "I find this infuriating!" This type of reading requires active participation with the text on the part of the reader, and writing these responses down can help a reader recall and build on these reactions to form a cogent response or an argument. Passively skimming a text for key words to jump out does not work for critical reading because the reader might miss important points that could change his or her response. Readings required for college courses are often complex and require a great deal of concentration for the reader to understand the information and interpret the argument being made, which makes "marginalia"—or notes in the margins—all the more important. A sure-fire way to effectively understand a text is to keep both one's eyes *and* one's analytical mind open to what is being read, while also jotting notes in the margins to keep track of the arguments and to sort through the complexity of the text. (For a sample annotated text with marginalia, see Appendix.)

To continue with Burke's description of the parlor, when people enter a conversation, they may hear some people making statements with which they agree and other statements with which they disagree, or perhaps statements with which they both agree and disagree. This idea of a back-and-forth conversation is in contrast with how people often define or think of the word "critical." The word "critical" is usually understood to be a negative approach, which can lead students to believe that they must disagree with or find fault with a text in order to *be* critical of it. As readers, we could very well find areas in a text with which we disagree, but we are not limited to disagreement or agreement.

In academia, "critical" refers to the scholarly analysis of a text, which involves understanding the writer's work and applying the reader's outside knowledge and experiences to help create meaning from the text, whether that includes agreement, disagreement, or both. For example, in "Why Women Smile," Amy Cunningham argues that women have learned to smile in order to appear submissive and to make others feel comfortable, regardless of their own feelings. She asserts that this is dangerous because women often hide their feelings behind fake smiles in order to come off as pleasant and accommodating. While a reader might agree that, yes, historically women's smiles have served a societal purpose to keep women in line with gender expectations, a reader might also argue that Cunningham ignores a crucial aspect about some of the evidence she uses. She references a study by Paul Ekman which differentiated between authentic smiles and social smiles, but she does not acknowledge that this study goes further to explain that many social smiles can help elevate an individual's mood, thus allowing for more genuine smiles. Now, while this is not the point of Cunningham's essay, it is still worth noting how a reader could refute her conclusion that "False [smiles] do nothing for us at all."[2] Additionally, for Cunningham, "us" implies women only, but a reader might also disagree with this distinction. I know from my own experience and observations that many men also use social smiles for networking and etiquette.

Through active reading, I have come to the conclusion that I would like Cunningham to explain further how women's social smiles differ from those of men. I can agree with much of Cunningham's argument about how women tend to smile more, while also showing disagreement in some of the claims she makes. Through analysis, I can respectfully disagree without making the generalized statement that Cunningham is completely wrong. Therefore, reading critically involves actively reading to help create meaning through interpretation and analysis. As I described earlier, it involves applying the reader's outside knowledge and experiences to help create meaning from the text, whether that includes agreement, disagreement, or both.

Another way to critically read and analyze so that you are creating meaning rather than simply accepting a writer's claims at face value is to ask questions while you read. Use the rhetorical triangle to help frame these questions: what is the writer's aim or purpose? What exactly is the writer arguing? What is the underlying message? What evidence does the writer use? Is the evidence credible and effective? Also, think about the writer's motives, how the writer handles information, and how the writer relays the information. What appeals are emphasized? Who can you say is the intended audience, and why? What

---

2. Amy Cunningham, "Why Women Smile," in *The Writer's Presence*, 6th ed. (New York: Bedford, 2006), 324–331.

can you say about the writer's style, and how does that affect your reading of the text? These questions will further help you to understand the writer's goals and intent.

Critical readers not only question the text but they also question their own reactions to the text, which further adds to the meaning-making process. They read themselves—their thoughts, emotions, and responses—critically at the same time that they read the text critically. They challenge their own assumptions by reflecting on both the reading and their reactions to the reading. A reader might ask: what biases do I see in my reaction? In other words, if, as a reader, you find yourself becoming angry or, in contrast, avidly nodding your head in agreement, it is probably a good idea for you to consider why you are responding in that way. You will have to ask what beliefs, preconceptions, or past experiences add to or affect your understanding of what you have read. It is important to remember that we all come to the table with outside knowledge and different personal experiences that color our reading. Thus, readers must be confident enough to form their own opinions based on evidence offered in the text and on what they already knew about the topic while also being open to changing their minds based on good use of evidence. Reading critically requires a balance between not immediately believing everything one reads and remaining trusting enough to be open to new ideas.

The following excerpt is from an essay by Gerald Graff entitled "Disliking Books at an Early Age." In his essay, Graff explains how, as a youth, he had been uninterested in literature because he could not relate to it. His interest grew only when his instructors began to teach the conflicting interpretations and analyses scholars and readers offer about texts. In other words, akin to Burke's description of the parlor, Graff began to hear and be interested in the different conversations about a text. Following the passage, I will offer an example of how to go about the critical reading process by responding to Graff's piece.

> To those who have never reconciled themselves to the academicization of literature, the seeming overdevelopment of academic criticism with its obtrusive methodology and its endless disputes among interpretations and theories seems a betrayal not just of literature and the common reader but of the professor's own original passion for literature. In a recent letter to an intellectual journal one writer suggests that we should be concerned less about the oft-lamented common reader whom academic critics have deserted than about "the souls of the academics and literati themselves, who, as a result of social and professional pressures, have lost touch with the inner impulses that drew them to the world of books in the first place."

What the writer of this letter cannot imagine is that someone might enter academic literary study because he actually *likes* thinking and talking in an analytical or theoretical way about books and that such a person might see his acceptance of "professional pressures" not as a betrayal of the "inner impulses" that drew him "to the world of books in the first place" but as a way to fulfill those impulses.

The standard story ascribes innocence to the primary experience of literature and sees the secondary experience of professional criticism as corrupting. In my case, however, things had evidently worked the other way around: I had to be corrupted first in order to experience innocence. It was only when I was introduced to a critical debate about *Huckleberry Finn* that my helplessness in the face of the novel abated and I could experience a personal reaction to it. Getting into immediate contact with the text was for me a curiously triangular business; I could not do it directly but needed a conversation of other readers to give me the issues and terms that made it possible to respond.[3]

On a first reading of Graff's text, it would not be surprising if many of the words are unfamiliar. Since the first step to reading critically is making sure I understand what is being said, it's a good idea to go ahead and look up words such as "academicization," "methodology," and "obtrusive." Perhaps I already have an understanding of a word based on my previous knowledge or association (this is referred to as the *connotation* of the word), but it often helps to review the *denotation* (dictionary definition) of a word as well. For example, I could again point out that "criticism" is a word that is usually thought of as showing disapproval of something; however, the denotation further states that criticism involves analysis and scholarly investigation, especially when dealing with written texts.

Next, I would summarize Graff's text in my own words so that I know I understand it. What is Graff arguing? What kinds of examples does he use to support his argument? I would start by noting that Graff strategically places an opposing argument before his own. He begins by acknowledging that many people disagree with what they consider the over-analysis of literature, or what Graff calls "the academicization of literature"—a reference to how we thoroughly study and break apart literature in the classroom. According to Graff, "naysayers" (those who disagree with the academicization of literature) believe that analysis can lead to the loss of passion for literature. Graff then

---

3. Gerald Graff, "Disliking Books at an Early Age," in *Falling Into Theory*, 2nd ed. Ed. David Richter (Boston: Bedford/St. Martin's, 2000), 44–5.

offers his own experience as a rebuttal to those naysayers, asserting that literary analysis can often be the means to an appreciation and passion for literature.

After making sure I understand what is being said in the text, I am now faced with the challenge of interpretation and analysis. I interpret much of Graff's argument as a rebuttal against those who think academics do nothing but destroy the "fun" of reading, and, as an English instructor, I recognize Graff's frustration. I am often frustrated when people think that my job is to destroy the joys of reading literature. I agree with Graff that analysis is part of the fun of reading. Furthermore, I get the feeling that Graff is also refuting the idea that reading literature is ever a purely "innocent" act. In other words, Graff is arguing that readers *always* approach a text with personal biases and opinions and that explicitly stating those biases allows for deeper understanding and further discussion among readers.

In order to further my interpretation and analysis, I also begin to make connections between Graff's essay and other texts I've read—and these connections, of course, are part of the "conversation of other readers" that Graff describes. For example, Michael Parker's "Talking Back to Books: In Defense of Marginalia" argues for a similar connection between readers and writers and argues that putting them in conversation with one another through readers' marginalia allows for more enjoyable reading.[4] He emphasizes not only the pleasure he gets from reading the marginalia left in books by their previous owners, but he further suggests that others' comments act as a guide for his own interpretations of what he reads. Like Graff, Parker values the back-and-forth of different interpretations and believes these various interpretations make the reading process more interesting. In addition to the connections I can make between Graff's essay and other texts, it is important to place Graff's essay into a broader context by considering the author himself. With a little research I can find that Graff is a professor of English who has also co-written, with Cathy Birkenstein, the popular composition textbook *They Say/I Say*, a textbook that furthers Graff's belief that students should be made aware of the ongoing conversations in academic discourse about all sorts of texts and topics. This background information about Graff's career as a writer and professor, along with Graff's own descriptions of his personal experience (look back at the passage when Graff states, "In my case, however"), enhance Graff's ethos. As a reader, I find him knowledgeable about his subject, reliable in his opinion, and approachable in his style. By reading carefully and critically, and by engaging with Graff's essay on a deeper level and with more background

---

4. Michael Parker, "Talking Back to Books: In Defense of Marginalia," in *Composing Knowledge*, ed. Rolf Norgaard (Boston: Bedford/St. Martin's, 2007), 380–385.

information, I have gained a better understanding of his argument and can now feel confident in any response I might have to the text.

The following list includes steps, or guidelines, for how to read critically. You've probably used many of these techniques while reading, perhaps without knowing that you were making yourself a more active reader. By making these steps more explicit, this list is intended to help you become more aware of your own reading process and to analyze and understand texts more fully, thereby giving you the opportunity to make the most out of what you read.

» Steps for Successful Critical Reading:

1. Take notes. This seems obvious, but many of us forget. Make sure to write your thoughts as marginalia (notes made in the open spaces of a hardcopy text) while you read. It helps to think of a text as a wall, ready for your graffiti. The margins are a perfect place for readers to make their mark, ask questions, and emphasize their responses.

2. If you don't get it the first time, try again. Read difficult texts (or at least difficult parts) more than once, and look up the meanings of words you do not know. It further helps to read confusing parts out loud. Just as reading your own writing aloud can help you "feel" where you need to work on rhetorical moves, reading others' writing aloud allows you to get a better understanding of the rhetorical moves in their texts.

3. Summarize in your own words. The best way to know for sure that you have understood what you have read is to try to summarize the argument being made in your own words. In order to do this, do not be surprised if you need to yet again pull out the trusty, dusty dictionary to be sure you fully understand the definitions of confusing words.

4. Reflect and respond. Try to take your summary a step further by making some conclusions about what you have read. How did you react? Describe and respond to the claims the writers makes. Do you agree, disagree, or is there a mix of both agreement and disagreement? Do you know any outside information or have you had any past experiences that contribute to your response?

5. Contextualize. Do a little investigating as to the background of the writer and the circumstances surrounding the text. For example, when reading Jonathan Swift's "A Modest Proposal," those who don't know the context of the essay assume that Swift's actual argument is for people to eat babies (yes, I'm serious!). After they do a little research, they begin to understand

that Swift's essay is satirical, meaning that it is social commentary situated in a specific time and place and in response to a specific social-political crisis.

6. Evaluate the text. If, as many rhetoricians insist, everything is an argument, then the reader can assume that anything he or she reads is open for debate. Therefore, it is a good idea for readers to analyze how the writer uses evidence to support his or her claims. Do you think the evidence used is effective? How about the way the evidence is used? In other words, is the structure of the text itself effective? Are you drawn to the writer's style, or do you find it ineffective or distracting? How are the appeals (ethos, pathos, and logos) used?

There are many ways to read critically, and these are simply a few that I have found work well for me. As you practice reading actively and with intent, you will find your own methods for understanding and interpreting what is being read.

Invention, Asking Questions to Find a Starting Point

Kathleen T. Leuschen

Tim has just received an assignment that requires him to write an essay on a topic he finds interesting. The trouble is that Tim, like many students, is fascinated by and curious about a variety of topics that range in both breadth and depth. Tim almost wishes the professor would have just told him what to write about so he could get it over with. Tim is so busy. How will he figure out what topic to write about for this assignment? How will he know what angle to take to fulfill the requirements of the assignment? How much research must he complete to develop a cogent argument? Instead of feeling overwhelmed, or choosing the first idea that comes to mind, or procrastinating until the very last minute, Tim can use the rhetorical canon of invention to help him choose a topic that is both interesting to him and that will efficiently fulfill the requirements of the assignment. The following explains one way that Tim can use invention to generate questions as he composes a rhetorical argument.

In the past, Tim has not taken the time to consider how he will invent his project. He just rushed through the process in order to complete the assignment only later to discover that his initial approach did not produce an effective rhetorical argument. Now, Tim understands that finding a starting point will shape the trajectory of his work. While reading Edward Said, Tim underlined the following quote: "There is no such thing as a merely given, or simply available, starting point: beginnings have to be made for each project in such a way as to enable what follows from them".[1] What Tim knows is that the kinds of questions he asks will shape the direction of his project. This means it is imperative for Tim to think about the composition of his questions as he writes them down. There are several elements to consider when composing questions: generality

> "There are several elements to consider when composing questions: generality and/or specificity, assignment requirements, and the stance from which he will begin."

1. Edward Said, *Orientalism* (New York: Vintage Books, 2003), 16.

and/or specificity, assignment requirements, and the stance from which he will begin. This is because the kind of question Tim asks will necessarily define the amount of research he will need to complete in order support his thesis. It will also determine the kinds of evidence, arguments, and persuasive techniques he should employ. The various elements that Tim will consider overlap in multiple ways.

First, when Tim is asking questions as a tool of invention, he considers the assignment requirements or the genre of what he is being asked to compose. For example, a rhetorical analysis assignment would require Tim to think about how the speaker creates and delivers a text to persuade a particular audience. A polemic essay assignment would require Tim to act as rhetor, imagine an audience, and craft a text that might persuade his imagined audience. Different genres of assignments will require different forms of questions to fulfill the assignment requirements. Moreover, the assignment genre will also help Tim decide how general or specific his questions should be. This is because general questions will require a breadth and depth of knowledge that will also necessitate extensive research and synthesis. More specific questions still require substantial research, but it will be more feasible for Tim to attend to the topic with depth, precision, and persuasion without writing an entire book length argument. Here are some examples of general and specific questions:

> *General Question:* Should students complete their homework?
>
> *Specific Question:* Should Tim write the first draft of his rhetorical analysis this weekend?
>
> *General Question:* Should schools go to a year round schedule rather than have summers off?
>
> *Specific Question:* Should the Council Bluffs Community School District move forward with its proposal to change the school calendar to six weeks in session followed by two weeks off instead of keeping their traditional calendar that has a ten-week summer break?

Notice a general question has a broad application, meaning it could be applied to a variety of concrete situations. A specific question refers to a particular subject and situation. Tim will choose the generality or specificity of his question according the assignment he was given.

It is important to acknowledge that when Tim composes questions, they are not simply general or specific; there are many levels of broad and narrow ideas.

The generality or specificity of a question is most usefully thought of as part of a continuum. In other words, it is only in relation to one another that questions can be identified as general or specific. Hence, the answers given to a specific or general question about the same topic are connected. If Tim answers that he should complete his homework this weekend rather than see a movie, go to a party, or play Wii, he would have logically answered the more general question above with a yes, he believes students should complete their homework. Here is an example of types of questions that move from general to specific:

General: Do all people have the right to access education?

More specific: Do immigrants have the same right to access education as U.S. citizens?

Even more specific: Should the government of the United States pass the Dream Act that allows the children of illegal immigrants to go to college?

Very specific: Should UNCG make provisions for Walburga to attend classes while she is working on securing legal residence in the U.S.?

The first question raises issues about the abstract. Notice how as the questions become more specific, the subject of the questions becomes about fewer and fewer people, places, or events.

Another element that Tim will consider when trying to find a place to begin his argument is to think about the stance or angle that he will take in his questions and answers. Again, Tim will consider the requirements of the assignment. If Tim decided he was very interested in writing about apples, there are various directions he could take that topic. He should consider some of these directions when composing questions. Tim could write about any of the following or other topics: the symbolism of apples in literature and art, the genetic makeup of an apple, the health benefits of humans consuming apples, and labor and wages issues concerning those who produce apples for the market. Each of the questions takes different perspectives about apples, and when Tim decides that he is most interested in the symbolism of apples in literature and art, he might compose more sub-questions that take him to more specific places. Another lesson Tim has learned from previous assignments is that the more specific he can be for a 4–6-page paper, the more space he has for his own voice and analysis. This means that even if Tim is concerned about reaching the page length of the assignment, a more specific topic will actually allow him to expound more on his argument about it.

Tim might create the following sub-questions for his interest in the symbolism of apples in literature and art:

> *General:* What are some of the ideas that apples symbolize in literature?
>
> *More Specific:* What are some of the ideas that apples symbolize in 21st-century literature?
>
> *Even More Specific:* What are some of the ideas that apples symbolize in 21st-century young adult fiction?
>
> *Very Specific:* What does the apple symbolize in the *Twilight* series?
>
> *Most Specific:* If the apple in the *Twilight* series symbolizes the desire for that which one cannot posses, what does this implicitly argue about femininity and sexuality?

After Tim has composed a variety of questions, he will turn to research to find some of the answers to these questions. According to the research he finds, he may adjust his question. Perhaps he finds that the apple in *Twilight* does not address issues of femininity and sexuality but does address issues of masculinity and sexuality. Tim may change his question as he continues through his work. In this way, his questions will shape the direction of his project, but the questions are tentative, meaning they too will be shaped and reshaped by the information Tim acquires as he endeavors to write.

Ultimately, it is important for Tim to take his time when using the rhetorical appeal of invention, but this does not necessarily mean once he has decided on a topic that he will not return to use other strategies of invention throughout his writing process. Asking questions in order to find a starting point and a trajectory for his work will help his writing process be efficient and assist his work in the other appeals.

Pre-Writing Strategies:
Ways to Get Started Successfully

Kristine Lee

One of the most challenging tasks we face is starting the work of writing. You may feel a sense of dread at the prospect of putting your thoughts down on paper, or you may be intimidated by the idea that writing must be perfect grammatically and syntactically. This may be your first college experience, and you may not be sure of the expectations from high school to this class. You may not yet have a structure in place that makes beginning less overwhelming. Thankfully, writing is always a learning process, and one of the best ways to develop your writing is to start the work with a blank slate. Polishing can definitely come later in the writing process. When you receive an assignment sheet or writing prompt in a class, you may be stressed about how to start the assignment, but there are a variety of strategies you can employ to make the process more productive. You may even consider using some of the support available for you on your campus, which can include meeting with the instructor or with a consultant at one of the Multiliteracy Centers to brainstorm ways to start. (For additional information about the Multiliteracy Centers on campus, please see Stacy W. Rice's chapter "The Multiliteracy Centers: Empowering Writers, Speakers, and Designers to Communicate Effectively.")

In high school or previous writing classes, you may have used a traditional Roman numeral or lettered outline to begin the writing process, but College Writing courses will expose you to a number of other ways to get started in addition to this one. Every writer has their own rhetorical choices to make regarding how to begin. There isn't just one way to begin the writing process, and each assignment might require a different strategy. As you get started, be flexible with trying a variety of strategies, be creative, and be sure to avoid procrastination. Here are a few helpful strategies to get you started:

> "As you get started, be flexible with trying a variety of strategies, be creative, and be sure to avoid procrastination."

- **Brainstorming:** This is one of the most valuable initial strategies for writers to use because of the low stakes involved. Brainstorming is a way of getting your ideas on paper, so you can arrange them for an argument later. It often allows the writer to make connections between ideas before the formal writing process begins, and provides an opportunity to think about what major topics should be covered. Before you ever write a formal paragraph on your essay or presentation, this process jumpstarts your thinking. Some writers brainstorm on paper, through conversation or visuals, or through other methods. As you brainstorm, you may make connections between texts, find evidence for tentative claims, locate page numbers and references to sources to back up these claims, or connect ideas to rhetorical purposes. As you integrate these brainstorming ideas, including transitions and ensuring logical arrangement of your ideas is key to the writing process. This way, your reader can see the connections you make as the rhetor between ideas and how these ideas build your argument throughout your text.

- **Listing:** When you are assigned an essay or other writing assignment, you may find that making a list is an effective starting place. For example, if you were assigned the topic of writing about an issue you are passionate about while including naysayers and privileging your own ideas, you could start by making a list of possible issues you could write about well. This rhetorical choice can make the writing more natural and strengthen your argument since you'll already have more to say and more evidence for your claim. You may also be more confident writing about these topics. For example, if I were writing a list of potential topics for a paper, it might look like this:

  1. Fair treatment of animals at shelters

  2. Access to healthy food, regardless of financial status

  3. The importance of acquiring education

  4. Incorporating technology in the classroom

Then I may add both sides of the argument and where I stand regarding this issue to my list. As a final step, I would narrow down my topic by considering which one I could write about thoroughly and effectively. I could use the list to rank which topics would be most effective for me as a writer, and especially emphasize the topics into which I could insert my voice easily.

- **Conversation:** Some writers benefit most from an oral conversation, and sometimes this is the most effective way to get your ideas flowing. You may find that having a conversation about the topic assigned can help you narrow down ideas, and adding another perspective of the person you're discussing your plans with may provide you with some additional points to consider. A few excellent resources for these kinds of conversations are your peers during peer review; the consultants at the Writing Center, Speaking Center, and Digital ACT Studio; and your instructor, though you are not limited to only these options. As you have a conversation together about your writing, you may find more direction. Consultants at the appropriate Multiliteracy Center, your instructor, and your peers can all ask questions to aid in making your argument more specific, as well as those that will help refine your points to support your argument. As you learn about the rhetorical triangle as an important consideration for your writing, it becomes evident that these conversations with others will allow you to better understand audience. Conversations with others will provide you with an actual audience for your argument and help you to anticipate potential reactions and/or objections.

- **Questions:** Some writers find that writing a list of questions can help them find a focused topic and/or ideas. The benefit of this practice is that it gives you an opportunity to think about the answers you may have to the questions you pose, and it gives you a starting point for finding credible evidence and sources to back up your answers. Asking questions is often the starting point for forming an argument that addresses your conclusions in your thesis. For example:

  - What are three topics that relate to the assignment?

  - Of these three, which one could I write about confidently, following research or preparation?

  - What is my thesis and why is it significant?

  - What parts of the text support my claims?

  - What supporting resources do I need?

Of course, you may ask yourself a variety of additional questions to help jump-start your writing. You may also ask your peers, instructor, or a Multiliteracy Center consultant to suggest some questions that could assist you with starting your writing process. If your instructor does not provide a specific prompt and wants you to write about whatever you like, asking questions may be a helpful way to find a topic. Here are some potential questions you may consider asking:

- What interests me?

- Will I be making an argument in this paper, or responding to something/someone?

- Is there a topic related to my major that I would like to write about?

- Who is involved in this topic I'm addressing? What is their stake in it?

(Refer to Kathleen T. Leuschen's chapter "Invention, Asking Questions to Find a Starting Point" for additional examples and information.)

- **Freewriting:** This method is very different from asking questions because freewriting helps the writer to dive right into the writing process rather than asking questions or listing beforehand. The well-known scholar Peter Elbow promoted this method of beginning the writing process, and you may discover that this is what gets you writing. Maybe you're having a difficult time starting because you're too critical of your own work, or you're not accustomed to writing drafts. It's easy to put pressure on yourself to create a "perfect" text on the first try, but drafting is all about developing your ideas and making changes as you write. For example, Suzanne Collins, author of *The Hunger Games* trilogy, and J.K. Rowling, author of the *Harry Potter* series, drafted their manuscripts several times before publication. These writers, among many others, found that drafting continually changed and developed their work, and sometimes getting started is the hardest part. Freewriting allows the writer to produce without impediment, and without worrying about a polished product. With this strategy, the writer has the freedom to write constantly without stopping, gliding from one idea to the next. Elbow describes a process where editing and producing writing are separate: "The main thing about freewriting is that it is nonediting. It is an exercise in bringing together the process of producing words and putting them down on the page. Practiced regularly, it undoes the ingrained habit of editing at the same time you are trying to produce" (Elbow 69). As writers, we have the tendency to worry about our writing being perfect from the start, but Elbow's act of

> "Freewriting allows the writer to produce without impediment, and without worrying about a polished product."

freewriting supports the idea that there is no perfect writing, and that the most effective way to begin may be ignoring the lower order concerns such as grammar and punctuation, at least initially. Freewriting is all about getting ideas written without the impediments of editing at the time of producing ideas. These polishing processes can occur in a later, more finalized draft. Following a freewriting exercise, you can go back and search for the useful ideas that support the argument you have formed and take out the information that isn't relevant to your claims. You may not use everything from your freewrite; in fact, it's possible that you might use very little of it, but this exercise may point you to new ideas that may have been left out of a more structured pre-writing exercise.

- **Outlining:** While freewriting may be freeing for some writers who respond to arranging texts later, outlining could be helpful for those writers that appreciate structure from the beginning of the writing process. At this point as writers, you are likely familiar with outlining, but this tool can be changed to model an efficient, organized structure for your text that arranges your ideas in a logical order. Some of you may have encountered the formal Roman numeral outline. Here's an example:

    I.   Introduction

    II. Body Paragraph 1

    III. Body Paragraph 2

    IV. Body Paragraph 3

    V. Conclusion

You may recognize this model from high school, but for College Writing courses, we're moving away from the five-paragraph essay and into crafting a more detailed piece of writing. As a result, the outline should become much more detailed. The following example demonstrates a more comprehensive outline you may use for a College Writing course. For this paper, the prompt is asking you to discuss the rhetorical effectiveness of Mike Rose's article "Blue-Collar Brilliance" by examining his use of the rhetorical appeals and triangle:

    I.   Introduction: Include background information about Mike Rose and what makes him credible.

        Working Argument/Thesis: "Blue-Collar Brilliance" is rhetorically persuasive due to the moves Mike Rose makes, including his use of the appeals and the triangle.

    II. Rose's Audience

        A. Other academics

            —Evidence from text along with analysis

        B. Students

            —Evidence from text along with analysis

        C. Blue-collar workers

            —Evidence from text along with analysis

   III. Rose's Context

        A. Personal experience

        B. Observation

        C. Family

   IV. Rose's Text

        A. Argument-centered

        B. Addresses the nay-sayer

    V. Conclusion

      —So what/who cares?

      —What can readers take with them from this text?

      —Why is it important to examine Rose's rhetorical moves?

As a form of pre-writing, outlining helps you with the successful arrangement of your ideas for a paper. Effective arrangement of your claims will make your points more clear, and will build your argument cohesively. (For additional examples, see Appendix.)

- **Webbing/Mapping:** If you are a visual learner, this could be a strategy that provides a clear structure for you. Although an outline can provide organization for a writer, a web or map can provide you with the opportunity to place ideas in a specific order and build on them by connecting parts of the web visually and spatially. A web or map of your ideas aids the writing process by allowing you to develop ideas visually. Placing your ideas in a web or map can help you to make logical connections between claims, center ideas around the argument, and organize sub-topics. (See Appendix for an example of a visual web/map.)

- **Reverse Outlining:** Some of you may find that outlining before writing a paper is not very helpful, but reverse outlining is a completely different process that may be a useful strategy since it focuses on outlining a draft that has already been completed. This method of outlining achieves a different aim since it happens after the writing process has occurred and not beforehand, and it relies on your choice of arrangement. One of the techniques many writers draw on is their familiarity with outlining, as demonstrated in the previous examples. However, drafting a reverse outline will require you to start with a completed draft of your paper. This may be an exercise you find beneficial during peer review. Creating a reverse outline gives you an opportunity to examine structure, locate places that may require further development, and determine if your paper has been sufficiently argued and supported. Here's how to start the process: look back through each paragraph of your paper and write a one-sentence summary of the main idea. Number the paragraphs on the draft to correspond with the numbers on your reverse outline for ease of use. After you've completed these steps, consider looking at these areas for improvement:

  - Paragraphs that could be broken down into shorter paragraphs or combined into longer paragraphs for organizational purposes.

  - Paragraphs that include too many topics for one area of the paper. In these cases, you may break these down into a few paragraphs and develop your ideas further.

  - Places where an idea is repeated more than once, or reiterated in the exact same way. Consider omitting or rephrasing to avoid repetition.

  - Cohesion is an important element of crafting a persuasive paper. If you find that there are places where it isn't clear where your paper is going, consider re-ordering your ideas.

  - Ideally, each paragraph should support the main argument of your text. If you find one that seems off topic, revise it to fit the topic—or you may strike it.

One of the best aspects of writing is the ability to make it your own from beginning to end—there is no one correct way to get started. Many writers have said that getting started is the hardest part of writing, and using these methods or others of your own to begin the writing process takes the pressure off of that first step to your final draft. You'll find that beginning writing, in

75

one way or another, keeps you from procrastinating and gives you a head start on the draft you'll bring for peer review. You may also have a variety of other strategies that you use for getting started, and you may consider discussing these in class or mentioning what you've discovered works best for you when another assignment comes along. You are, by no means, limited to this list of suggestions. The most important thing is that you find a method that aids you in creating ideas for writing.

"There is no one correct way to get started."

» Works Cited

Elbow, Peter. "Freewriting." *The Arlington Reader: Contexts and Connections*, Third Edition. Eds. Lynn Z. Bloom and Louise Z. Smith. New York, NY: Bedford, St. Martin's, 2011. 67–70. Print.

Rose, Mike. "Blue-Collar Brilliance." *They Say/I Say, with Readings*, Second Edition. Eds. Gerald Graff, Cathy Birkenstein, and Russel Durst. New York, NY: W.W. Norton and Company, 2012. 243–255. Print.

How the Thesis Guides Effective Writing

Charlie McAlpin

What is a thesis? We hear this word thrown about constantly in our classes—"make sure you have a strong thesis"—but few students feel comfortable with their ability to explain what exactly a thesis is and why instructors emphasize it. *Thesis* is like one of those words we encounter in a novel that we could not really define if prompted, but we basically understand it in the context of the sentences surrounding it. But we need to pay more attention to this word, *thesis*, because it embodies the whole project of an essay. The thesis frames your discussion, gives it purpose and energy, keeps both you and your reader focused on the essay's significance, and invests power into your conclusions. By taking some time to figure out how a thesis functions within the larger context of the essay, we become more active agents in its construction and offer a more persuasive product to our audiences. The writing process also becomes less mystifying, more empowering, and, yes, more fun.

A thesis is an argument. "Make sure you have a strong thesis" means "make sure you have a strong argument."[1] Instructors insist on a thesis because they don't want stale book reports. They want you to bring in your own voice and make claims. Professor Smith knows what happened to the Cherokee nation in Georgia; she wants to see what you can say about it. She wants you to introduce your perspective, to join the exchange of ideas that embodies the ideal of higher education. She wants to see your interpretation of the material.

You are probably comfortable with this kind of discussion about the thesis. It may be as much as anyone has bothered to tell you about the meaning behind this complex word. But this chapter's argument—my thesis—claims that the term embodies much more significance when we think about its function in the essay as a whole. By exploring the myriad ways that a "strong thesis" can make an essay persuasive for our audience, we empower ourselves to construct more compelling arguments.

---

1. Bear in mind that the technical academic definition is a little different: *thesis* simply means a unique perspective on an issue, and the pithy declaration in your introduction is your *thesis statement*, which outlines that unique perspective. By defining *thesis* as *argument*, we are relying on a broader definition that lends more clarity and force to these terms.

Examining the history of the word *thesis*, its etymology, will help us to understand its use in guiding our arguments. According to the *Oxford English Dictionary*, *thesis* is an ancient Greek word that described the "setting down of the foot or lowering of the hand in beating time." In other words, it meant keeping a beat like a bass drum. This definition is instructive in two ways: first, it indicates that a thesis comes down hard, forcefully, and clearly. Second, it implies repetition; the thesis does not simply represent an emphatic introduction but also a steady prominent rhythm. Thus, we can characterize the argumentative thesis as something that must both begin clearly and also reappear regularly throughout an essay.

A clear and engaging thesis introduces a persuasive essay, but it is rarely easy to invent such a thesis. As you decide what to write about, keep "a thesis is an argument" in mind. Scholarship is a conversational exercise. Instead of writing to the void, persuasive scholars show how the thesis conflicts and agrees with other people's arguments. We research secondary sources so we can enter this conversation, learn from it, and allow these voices to illuminate our own ideas. Nobody expects us to be spontaneous geniuses, nor would such an attitude benefit a community of thinkers. But by conceptualizing the thesis as an argument, we let others help us decide what is worth arguing and how to argue it.

"An essay must begin with a strong thesis—a compelling argument—because our readers need to know what to expect from the following pages."

An essay must begin with a strong thesis—a compelling argument—because our readers need to know what to expect from the following pages. As you write, think of your reader as someone to whom you owe a debt. You can start to repay that debt by making a substantial down payment, and that is your opening thesis statement. The thesis tells your reader what you will argue throughout the paper and thus provides an overarching logic that will contextualize the body of your essay. By extension, the thesis should also imply or even explicitly state the major pieces of evidence that you will discuss in your essay. Your goal here, in the first or second paragraph as a general rule, is to set your foot down forcefully and establish the beat.

For a thesis to come down with force, it needs to be clear and concise. Your reader should be able to identify the argument and predict the discussion's trajectory. If a thesis is vaguely or sprawlingly constructed, it will lose its force and leave your audience feeling off balance and disoriented. Unclear theses are especially problematic in speeches, where audiences cannot take the time to read the thesis statement carefully. I frame this problem in terms of our audience, but it applies to us as writers as well. If we can't condense our thesis into a compact kernel of potential energy, then we won't be able to effectively break it down and persuasively argue its parts. Overly broad theses will send you flying past your page limit, falling into weak generalizations, or simply feeling lost about how to proceed. On the other hand, excessively minute theses that can be proven in a page or two will cause different problems. The trick is to find that happy middle ground where you can persuasively work through your argument's components in the space provided. Thus, a clear and concise thesis both provides the writer with a guiding framework for the essay and also makes the audience comfortable with that framework.

Oftentimes we leave our thinking about the thesis right there in the first couple of paragraphs, but the best essays revisit it continuously. Most of us have gotten to that point in a paper where we stop, realize we have no idea what we are saying or how to proceed, and panic. You can deal with this common dilemma in several ways: go back to your notes, your primary text, or your secondary sources for new ideas and clarifications. However, one of the most helpful strategies is to go back to your thesis. As you become lost in your mental gymnastics, your thesis remains apart, clear and forceful, keeping a steady beat. If you look back at your thesis and figure out how you want to proceed, that's great, but the larger point here is that *your audience may have become lost, too.* Do we expect readers to also go back and find the thesis for clarification? Probably not. We are the writers. That is our job.

The example of writer's block functions to prove a larger point. We need to remind both our audience and ourselves how the discussion relates to the thesis—throughout the essay—and it is our responsibility to do the reminding. We call this *signposting*. Whenever you have pursued a train of thought for a couple of paragraphs, or a couple of pages, and begin to transition to a new argumentative point, take the time to figure out where you are positioned in proving your thesis. Ask yourself how that point fits and how your next point will build upon it, and spell out that intersection for yourself and your audience.

Look two paragraphs back, for example, at how the first sentence carefully shifts our discussion from the introduction to the body of an essay, support-ing my thesis by claiming that this is where some of the thesis's really crucial work happens. The "keeping a steady beat" metaphor also provides a recurring signpost, designed to remind you of the thesis's relevance throughout an essay. The exercise of signposting thus keeps writers focused on the thesis so we stay on track, avoid tangents, and hit all the necessary elements of our argument. It also keeps audiences oriented and engaged, helping them place our current evidence and analysis into the context of the essay's larger claims. Signposts are especially important in speeches because listeners will easily lose track of these claims. So while your thesis establishes the beat, signposts keep it loud and steady.

Common knowledge dictates that the conclusion should restate the thesis, and this rule commonly strikes writers as oppressively dull. But this frustration cools when we think about the thesis as a continuous process throughout the essay. If our thesis is a kernel of potential energy, then our analysis is working to make that energy kinetic—to make the kernel pop. Our arguments apply pressure to the thesis and expand it, adding complexity and definition. It is a turbulent process, which is why we signpost to control the progression. Now, should we spend our final paragraph—our big finish—simply copying and pasting what we wrote in the first paragraph? Of course not. That would be a travesty to our hard work. But our essay has excitingly shaped and colored that thesis, and the conclusion needs to tie all of that together.

"Restate the thesis" is a weak shorthand for a crucial exercise. The conclusion must remind the audience where the argument began, but it should also embody the complexity that we developed throughout. It needs to pull our thesis and our signposts into one final statement, a closing argument that encapsulates what came before but opens up to larger implications as well. Don't literally restate the thesis, but tie it together as a kind of summary on which you can build some final thoughts that speak to the major implications of your argument. Think of it as a coda, a chance to revisit the rhythm of your thesis, and end it with a final, emphatic bang.

All effective arguments take a side, and this one is no exception. This chapter treats the writing process linearly: you develop a thesis, write your analysis, and finish with a conclusion. Many of us write exactly this way, but many of us do not. Other writers, including plenty of your professors, avoid writing the introductory paragraphs until after they have written the rest of the essay because only then can they adequately understand what the thesis actually *is*. Neither process is right or wrong; writers simply conceptualize the planning and revising processes differently. If you relate more to the latter process, then think of this advice in revision terms: figure out what your thesis was and condense it for the introduction; find the hazy areas of your argument and revise them, then signpost them; finally, rewrite your conclusion to reflect these changes.

Regardless of your process, the final product will only reach its full persuasive potential if it achieves the level of concision and organization that this chapter suggests, and you can only achieve that clarity by focusing on the primacy of the thesis throughout your essay.

Arrangement as Rhetorical Composing

Chelsea Skelley

Imagine three works of art: a painting, a film, and a piece of music. Each requires the artist to carefully arrange the content to be effective for the intended audience. A painter deliberately composes a painting, paying special attention to where and how each element or brushstroke works best for his or her purpose. A director, with the help of a producer and editor, meticulously crafts a final film that evokes the appropriate responses from the viewers, making the audience laugh, cry, jump in their seats, feel relief, or a combination of these and other feelings. A composer painstakingly arranges a piece of music, adapting the piece to suit various musical instruments by adding new material, transitions, and other elements. In each of these cases, the artist conscientiously composes his or her work to ensure that it is compelling. The same principle applies when you as a rhetor compose a written, oral, or visual text. In fact, the musical composition analogy is helpful to keep in mind when drafting an essay. If the thesis statement of an essay serves as an "emphatic beat" and "a steady prominent rhythm" as McAlpin states in "How the Thesis Guides Effective Writing," then using the proper arrangement will determine whether or not you effectively communicate your ideas and arguments to your intended audience(s). As the composer of an essay, you should apply the same careful attention to make sure that your audience can follow your train of thought and understand your points, just as a music composer arranges music for specific instruments, musicians, or genres.

Before discussing some basic organizing principles to use when drafting a piece of rhetoric, let's more thoroughly explore what the canon of arrangement involves. Arrangement typically refers to organizing an oral, written, or visual piece of rhetoric in order to successfully persuade an audience. In classical rhetoric a speech is typically divided into six parts: 1) Introduction (*exordium*); 2) Statement of facts (*narratio*); 3) Division (*partitio*); 4) Proof (*confirmatio*); 5) Refutation (*refutatio*); and 6) Conclusion (*peroratio*). The introduction should put forth your topic and typically, as argued by the Roman rhetor Quintilian, should establish your credibility, building trust with the audience.

Do not underestimate the importance of drafting a compelling introduction. Remember that an audience often determines their initial opinion about your quality as a rhetor and the merit of your ideas during the introductory paragraph. During the statement of facts, provide enough background information to ground your audience. This is key since if you simply state your argument without contextual information, your audience may understand your point but not the importance of what you are trying to argue. After stating your facts, move into your argument by summarizing the points you plan to explain. This serves as the division section of your speech or essay. It is helpful to consider this section a roadmap, outlining where you plan to take your audience, which makes it easier for them to follow your logic.

Following the division, the proof section is the main body of the essay wherein you will make your key argument. Typically using logos, you will build your argument, carefully moving from point to point while connecting to the ideas discussed in your statement of facts. This will ensure that you are making well-grounded, reasonable arguments. Once you've convincingly stated your case, address the weaknesses of your argument in the refutation. Initially this may seem damaging to your argument and overall ethos, but addressing your naysayers gives you a chance to show the audience that you have considered the opposing side, and it allows you the opportunity to counter their points. Sound arguments show the audience that you, at least, acknowledge what the opposition has to say, which in turn builds your ethos as a rhetor. Finally, you should conclude your paper concisely, yet powerfully, by summing up your argument. For classical rhetoricians, the conclusion serves as the most appropriate section for using pathos to memorably appeal to your audience's emotions. As you can see from this classical model of arrangement, Roman rhetoricians assigned specific rhetorical appeals to each part of an oration for maximum effectiveness, using ethos in the introduction, logos in the statement of facts, division, proof, and refutation, followed by pathos in the conclusion.

This basic structure for an essay or speech is quite effective, but it may seem too prescriptive and formulaic. It is important to remember that there is no hard and fast rule that says you cannot alter the organization of your writing to suit your needs and those of your audience. In fact, you may find that given specific audience expectations, subject matter, genre conventions, etc. you *should* organize your essays differently from this standard model. For example, if you really want to drive a few points home, you would repeat your main points for emphasis before moving into the refutation. Or if you know that the counter arguments to your argument are particularly strong, you may wish to address those in your refutation before your proof section. You will find that as your ideas and argument take shape, your arrangement will change as well. The thing to remember is that arrangement is quite flexible, and it is up to the rhetor to decide what is best given the distinct rhetorical situation.

Now, given this basic framework for rhetorical arrangement, you may ask, how do I choose the best arrangement for my purposes? To do so you should consider a few rhetorical modes and principles for organizing your ideas, meaning you should find a few ways that will help you develop and articulate your arguments as effectively and logically as possible. For example, you might choose the quite common compare and contrast mode to discuss standardized tests versus essay format exams. Or the familiar cause and effect structure might help you make a claim about the effects of social networks on one's thought and communication processes. You may find a genre that requires you to use a process structure, outlining step by step how something happens or how one should do something, like how to upload a YouTube video. Or an assignment may call for you to define an idea, moving from a broad definition to a more distinct, narrower concept. For example, you could choose this mode to explain how you think marriage should be culturally and/or legally defined. Other essays might require you to narrate an event, such as a first-hand literacy narrative in which you describe a time when reading or writing greatly affected your life. As a scholar, you will find these common rhetorical modes helpful in drafting and developing various types of arguments, even when used in various combinations.

In addition, a few organizing principles will also help you to successfully arrange your thoughts. These include ordering your ideas chronologically, spatially, climactically, or topically. Chronological order relates to time, meaning that you arrange your ideas in the order that they occur, a particularly effective arrangement for narration and process essays. If you write about a historical event such as the Civil Rights Movement, for example, you might logically choose to relay the major events of the movement chronologically. Spatial organization is quite useful for a variety of topics as you lay out your ideas or items based on physical relationships. For example, if you are tasked with describing a house, you would move your audience spatially around the structure moving room-to-room, paragraph-to-paragraph as if you are giving them a tour. Or you may find this organization effective for arranging your thoughts about social issues. For example, if writing a paper about immigration policies in the United States, you can orient your audience spatially by outlining different states' immigration policies, spatially noting the differences between southern and northern border-states. When arranging your ideas climactically, you typically present them in order of importance. You may move from least important to most, from general ideas to very specific, simplest to most complex, most familiar to least, etc., depending on what you wish to emphasize.

Using topical arrangement, you order your ideas in relation to the topic itself. For example, you could write a review about a specific product, first briefly outlining the manufacturer, then describing the product itself, followed by a review of its merit, concluding with the product's availability through specific vendors. Both climactic and topical arrangements are quite common and can be used for multiple genres and assignments.

Having all these various modes and principles at your disposal, the key aspect to remember when outlining your ideas is to make sure you logically move from idea to idea, and, more specifically, paragraph to paragraph. When moving from one paragraph to the next, pay careful attention to your use of transitions, making sure that you use the most logical and suitable words or phrases to guide your reader. Consider these phrases as road signs helping direct your audience so that they may easily follow along. This often proves tricky if you are uncertain about the logical relationship you are trying to establish between your ideas. For help in choosing the appropriate transitions, Table 1 on page 85 (adapted from UNC Chapel Hill, Michigan State, and Southwest Tennessee Community College) may be of some use. Using this table as a guide will aid you in selecting the proper words for the rhetorical move you are making in the next paragraph. For example, when writing a review, if you discuss the new, innovative features of a smart phone in one paragraph, then, in the following paragraph, outline the much improved battery life, you do not want to use "however" as a transition. This implies a contrast; rather, you would use a transition like "additionally." Choosing the most suitable transitions to best arrange your work will not only make it simpler for you to think about, develop, and remember your arguments, it will also help your audience more easily and logically follow along and understand your train of thought. This will help you maintain a sense of coherence throughout your essay.

All of these tools will help you to develop and organize your numerous arguments for various rhetorical situations. Depending on your audience, genre, assignment, and numerous other factors, this chapter offers you a starting point for formulating your ideas. Careful arrangement allows you, the rhetor, the opportunity to powerfully engage with your audience in a multitude of creative ways. But keep in mind that as your ideas develop, your arrangement will adapt and change as well. So, do not hesitate to shift your ideas around. Experiment with various modes and patterns of organization. For practice, make multiple outlines to test out which will be most effective. Or reverse outline your draft if your writing process leans towards a nonlinear method of writing first and organizing after. These organizational strategies will help you formulate and hone your argument as you try out different arrangements.

Table 1.

Logical Relationship	Transition
Additional Support or Evidence	additionally, again, also, and, as well, besides, equally important, indeed, further, furthermore, in addition, moreover, then
Cause and Effect	accordingly, as a result/consequence, because (of), consequently, for this reason, hence, so, therefore, thus
Concession	admittedly, albeit, although, be that as it may, but even so, despite (this), granted, in spite of (this), nevertheless, even though, nonetheless, notwithstanding (this), on the other hand, regardless (of this), though
Conclusion/ Summary	finally, in a word, in brief, in conclusion, in the end, in the final analysis, on the whole, thus, to conclude, to summarize, in sum, in summary, consequently, hence, in short
Digression	by the way, incidentally, to change the topic
Dismissal	all the same, at any rate, either way, in any case/event, whichever/whatever happens
Emphasis	above all, even, even more, indeed, in fact, of course, more importantly, truly
Elaboration	actually, by extension, in short, that is, to put it another way, ultimately
Example	for example, for instance, namely, specifically, to illustrate
Exception/ Contrast	but, however, in spite of, on the one hand ... on the other hand, nevertheless, nonetheless, notwithstanding, in contrast, on the contrary, still, whereas, yet
Importance	a more effective..., best of all, even more so, frequently, more importantly, occasionally, still worse
Place/Position	a bit further, above, adjacent, below, beyond, here, in front, in back, nearby, to the right/left, there
Resumption	anyhow, anyway, at any rate, to get back to the point, to resume, to return to the subject
Sequence/Order	first, second, third, next, then, finally, another
Similarity	also, in the same way, just as ... so too, likewise, similarly, along the same lines
Time	after, afterward, at last, before, currently, during, earlier, immediately, later, meanwhile, now, recently, simultaneously, subsequently, the following day, then

The Play of Style

Ann-Marie Blanchard

Our writing style evolves every time we put a word on the page. Daily, we perceive the world in new ways, and these experiences inspire us to see the world differently; hence, the person we are each time we come to the page is a little different than the person we were in previous writing sessions. Our style is not fixed, nor are we "stuck" with one style, nor does anybody own a style that nobody else can explore. Although I am suggesting style is forever changing, it is also founded on our history: the family we were born into, the kids we played with in our neighbourhood, the personality of our hometown. It is when we bring our past experiences to the page that our writing is often the most vibrant as we connect with what we know and the diction that comes to us most naturally. Our style will continue evolving as we have new experiences, and part of the fun of writing is found when we take stylistic risks, by trying out something we have never done before, and by enjoying the freedom and fluidity of performing unlimited stylistic choices.

As students of rhetoric, we must consider the five rhetorical canons: invention, arrangement, style, memory, delivery. Each canon offers insight into the steps taken by a rhetor. I believe style is one of the more exciting rhetorical phases, as you get to have fun with your piece by artfully playing with ways to share your ideas. However, before we look further at the ways you can play with your style, let us first consider what style is and why it is a core component in every rhetorical situation.

Style is easy to understand when thinking of the way we dress, but it can seem more challenging to pinpoint in writing. When getting dressed for class, are you more inclined to throw on a sweater or spend an hour preparing yourself before class? Think now about what these choices regarding your self-presentation say to the people you see throughout the day. What might people think about you by interpreting your style of dress, e.g., that you're a hipster because you're wearing your grandmother's vintage sweater? What does that say about you? The clothes you choose to wear persuade people to assume certain things about your personality. And just as we dress to communicate to others, writers write because they have something to say, and that which they wish to say can be said in an infinite number of ways. Style, then, is the way in which the author chooses to say what it is they have to say, and through these words he/she fosters a certain kind of relationship with their reader.

To demonstrate, let's look at two passages by Nathaniel Hawthorne.[1] Hawthorne writes two accounts of a situation, one fictionalised, the other a personal account, and as you'll see, he chooses very different ways to tell the story. In *Our Old Home* a gentleman travels through Liverpool and stops at a workhouse, where he meets a sickly child that won't leave him alone. The narrator says, "So I watched the struggle in his [the gentleman's] mind with a good deal of interest, and am seriously of the opinion that he did a heroic act…when he took up the loathsome child and caressed it as tenderly as if he had been its father" (218). Hawthorne, as it turns out, fictionalised this moment from his own life, as seen in his personal journal: "We went upstairs into another ward; and on coming down again there was this same child waiting for me, with a sickly smile around its defaced mouth, and in its dim-red eyes…I should never have forgiven myself if I had repelled its advances" (219). As these accounts demonstrate, Hawthorne changed the way he tells this story to produce two very different accounts of the same instance. In the first account, there are words like "heroic," "caressed," and "tenderly," which romanticise the event in a way that is less confronting for an audience. In the second account, the word choices emphasize the child's sickness: "defaced," "dim-red eyes." There's nothing cute about the way this story is told, and yet the story has much more power because Hawthorne does not shy away from the child's sickness, or portray himself as a saintly figure, but instead chooses words that are harsh, pointed and authentic. As you can see, the way Hawthorne told this story changed, as the genre and intended audience influenced him to make different stylistic choices.

Writers make many technical choices that ultimately create their style, such as grammar, figurative language, syntax and diction. You have seen the impact of Hawthorne's varied word choices and how this produces different effects. The culture we grow up in influences our speech (word choice/phrases), and this style of speech we perform is called diction. In the following excerpt, Narritjin Maymuru, an indigenous Australian, writes to the director of Aboriginal

---

1.   In choosing Hawthorne's texts as prime examples to demonstrate style, I am indebted to Flannery O'Connor's work *Mystery and Manners* wherein she compares Hawthorne's two accounts. O'Connor, Flannery. "Introduction to a Memoir of Mary Ann." *Mystery and Manners*. Ed. Robert Fitzgerald and Sally Fitzgerald. New York: Farrar, Straus and Cudahy, 1979. 213–228. Print.

Welfare in the North Territory to speak out against the mining companies that are destroying his clan's sacred land:

> Mr Gise who looking after for all the Aborigines in the N.T. We want to help us belong to this country Yirrkala, please Mr Gise? Because the Maining campany will be here soon. All the Aborigines in Yirrkala are wondering about this country. What we are going to do Mr Gise? You think us a funny? or you think us a good people. You going to help us Mr Gise? or no.[2]

Maymuru, an indigenous Australian, was unable to write in his first language to communicate with the authorities of the territory, and so he melds the native rhythms of his tongue with English, producing a truly unique and provocative style. The very fact that this letter is not written in Standard English (the preferred dialect of the academy) is exactly why it catches our attention and draws us in to the suffering of these people who fear their land will be stripped by the mining industry. Fresh language catches our attention because we are so accustomed to clichés and catch phrases—the same old. Reading something unexpected wakes us up and helps us to connect more deeply with the author and the purpose of their piece.

As Maymuru's piece demonstrates, you can take the diction that comes naturally and create hybridised styles by engaging with new rhetorical approaches. Why am I telling you this in a chapter about style in the academic world? Because although the academy encourages that we write in Standard English, there are ways of combining your dialect with the shared dialect in thoughtful and inventive ways to build your style. I, as an Anglo-Saxon Australian, have had to reconsider my oral and written style once I moved to the USA because some words I would normally choose wouldn't be understood. For example, "Hey, do you wanna catch up this arvo?" would be more easily understood if I simply said, "Hey, are you free this afternoon?" Just as I need to make choices about adjusting my colloquialisms, I also have to consider how transparent my language will be in an academic setting. In this chapter I wrote, "are you more inclined to throw on a sweater or spend an hour preparing yourself before class?" Australians tend to call sweaters "jumpers," but knowing my audience will largely be Americans and American immigrants, I chose to use a shared word that would likely be understood by everybody. In this sense, what comes naturally isn't always the right style for the moment; in fact, it is often more effective to vary our style depending on each audience we encounter. In the academic world, we experience a melting pot of cultures, races, religious beliefs

2. Maymuru, Narritjin. "Letter to Mr H.E. Giese, Director of Aboriginal Welfare, NT." *The literature of Australia*. Ed. Nicholas Jose. New York: W.W. Norton and Company, Inc, 2009. 615. Print.

and much more. Our audience expands, so we must question how to best take what comes naturally, as a writer, and tweak it slightly to reach a wider audience. Think of it as inviting new readers into your work so that they can hear your story, your beliefs, your new ideas.

Along with diction, another important element of style to consider is syntax. When reading the following excerpts examining death, ask yourself the question, "How do these pieces make me feel?" C.S. Lewis opens *A Grief Observed* with, "No one ever told me that grief felt so like fear. I am not afraid, but the sensation is like being afraid" (1).[3] On the other hand, Sloane Crosley begins "The Pony Problem" with, "As most New Yorkers have done, I have given serious and generous thought to the state of my apartment should I get killed during the day…I never should have left, the bed has gone unmade and the dishes unwashed" (1).[4] As you can see, when placed side-by-side each author's syntax reveals two very different styles, one sincere and vulnerable, the other playful and entertaining, which ultimately make the reader feel very differently. Lewis opens his piece with sentences that do not distract from the deep questions about grief and fear that he wishes to interrogate. There is a sense of focus and a lack of flourish. Sometimes, the simplest sentence can be the most profound because in being stripped down, the sentence can strike the reader with a great deal of impact. A bare-bones sentence, however, is not always going to serve our style. Unlike Lewis, Crosley wants to set a tone that is inviting, energetic and humorous, which she does by writing lengthier sentences, tongue-in-cheek adjectives ("generous thought") and using more sophisticated language that is funny because her topic is not formal but comic. Often as writers we tend towards sentences that feel safe and we avoid venturing out of our syntactical habits. If you're more of a Lewis, perhaps it's time to try a Crosley approach or vice versa.

Writing with style requires courage, just as bringing our experiences to the academy requires courage. When we are timid, our style suffers, as we start to play it safe with what we say and how we say it. We don't want to assert anything too strongly, in case somebody might disagree. Or, we state things so decisively that we alienate our readers. Consider the courageous title of Sue Hum's academic essay: "'Yes, We Eat Dog Back Home': Contrasting Disciplinary Discourse and Praxis on Diversity."[5] Hum does not shy away from popular assumptions about her culture. Courageously, she employs humour to open up the topic of diversity, and then in the subtitle she uses academic discourse

---

3. Lewis, C.S. *A Grief Observed*. New York: The Seabury Press, Inc., 1976. Print.

4. Crosley, Sloane. *I Was Told There'd Be Cake*. New York: Riverhead Books, Inc. 2008. Print.

5. Hum, Sue. "Yes, We Eat Dog Back Home: Contrasting Disciplinary Discourse and Praxis on Diversity." 19.4 (1999): 569–589. Web. 1 Feb. 2014.

to target her chosen audience of scholars. In saying "yes," Hum affirms her culture, rather than defending a norm that other cultures do not understand or respect. This is, therefore, a celebration of her narrative and the narrative of her people. Hum could have chosen not to give her essay the title, "Yes, We Eat Dog Back Home," but instead she discovers a way of uniting her culture with the academy.

Two lessons can be learned from Hum's title: the importance of mining your own experiences and the power of putting your own unique thoughts forward in a fresh and provocative way. Pamela J. Annas states, "People write well—with passion and color—when they write out of their experience and when that experience is seen as valuable so that they have the confidence to write it" (361).[6] Once in an academic setting, it is easy to belittle our personal histories and to consider our beliefs unimportant since there are already so many distinguished thinkers surrounding us. However, just as Annas states, profound writings come from those who engage with their own experience and write about what they care about—what others need to know about. Not all classes will allow for narrative papers; however, writing from your experience does not necessarily have to be a particular story from your past. Rather, you might simply focus on what your life has thus far taught you, and then you can find ways to pursue the topics that you feel the most passionate about. In finding that which you really care about, you're bound to write with more ease and enthusiasm.

Practically speaking, the best time to think about your style is not when you write the first draft of your paper. As previously mentioned, often when we attempt to put our words down for a scholarly audience, we freeze. A great way of finding your style and the way you want to perform for a particular paper is to begin your essay with a discovery draft, which is a free-write where you put all your thoughts down on the paper without going back to check your grammar or train of thought. Just throw it all down as it comes to mind. Don't rush. Just write as fast as your hand will move (and yes, it's often great to do this the traditional way, pen-to-paper, so that you experience the tactile act of choosing your words). Even once you turn to your next draft or two, I would avoid spending too much time considering your style, but once it comes to your final drafts, it's time to take each of your words and sentences to task.

Before an outside audience reads your text, try to remove yourself and play the role of reader. A good way to do this is to put your writing aside for at least twenty-four hours so that when you return to it you can have fresh eyes and

---

6.   Annas, Pamela J. "A Feminist Approach to the Teaching of Writing." *National Council of Teachers of English.* 47.4 (1985): 360–371. Web. 1 Feb. 2014.

the clarity of a good night's sleep. Once you have edited to the best of your ability, you can then turn it over to a wider audience, such as peer editors, consultants, or your professor during office hours to talk over certain sections. In peer reviews, you might get feedback that surprises you, such as "the author sounded really annoyed," "I didn't like some of the casual words they chose," "this paper feels really impersonal." When writing an essay, the author has a sense of the style they wish to create for the piece, but often a reader might have an unexpected response. Listen to the language used by your readers and ask them specific questions about how they felt reading your piece, such as empowered, saddened, informed, and decide if this fits with your original intent. Return again to your text, and see what stylistic choices you can make to strengthen your argument.

When you face the page, put aside all your assumptions about the kind of writer that you are, good, bad or indifferent, and try taking some risks. At times, you might not like what you produce, but there will be days when you write a sentence, a paragraph, a page, that is nothing like anything you've ever read before. This is why we write. For those moments when style sings.

Understanding Tone and Voice

Lilly Berberyan

Whenever you write something, whether it is an essay for your history class about the Civil War or a casual email to a group of friends inviting them to dinner, you inevitably find yourself dealing with matters of tone and voice. As you consider how you would address the aforementioned scenarios, you are already making the kinds of choices that will lead to the most effective tone and voice in a given rhetorical situation, helping you strengthen your skills as a rhetor.

Even though tone and voice are often conflated in discussion, it might be helpful to think of tone as the kind of mood that a piece of writing might evoke, while voice is the set of specific characteristics that make your writing uniquely different from that of others. In other words, voice is *your personal arsenal* of diction, syntax, and grammar, while tone is *how you use this arsenal* to create a particular mood. Another way to think about tone and voice is through the analogy of attire: When you wake up in the morning, one of the first decisions you make is what to wear based on an anticipated prognosis of your day and the contents of your wardrobe. Your chosen items of clothing constitute your voice as a dresser; the specific items you choose on a given day in response to the different situations you anticipate can be characterized as your tone. In other words, you are limited to what pieces of clothing you own (vocabulary and grammar skills). At the same time, how you utilize what you have—such as ending a sentence in an essay with a period as opposed to the exclamation mark you might use if you were sending a text message to a friend—becomes a matter of tone. Thus, you might wear a shirt with a pair of jeans when heading out to the movies to convey a casual dressing tone; however, you could also wear that same shirt with slacks to convey a more serious tone for an interview.

The analogy of clothing is quite apt in describing tone and voice when considering a specific writing assignment. After analyzing the assignment sheet, you and your classmates may choose to write about the same topic and decide that you will use a serious academic tone. While you might all use the same tone, your essays will be vastly different because your voices will differ. As you work to develop your tone and voice for a specific writing situation, consider the rhetorical triangle: knowing your audience's expectations for a given subject will help you tremendously in establishing your ethos as an author.

» Tone and Voice: A Rhetorical Situation

To better understand how your rhetorical situation influences your tone and voice, consider these examples from *Newsweek* and *Health Communication* discussing the correlation between the MMR vaccine and autism. As you read the following samples, be sure to assess the tone and voice in each by considering these questions:

+ What is the author's purpose?

+ What kind of vocabulary, syntax, and grammar are part and parcel of this author's lexicon?

+ Does the author use neutral or emotionally charged language?

+ What is the mood conveyed by the author?

+ How do I feel about the subject after reading a specific text?

+ How does the author's intended audience influence the tone and voice in a piece of writing?

First, let's look at a portion of an article from *Newsweek* about allegations of the MMR vaccine and supposed links with autism:

Andrew Wakefield, the sham scientist whose now-retracted 1998 paper led millions of parents to believe in a link between autism and the measles/mumps/rubella vaccine, has just lost his license to practice medicine in Britain. [...] If the first principle of medicine is "do no harm," Wakefield should have lost his license a long time ago. To say that his autism study was discredited isn't strong enough. Wakefield apparently lied about the young patients he reported on in his paper; his descriptions of their conditions didn't match up with records kept on file at his hospital. He also lied by omission, neglecting to reveal a huge conflict of interest: he had been paid about a million dollars to advise lawyers of parents who were worried their children had been injured by the vaccine. According to the *Guardian*, Wakefield "tried out Transfer Factor on one of the children in his research programme but failed to tell the child's GP. He took blood from children at a birthday party, paying them £5 a time." Ten of Wakefield's co-authors eventually renounced his study, and *The Lancet*, the journal that had published it, formally retracted it in February. Unsurprisingly, follow-up studies in 2002 and 2005 found no link between autism and the MMR vaccine. By then, though, it didn't matter: Wakefield's paper had gotten too much traction among the general public. Vaccination rates in Britain plummeted, and kids started to get sick. In 2006 a 13-year-old boy died of measles, the first victim in Britain since 1992. (Carmichael)

In analyzing the excerpt, you will note that the article's overall voice is geared towards the general public; names that could be confusing to readers are contextualized, examples are thoroughly explained, and diction that could possibly be confusing to the reader is eliminated. For example, rather than use the shorthand MMR that professionals in the medical community use to refer to the grouping of "measles/mumps/rubella," the author uses the full names of these diseases. Overall, the article seems to be focused on discussing the impact of Andrew Wakefield's study on public perception of vaccinations. While the author's voice is geared towards informing the magazine's readers about an issue that they might not be familiar with, the tone of the article has a more targeted role: that of discrediting the subject of the article—Andrew Wakefield. The author's use of the phrase "sham scientist" to describe Wakefield, her argument that Wakefield's work has caused harm to patients, and the examples of falsified data all work to discredit Wakefield. In this case, her tone changes in accordance to what she would like to convey to her readers—an attitude that would make her readers doubt Wakefield's credentials and his work.

By contrast, an article that originally appeared in *Health Communication* magazine discusses the same topic using a different tone and voice:

Numerous epidemiologic studies subsequently failed to support an MMR-autism link (Gerber & Offit, 2009; Miller & Reynolds, 2009; see also Institute of Medicine, 2004), and criticisms of the study's methods, ethics, and conclusions remained prevalent. Notably, 10 of the study's 13 authors issued a retraction of the MMR-autism interpretation in 2004 (Murch et al., 2004). At the same time, allegations of Wakefield's professional misconduct were publicized by *Sunday Times* investigative reporter Brian Deer (2011a; 2001b). In June 2006, the UK General Medical Council (GMC) formally accused Wakefield of failing to attain ethical review board approval for the study and of failing to disclose that he had received compensation from a lawyer representing several children in the study whose families were involved in autism-related litigation against MMR manufacturers (Offit, 2008). In January 2010, the GMC found him guilty of these charges and revoked his British medical license (Whalen, 2010). One month later, *The Lancet* retracted the original 1998 articles in its entirety. Finally, in January 2011, the *British Medical Journal* published a series of articles that summarized many of the prior accusations and demonstrated how Wakefield falsified data to strengthen the apparent MMR-autism link (Deer, 2011a, 2011b; Godlee, Smith, & Marcovitch, 2011). (Holton et al. 691)

The article is written by several authors and consequently captures a collective voice, which in this case is serious and academic. The general audience of the article knows enough about the subject matter that the authors do not have to spend time contextualizing who Wakefield is or how he relates to autism. Right away, you'll notice that the second example seeks to demonstrate the lack of credibility of Wakefield's study, but does not ever resort to the ad hominem fallacy of attacking Wakefield personally. Rather, it argues that there has not been a clear link between the vaccinations and autism and supports its arguments by relying on studies rather than launching a personal attack against the author. Both the voice and the tone in this excerpt are serious and academic; the voice of the article follows the conventions of scientific writing. Unlike the first excerpt, the authors of this example are concerned with conveying a more formal tone and taking part in academic discourse (e.g., the authors' explanation of abbreviations, such as the "GMC" shows that they are interested in educating their audience when applicable). You'll note the abundance of APA citations throughout the excerpt; these citations help support the authors' credibility while simultaneously enabling the article's audience to find out more about the presented evidence and further engaging in academic discourse. Following the conventions of academic writing, the authors of this article have abstained from making overtly biased statements regarding Wakefield and instead focus on the shortcomings of his study and the surmounting evidence against his credibility.

The two excerpts discuss the same topic, but the authors approach their subject matter from vastly different perspectives. The tonal and vocal differences between the two texts are partly motivated by the authors' perception of their audiences; while the first example is targeted towards a general audience, allowing for a casual tone/voice, the second example is meant for an academic one, necessitating a more formal tone/voice.

» Tone and Voice: Oral Communication

Throughout your college career, you'll be asked to deliver your work both orally and in writing. Oral communication takes various forms, including oral presentations, podcasts, feedback you deliver to your classmates during workshops, and class participation. Like written communication, oral communication is a skill that can be perfected with practice. Whenever you speak up in class, whether during an oral presentation or making a comment in class, you might find yourself elevating the tone of your language. You might find yourself enunciating for clarity, eliminating filler words, and expressing well-thought-out ideas.

Let's briefly go back to the analogy of clothing. Consider what you might choose to wear on a day when you have to deliver a presentation. You will likely choose an outfit that is somewhat formal. Along with your attire, you'll also want to adapt a more formal tone to deliver information to your instructor and your classmates. From the words you choose to the way you convey yourself while presenting in front of a class, you'll need to convey professionalism. The advantage of oral communication over written communication is that the former allows you to gauge your audience's reactions as you go through your presentation. Looking at your audience will allow you to determine if your audience is confused or bored and if so, you can adjust your delivery accordingly.

Another example of oral communication that you might engage in throughout your college career might be the conversations you have with your peers during workshops. Your peers might be your friends, but while you're discussing your writing with each other, you'll find yourself in a position where you have to generate thoughtful and helpful feedback. Thus, the comments you generate for your peers will have to be more formal in tone and go beyond qualitative statements like "this is good" or "this is bad."

» Tone and Voice: Written Communication

While you may not think of tone or voice during the initial stages of your composition process, you should take the time to consider how your writing comes across to your audience when revising your work. Mastering tone and voice and incorporating them into your writing process will help you control how your writing comes across to your audience, guiding the kinds of reactions that you want to elicit from your audience. As you work to develop your tone and voice for a specific writing situation, consider the rhetorical triangle: knowing your audience's expectations for a given subject will help you tremendously in establishing your ethos as an author. (For more information about how to develop your credibility as an author, see Christina Romanelli's chapter "Writing with the Rhetorical Appeals.")

Cultivating and fine-tuning your voice will instill a sense of continuity in your writing. Voice can be acquired and perfected through practice, but you will want to start out with the voice that comes to you naturally and proceed to fine-tune it in each writing project. For example, if you notice that your voice tends to be redundant, you will learn to take out unnecessary words and phrases in your editing process. In a typical week, you may be prompted to complete a number of writing tasks—anything from writing an entry on your blog to researching the effects of caffeine on the human body, and knowing how to manipulate your voice to best fit the requirements of the assignment will help you become a more effective and proficient writer.

Tone varies from one writing project to the next. Tone captures a specific mood expressed through language, conveying the writer's attitude toward a specific subject. You can manipulate tone through the use of words or syntax. As evidenced in the first example on pages 93–94, the simple addition of the word "sham" to "scientist" conveys the author's bias toward her subject and establishes a disparaging tone throughout the excerpt.

As you work to cultivate an effective tone or voice, be sure to keep in mind the various elements of the rhetorical triangle. (For more information about the rhetorical triangle and the relationship between text and audience, see Jacob Babb's chapter "An Introduction to Rhetoric and the Rhetorical Triangle.") Consider such questions shaped by the rhetorical triangle as:

+ What is your relationship with the text?

+ What would you like for your audience to learn about the text after reading your work?

+ How much detail do you need in order for the text to make sense to your audience?

Some additional questions you might want to ask yourself as you write include:

+ Do I need to address this topic in a specific tone or voice?

+ Will my audience easily detect what tone I'm using and is it important that they do?

+ To what purpose am I using a specific tone?

+ Does it achieve this purpose?

+ What do I want my readers to learn, understand, or think about as they read my work?

Your voice and tone can play a crucial role in getting your desired message across to your audience. As you work to develop and improve your writing abilities, it is important to keep in mind just how your writing comes across to your audience. Cultivating and improving your abilities to shape your tone and voice will help you deliver your message to your audience exactly as you want it to be understood.

» Works Cited

Carmichael, Mary. "The 'Autism Doctor' Isn't a Doctor Anymore. Does It Matter?" *Newsweek*, 23 May 2010. Web.

Holton, Avery, et al. "The Blame Frame: Media Attribution of Culpability About the MMR–Autism Vaccination Scare." *Health Communication*, 27.7 (2012): 690–701. Print.

It's All—Well, a Lot—in the Delivery

Brenta Blevins

» Defining Delivery

In antiquity, rhetoric focused on delivery through oral speech. In your writing-focused college classes it may be easier to think of rhetoric as primarily written. However, rhetoric isn't an either-or. Rhetoric encompasses the spoken, the written, and the visual—as well as the combination of these modes in compositions called "multimodal." Delivery is how we perform and speak, the medium and genre we choose, as well as stylistic considerations and more. The canon of delivery guides rhetorical decisions about how best to convey messages in specific rhetorical situations, whether delivered via spoken, written, visual, or multimodal compositions. (For more discussion of the canons, see Will Dodson and Chelsea Skelley's "The Canons of Rhetoric as Phases of Composition.")

» Spoken Delivery

In speech, delivery is clearly spoken, but it can be so much more. For example, tone alone can convey much of a message. Even when using the exact same words, the tone in which those words are pronounced can convey very different meanings. Saying "I'm fine" with a testy pronunciation or a happy tone conveys whether the speaker intends the audience to receive the text as sarcastic or literal. Body language is another tool that can help deliver intended messages. Speaking with a smile or a serious expression affects the delivery of the text. Pausing or making gestures can elicit specific emotions from the audience to emphasize your point. And delivery is key for establishing ethos with the audience, building trust and rapport with them. If a speaker has innovative ideas but ineffective delivery, the message and the speaker's ethos get lost. (For more information about tone and voice in relation to delivery, see Lilly Berberyan's chapter "Understanding Tone and Voice.")

» Written Delivery

Writing is also concerned with delivery. Determining whether to write up a bad day in the chemistry class in an email, an essay, or a lab report is a delivery decision, depending on your audience and their expectations. If the information is delivered in an email, the write-up might contain a few sentences, while a lab report requires a more structured format. An essay requires paragraphs and citations. An MLA-formatted essay, for instance, requires a particular format, with a recommended font and specific margin sizes, and specifications for in-text and Works Cited citations if the writer is to establish ethos with the audience. Even casual communication is affected by delivery. In a brief text message, for example, even the presence of punctuation is a delivery decision. Whether we write, for example, in an instant message that we are "okay," "okay.", or "okay!!!!" provides different messages for the audience.

» Visual Delivery

Information can be delivered through visual images like photographs, drawings, charts, tables, and more. The type of image conveys mood. For example, the use of cartoon figures conveys informality, while using graphs with numbers conveys a more serious tone. Color represents another delivery decision. Choosing black and white images might create a more formal environment, while choosing to use school colors can be an appeal to pathos. Spatial arrangement of the content is also a delivery decision, guiding the audience to look at some material first before looking at other material. This list is clearly not exhaustive. (For a more detailed discussion of rhetoric and visual media, see Zach Laminack's chapter "Rhetorical Analysis and Visual Media.")

Let's take a closer look at visual delivery by examining the relationship between color choices and delivery. Consider the difference between the two text boxes:

I'm so happy

I'm so happy

The black and white image uses more traditional textual colors and thus may provoke an ironic response, while the pink block may catch the audience's attention and evoke an emotional reaction, like lightheartedness. Colors can suggest different moods; therefore, rhetors should ensure that the color usage of fonts or images aligns with the intended emotional impact to maximize the text's rhetorical effectiveness.

Designers should consider their audience in their visual decisions. The headings in this textbook, for example, are a different color than the body text to guide the audience's attention to major sections of the text. Similarly, this textbook's pages use color along their edges to help group like chapters together within similar content areas. While a means of gaining the audience's attention, color decisions should take into account that some color choices can make text less accessible. For example, it is much easier to read certain color combinations than others; consider the following example:

Yellow text on a white background

Or

Blue text on white background

As this textbook and many other books demonstrate, readers are accustomed to and comfortable reading large amounts of dark text on light backgrounds.

Color and other visual choices should be carefully weighed to maximize the rhetorical effectiveness and thus should avoid an unintended audience response and/or undercutting one's rhetorical purpose. The content in a presentation, such as a PowerPoint or Prezi, may be excellent, for example, but the visual delivery can detract from the argument because of something as seemingly simple as the color of the font. Poor visual choices can make it challenging for the audience to receive the message. A font color that is difficult to read, crowding too many images or too much text on a slide, or not using standard MLA formatting for an essay can weaken the overall argument by detracting from the rhetor's ethos. Keeping the audience in mind when making visual choices can guide the rhetor toward effective rhetorical designs.

» Multimodal Delivery

Multimodal compositions combine a variety of communication modes including speaking, writing, and visual design. For example, multimodal compositions such as presentations, Web pages, wikis, videos, and even Facebook posts, may all call for authoring text, as well as audio, still images, moving images like animation and video, and much more. In making careful rhetorical decisions about font, color, image, music and even pacing, designers can take such compositions to a new level of "show, don't tell." (For more detail about how moving images like video and film function rhetorically, see Dan Burns's chapter "Analyzing Film Rhetoric.")

» Considering Delivery in Assignments

Let's take a look at some delivery decisions you may face in a College Writing class. One common assignment students receive is the linked assignment. In this assignment, students are responsible for writing an essay and then making a presentation related to that content while using a visual aid. For such an assignment, you need to make rhetorical decisions shaped by the delivery of each particular text. In this section, we'll examine some of the delivery decisions involved in a rhetorical analysis of *Narrative of the Life of Frederick Douglass* in both essay and presentation format.

For the essay, a student in a College Writing class will likely begin with an MLA-formatted essay (see Figure 1). While writing, the student considers the audience's expectations and visually establishes ethos through the arrangement of text, such as having appropriately formatted paragraphs and headings, and otherwise adhering to applicable MLA conventions. The student knows that each essay paragraph will develop a portion of the argument, starting with one point and including specific textual evidence in a logos-building move, as well as offering analysis of that evidence to support the argument. To enhance authorial ethos, the student will cite any use of textual evidence both in-text and on the Works Cited page at the end of the essay.

Christopher Smith

Prof. Moore

ENG 101

28 January 2013

Conflicting Christianity: Arrangement, Logos and Pathos in *The Narrative of the Life of Frederick Douglass*

In his landmark work *The Narrative of the Life of Frederick Douglass*, the author offers two conflicting

forms of Christianity, each with its own purpose. Through personal recollections and thoughts, Douglass describes

both real and false versions of religion and generally, the real or "true" form of Christianity he practiced as well as

some whites opposed to slavery. The false form of religion, "the hypocritical Christianity of this land," is practiced

by whites and is a complete bastardization of the true ideals behind genuine Christian thought (95). Douglass

deliberately structures his narrative by interspersing discussions of religion that show slavery and true Christianity as

opposing forces that cannot simultaneously exist. Further, he logically argues that if there is a "real" or "pure"

Christianity, the existence and practice of slavery wholly and inevitably corrupts it. Through his careful, logical

juxtapositions and appeals to pathos, Douglass' narrative moves beyond a traditional religious exposition of the evils

of slavery to make an overt political statement about his current political and personal exigence.

Figure 1. **A Written Essay Analyzing** *Narrative of the Life of Frederick Douglass*

Once the essay is completed, the student then plans a speech to deliver in conjunction with a PowerPoint presentation. Because the audience will be listening, the student realizes they will not be able to remember the same level of detail found in the essay, when the reader can slow down, look up unfamiliar words, and re-read to ensure comprehension. To aid the audience's memory in the spoken presentation, the student decides to place the argument's key points visually on a presentation slide. In addition, the student considers the appropriate tone, volume, pitch and body language to deliver the speech given the subject matter, audience, time, space, and other constraints. Further, the student plans a speech that will provide good verbal cues to enhance the presentation by helping the audience follow the orally delivered text.

The student knows that rhetors can gain credibility by crediting the works used to develop a text's content. (See Charles Tedder's chapter "Academic Integrity" and Ben Compton's chapter "Rhetorical Elements of Academic Citation" for more information on how student rhetors gain credibility through their citations.) While written texts use in-text and bibliographic citations to document their sources, the student delivering an oral speech names the authors, texts, and dates of texts, and also lists at the end of the presentation all citations on a Works Cited page. In the same way the student includes citations in the written text, he or she knows that material used within the presentation affects his/her ethos. While most know that copying text off the Web is inappropriate, reusing images, music, and/or videos without giving credit is likewise unacceptable. Because of this, the student decides to locate an image freely available through Creative Commons, and cite the use of that image.

To take advantage of the multimodal format, the student decides to include a visual image of Frederick Douglass. The student conducts research to locate images of Douglass, paying careful attention to each potential text's overall composition and framing, noting Douglass's expression, body position and eye contact, clothing, and more. Because the slide's topic is focused on ethos, the student locates an image of Douglass that seems to represent the ethos that he is striving to invoke in his narrative.

The Narrative of Frederick Douglass

- Ethos
  — Describes his personal experience
  — Specifies names, dates, places to build credibility
  — Cites authorities that his audience would recognize
- http://docsouth.unc.edu/neh/douglass/menu.html

Courtesy of the Library of Congress, LC-USZ62-15887

Figure 2. A PowerPoint Slide Analyzing *Narrative of the Life of Frederick Douglass*

Again taking advantage of the digital nature of the multimodal presentation, the student also decides to include a hyperlink for reference during the presentation and for later viewing through the class's discussion board. Including an authoritative website hyperlink both increases the delivery capabilities by linking to other electronic resources and affects the student's ethos by demonstrating credible research.

For optimum delivery, the student designs the multimodal compositions to utilize technological effects that augment rather than detract from the message, for example, making sure the images are an appropriate size in relation to text. Likewise, a good visual design in a multimodal composition recognizes that yellow text on a white background is hard to read, showing inadequate consideration of the audience. As another example, consider the differences between these fonts:

This is one font choice.

This is another font choice.

This is another font choice.

Which font adds the most ethos to a persuasive piece, suggesting a rhetor who respects his or her audience? The answer depends on the rhetorical situation and the rhetor's ability to respond to the audience. A whimsical font, as long as it is easily readable, may be appropriate for rhetorical purposes such as addressing a younger audience or to evoke a "fun" context. More traditional fonts appeal to more serious audiences or for professional rhetorical situations. For this presentation, the student decides to use a font that treats the serious topic with a font that mirrors the text's tone, and thus uses the bottom font choice.

» Revision

The rhetorical canon of delivery can guide purposeful design decisions, choices that determine how a composition fulfills one's rhetorical purpose. These delivery decisions, which extend across the spoken, written, visual, and multimodal text, can all be used to show respect for the audience. As with traditionally written essays, texts using other delivery modes should be reviewed and revised upon completion of early drafts.

Revision of texts should account not just for content choices, but also for rhetorical effectiveness of the delivery. For example, in reviewing a spoken text, the author or reviewers should take into account the audience's short-term memory and whether verbal signposts guide the audience, whether sentences are accordingly concise, whether the verbal delivery is well-paced and appropriately pitched, and how body language enhances the presentation. Reviewing a visual text should take into account whether the design enhances or detracts based on color choice—which could include readability, whether clarity is maintained, and whether the spatial arrangement of materials is effective. Reviewers of multimodal compositions should take into account whether the thesis is supported throughout the *entire* composition, whether focus and a coherent organization are clear and maintained throughout the piece, and whether there is any feedback to provide based on spoken or visual delivery.

University resources can also provide feedback to improve the final delivery of all texts. The Writing Center can provide responses to written materials, while the Speaking Center can aid in refining the delivery of speeches. Students can take digital projects to the university's Digital ACT Studio to gain feedback for revision. The consultants in these locations serve as informed audiences, and by providing collaborative consultation they can help rhetors make rhetorically effective choices. (For more information about the centers that can help guide your creation and revision of written, spoken, and multimodal texts, see Stacy W. Rice's chapter "The Multiliteracy Centers: Empowering Writers, Speakers, and Designers to Communicate Effectively.")

Revision Is Writing

Matt Mullins

Writing is a thinking process. Let's face it, if your professors did not ask you to write papers about the rhetoric of advertising, the ethical implications of cloning, or the effects of global warming, you might not ever think very deeply about these ideas. But why do you have to write papers and give oral presentations? Why can't you just address these problems off the top of your head in class? In all likelihood, you need time to think about these ideas and to find out what others think about them before you can ask questions about the subject that will enable you to provide some important answers. Thus, your professors ask you to write about these issues, knowing that the process you will go through to produce an essay will force you to engage with the material on a deeper level than you would otherwise. But does anyone think in perfectly formed five or ten page papers? I know my thoughts don't come to me that way. I think in disjointed phrases, keywords, and only sometimes in complete sentences. Therefore, I never write anything in a single draft, and that includes this chapter. The advantage of writing is that you have the opportunity to take your scattered and unorganized thought process and shape it into something clear and coherent. While it might seem nice to be able to sit down and just pound out a paper word-for-word in a single sitting, it is often in the stages of revising your writing that you will learn the most.

This chapter is about revision, but to learn how to revise you have to know what revision is, and to know what revision is, you have to understand what it is not. "Revising" and "editing" are terms that are often used interchangeably. However, there are significant differences between the two. Revising is typically concerned with rethinking ideas in your writing, while editing is typically concerned with correcting errors in your writing style. Here's an analogy that will help you distinguish between revising and editing: let's say you're interested in selling a house. You have an inspector come take a look at the structure of the house. The inspector informs you that the foundation is sound, and that it could withstand a devastating storm of virtually any proportion. The interior is also impressive. Every room has beautiful hardwood floors, the kitchen is spacious with brand new appliances, and the entire house is bright with natural light streaming in from big picture windows throughout. But the exterior is a different story. From the street, it's evident that the paint is chipping, there are weeds and vines growing on one side of the house, and the gutter above the front door is hanging loose. While none of these problems has anything to do with the home's foundation or with its interior appeal, it's unlikely that you'll ever get anyone inside to learn about these important features based on the house's outward appearance.

Revising and editing have a similar relationship. Revision addresses the structural soundness, or the ideas, in your writing, while editing takes on the cosmetic, or surface, level of your writing. It's obviously most important that your structure is safe and sound; after all, you can't live in a house that's about to sink into the ground. You can live in a house with an ugly exterior if the inside is safe and comfortable, but when it comes time to sell that home, or even just to bring someone over to see it, the outside needs to be clean as well. When you revise your writing, you are reading your own work to interrogate and scrutinize your ideas, your argument—your thought process. When you edit your writing, you are reading your own work to make sure there are no surface-level errors like misspelled words, formatting problems, or grammatical mistakes. While this chapter is primarily focused on revision, there are a few simple steps you can follow to improve your writing through editing. For starters, you should try reading your work aloud. Once you've read through your work yourself, you might ask a friend or classmate to read the work aloud to you. Hearing the words on the page will help you identify and address editorial problems that might distract your reader. Most importantly, you should give yourself enough time between the first draft and the due date to take a few hours off before you begin editing.

Unlike editing, revision is concerned with more than just surface-level problems in writing. Revision should focus on rethinking what you are trying to say in your writing. In her essay on revision entitled "Between the Drafts," Nancy Sommers says, "It is deeply satisfying to believe that we are not locked into our original statements, that we might start and stop, erase, use the delete key in life, and be saved from the roughness of our early drafts."[1] Sommers is drawing a comparison between our ability to revise our writing and our ability to revise the way we think about the world. When you revise, you look at your writing again and often make changes based on things you didn't see before. Sommers suggests that life works similarly. We always have the opportunity to look at things we think and believe and to reinforce or change those thoughts and beliefs based on where we are at that moment. During the revision process, you reexamine your thoughts more deeply and, just as importantly, give your readers an opportunity to do the same.

Whenever you write, you should also revise because you will necessarily know more about your subject when you've completed an entire draft of your essay than you did when you first began. It stands to reason that the conclusions you reach by the end of a paper might significantly alter what you said in your first paragraphs. You're at a different place in your thinking. So when you revise, look at your ideas again to see if you need to make changes based on where you are now. To return to our house analogy, in revising you are inspecting and securing the foundation, the structure of your writing, making the interior of your work comfortable and easy to understand. You may even make substantial changes, remodeling your writing. During this revision process, you'll surely see cosmetic problems like misspelled words or unnecessary commas. You'll be able to edit these mistakes in such a way as to remove surface-level distractions from your writing, inviting your reader inside to consider the ideas you're thinking about. But it's important to remember that no amount of surface-level repair work can make up for an unstable foundation. If there are no ideas in the writing to begin with, even the best editorial work can't cover over the absence of a solid structure.

> "Unlike editing, revision is concerned with more than just surface-level problems in writing. Revision should focus on rethinking what you are trying to say in your writing."

In contrast to the simple steps to editing mentioned previously, revision requires asking yourself tough questions. These questions are intended to help you make sure your writing contains solid ideas: what am I ultimately trying to say? What do I want my readers to do with my ideas? Do I want to persuade my readers? Am I assuming anything in my writing that I do not state

---

1. Nancy Sommers, "Between the Drafts," *College Composition and Communication* 43.1 (February 1992), 23–31.

explicitly? All of these questions assume one thing in common: time. Writing is truly like any other undertaking. If you want to do anything well, you have to invest quality time, and you have to practice. Even the most gifted athlete in the world would suffer serious injury if he or she walked onto the field in the middle of a *Monday Night Football* game without practicing and with absolutely no knowledge of football whatsoever. In the same way, writing is not about natural ability or some mystical power that some people have and others don't have. Writing is about time, exposure, and practice. The best way to practice when it comes to writing is to revise. Think of revision as the stage of your writing where you put in some serious time. Novelist and non-fiction writer Anne Lamott says, "Very few writers really know what they are doing until they've done it."[2] As I've already suggested, if you're writing an essay on a subject you know very little about, you're much more of an expert when you're finished writing than when you began. If you only spend time on a first draft, you miss out on the part of the writing process in which the most productive thinking takes place: the revision. Think of the first draft as your chance to develop your thoughts on your subject, and then push yourself to

> "Writing is about time, exposure, and practice."

see if your thoughts make sense by revising your writing. With each successive draft, you'll find that you know a little more and that writing is giving you opportunities to think that you might not have taken advantage of otherwise. Revision is writing, and writing is a thinking process.

---

2. Anne Lamott, "Shitty First Drafts," in *Language Awareness: Readings for College Writers*, edited by Paul Eschholz, Alfred Rosa, and Virginia Clark, 9th ed. (Boston: Bedford/St. Martin's, 2005), 93–96.

3

Rhetorical
Research

The Genre of Academic Discourse

Craig Morehead

Academic discourse is the language that scholars use to communicate in their special fields of study. Every academic discipline has its own academic discourse that determines the rules, styles, formatting, theoretical models of analysis, vocabulary, and research requirements and expectations for communicating in that field. These conventions largely reflect the values and methodologies developed over time in each field. For example, writing an interpretive essay of a work of literature, designing an analysis of data for a biology lab report, working up visual representations of Noh drama theater masks, and conducting a speech on a medical research trial all follow different modes of academic discourse. The terms used to refer to important elements will vary based on content, as will the expectations for use of data, external sources, and personal voice. That said, some disciplines are closely related and even have some measure of overlapping content and conventions. So, it is safe to say that the boundaries of academic discourse are not rigidly fixed, but rather that they are in constant flux and continually reshaped and remade as those within the disciplines redefine the accepted academic discourse for their fields.

Academic disciplines are largely defined by their content of study, their analytical methodologies, and their means of communicating their findings and arguments. Vocabulary is but one of the markers of an academic discipline. Scholars often use specialized vocabulary for their particular discourse because these words or phrases carry with them a specific set of contextualized ideas that resonate within their fields. Consider what ideas are loaded with these terms and what disciplines might use them: non-Euclidean geometry, Existentialism, noble gases, asset protection trust, parataxis, negative space and paresthesia. Obviously, these terms aren't used in everyday conversation, but they are used in the academic discourse of each of their respective fields because they serve to describe and communicate specific ideas quickly and efficiently to those who are familiar with them in their given contexts. They allow the practitioners in each field a kind of shorthand communication that both sets the boundaries of a field (usually, only insiders know and use the field's specialized vocabulary when talking to one another) and focuses language to the specific rhetorical concerns of a field. So, the condition of "a burning or prickling sensation that is usually felt in the hands, arms, legs, or feet, but can also occur in other parts of the body"[1] is reduced and contained by the term paresthesia for those in the know (presumably the medical community, specifically the dermatological branch).

It takes a lot of time, work, and practice to learn what is expected for academic communication, but it is important to learn to enter the disciplinary conversations even if you don't plan on becoming a professional scholar. The ideas and methods of academic discourse are practiced and valued outside of the academy. While there are various modes of writing and ways of expressing yourself, the majority of the writing expected in college falls under the broad category of academic discourse. This chapter is not designed to introduce the general expectations for each academic discipline; rather, its purpose is to broadly outline some of the "habits of mind"—mental patterns—that scholars value and those practices in which we must engage in order to enter disciplinary conversations. To be successful in academic discourse, a scholar must display certain general habits of mind: intellectual curiosity, critical thinking, and creativity.

> "The goal of all academic discourse argues for new ideas, new answers, or even new questions."

» Intellectual Curiosity

All academic discourse centers on answering questions and refining ideas. Therefore, the goal of all academic discourse argues for new ideas, new answers, or even new questions. Scholars display their intellectual curiosity by first asking questions. This may lead to the discovery of a new question or a reformulation of an old question, but in any case, the academic endeavor starts with something puzzling, rather than with something we already think we know or understand.

In order to answer questions, academics begin with open minds and attempt to learn what questions others have asked and what answers they have provided. Entering a conversation is a good way to think about academic communication. In order to enter a conversation, we have to know two basic things: who is talking and what has already been said. This is why scholars rely heavily on reading and research. Basically, there are two kinds of research: the research

---

1. "NINDS Paresthesia Information Page," National Institute of Neurological Disorders and Stroke, National Institutes of Health, 12 Apr. 2007 <www.ninds.nih.gov/disorders/paresthesia/paresthesia.htm>.

one does to familiarize oneself with what has been said about a subject and the research that produces new data and ideas that contribute to the pool of knowledge about a certain subject. It is important to note that the first kind always precedes the second, meaning that even though you may be conducting new polls or experiments and putting forth new arguments, ideas, and data, it is expected in academic discourse that the new research joins the existing conversation by relying on and referring back to the established research that has come before, even if only indirectly.

Thus, academic discourse is founded on research. Scholars read widely in their field to recognize what trends of thought and analysis have been used to examine and interpret information, data, and ideas. Reading widely means reading from a number of varied sources in order to gain a broad context for entering the conversation. Reading widely helps contextualize our ideas within the larger conversation. Contextualization explores and situates the reasoned significance of the intellectual and material evidence in relation to our own ideas. Furthermore, reading widely for context doesn't mean that we use or quote everything we read; the assumption is that the more background we have, the more informed we are about the topic and the more nuanced and creative we can be in putting forth our arguments. Typically, scholars read much more than they will actually cite or use in an individual project. It is not unusual for a scholar to read an article or book and not use it to support an argument. But simply because that particular research isn't used directly in the project doesn't mean that it wasn't useful for constructing the argument; it might have provided essential background information, offered a way of thinking about the project, or led to another useful source.

Research is used in academic discourse in several ways: it establishes credibility and contributes to ethos by demonstrating familiarity with the current conversation; it provides information and ways of thinking about the questions we want to answer; and because academic discourse values producing *new* knowledge and ideas, research ensures that we are not essentially repeating what has already been said.

» Critical Thinking

Since academics like to rethink issues to expose new ways of approaching certain topics and to argue for how those new ways of thinking will reshape our ideas and our world, they are careful not to take established ideas and information as fact. In this way, academic discourse also relies on critical thinking. Critical thinking entails questioning assumptions and opinions, reflecting on origins and consequences of ideas and events, attending to nuance to expose complexities, and analyzing and synthesizing multiple viewpoints. It requires scholars to be active participants who read and interpret the research rhetorically and skeptically, rather than passive receivers of information. A scholar will not take something someone has said before as fact without questioning it, testing it, refining it, and ultimately rejecting it or using it to form new ideas.

Academics absolutely love exposing the subtle nuance and complexity of a seemingly straightforward issue. They do not value this process simply because it gives them a chance to perform some mental gymnastics but because, more often than not, issues don't break down into an either/or, two-sided problem. We all know that there are multiple answers to most problems and as many ways to get to the answer as there are possible solutions.

Recall that the goal of academic discourse is to argue something new or create new knowledge, usually in response to a question and driven by intellectual curiosity. Academics conduct research on all manners of solutions posed in attempts to answer those questions, and because they look at those sources critically, they find those answers lacking in some way and in need of refinement. In order to use previous ideas to construct new ones, scholars must be attuned to the ways in which the authors have constructed their arguments. They must weigh the evidence, the claims, the assumptions, the perspectives, the motives, the values, and the language of the argument—the process of rhetorical reading—in order to identify not only what the author has to say but also to infer how the way it is said affects the message. This allows the scholar to parse what is useful in the argument and what is flawed so that previous ideas can be culled and refined to form a more nuanced and, therefore, better argument.

> "Critical thinking keeps us from regurgitating predetermined and preconceived opinions and phrases without thinking our own thoughts."

Critical thinking keeps us from regurgitating predetermined and preconceived opinions and phrases without thinking our own thoughts. It also ensures that we do not generalize, thereby blocking our attention to detail and complexity, leading us to stop short of thinking through an issue as much as we should and failing to account for the dissonance, or gray area, of an issue. Critical thinking drives scholars to get closer to an accurate conception of the way things work and to locate and explore problems in ways that others have failed to see.

» Creativity

Scholarly work values creativity because scholars try to answer difficult questions and make new arguments based on prior knowledge and new evidence. Scholars ultimately seek to create new ways of thinking about the world that reflect a more accurate and nuanced view of the way ideas, organisms, institutions, texts, and material objects interact with and influence each other. They use argument as a principle means of expression because they seek to convince others that their way of thinking about a subject is new and different from established ways of thinking about it. Scholars know that as the process of academic scholarship progresses, their ideas will be scrutinized and accepted, rejected, or refined by others. The merits of the argument will be debated and a conversation based on relevant conversations already taking place within the field will begin. This is why it is important to think of yourself as participating in a conversation when engaging in academic discourse.

While some scholars prefer to stay within the boundaries of their specialized academic disciplines, many more scholars borrow ideas from other disciplines, practicing a process known as interdisciplinary study. This means that a literary scholar might borrow ideas from philosophy, sociology, economics, and even chemistry to produce a new argument about *Moby Dick*, while still operating under the conventions of the specific academic discourse. Consider how the ideas of the other disciplines would make for an interesting and new interpretation of the novel.

> "Scholars ultimately seek to create new ways of thinking about the world that reflect a more accurate and nuanced view of the way ideas, organisms, institutions, texts, and material objects interact and influence each other."

Whether scholars engage in interdisciplinary research or not, their new arguments are still founded on research. They are careful to use research critically to inform and support their arguments; they don't let someone's research speak for itself without analysis and interpretation. Scholars emphasize their own voices and ideas over those of others because they are trying to establish new information and ideas of their own. This is why scholars synthesize research with their own arguments rather than simply summarizing what someone else has said. They are careful to integrate the arguments and data of others while offering their own interpretation of what the research means and how it relates to their argument.

Scholars make new, interesting, and complex connections between established ideas by thinking critically in order to offer more cogent answers to the questions they are seeking to answer. Of course, intellectual curiosity, critical thinking, and creativity are only three of the general habits of mind that scholars value, but if you work hard to foster them, you will find yourself adeptly entering and contributing to the lively and rewarding conversations of the academy and of the world at large.

Finding a Conversation
to Find Research

Courtney Adams Wooten

Billy has just received an assignment from his College Writing instructor to write a ten-page paper with sources about education. From the research session his class went to at the library, he knows that he needs to find scholarly sources. So he first goes to a library database, ERIC,[1] to find research for the essay. He types in "education" as a search term, but ERIC returns with 962,140 hits. Billy knows that he cannot look through all of these resources to write his paper. So he decides that he will try to narrow down his topic; eventually, he decides to write about bilingual education. So he types "bilingual education" into ERIC and still receives 11,198 hits for this subject. Suddenly, Billy feels overwhelmed—how is he going to look at all of these sources and write a paper in just a few weeks?

All students find themselves in this position at some point or another, whether it is in a College Writing course, a speech course, or a fourth-year psychology class. Although the length of the assigned essay is certainly a factor, the amount

---

1. This is the Education Research Information Center database, which contains many articles focused on topics in education.

of research required before even beginning to draft an essay with sources causes many students to doubt their rhetorical abilities as soon as they receive this type of assignment. In order to overcome these doubts, students need to make an important shift in thinking about research, from viewing this process as "filler" to reach the correct page or time length and to fulfill the professor's research requirements to seeing this process as joining a conversation. This shift will help you to understand the role research has in showing you how to narrow your topic, how to write a specific thesis, and how to incorporate research into your essay or speech as you develop this thesis.

Usually, students approach research in a straightforward way: find the required number of sources to back up what they think. With this model of thinking, students may write the entire essay or plan the entire speech before finding sources that merely repeat what they think, or they may find sources and write a paper or a speech based on what these sources say rather than what they themselves think about the topic. Research is "finished" when they have used the required number, whether that is two, five, or ten sources. Following this model to include research in essays and presentations fails to incorporate research into your ideas; instead, research is a prop for already-formed ideas or a boundary within which you must force your ideas. Rhetoric devised in this way often sounds boring or disengaged and it raises questions—are your ideas important? Can other people talk about your ideas? In order for an audience to engage with your work, they need to know where you stand on the issue and how you are speaking to other people who are also talking about this topic. Audiences need you to become a part of a conversation.

Returning to the previous example will illustrate how research can be used as a conversation. At this point, Billy knows that he has a problem. He has a topic but too much research to read; he knows he needs to narrow down his topic so that he can look at a smaller amount of research. Simply choosing several sources from the over 11,000 available would result in a lack of focus for his essay, and, with this many sources available, it would be impossible for him to sound knowledgeable about the topic. Billy isn't quite sure, however, how to narrow down his topic. He could just start typing in random keywords with "bilingual education" to see what he comes up with, but that could take up a lot of time and he isn't sure what he could try to narrow the topic to.

Billy begins to look over the first few pages of sources found as he desperately searches for a way to narrow his topic. Looking at the titles, he suddenly notices that many of the sources discuss bilingual education in relation to specific places. Texas and California are often mentioned. Having been born in North Carolina and knowing that bilingual education is a topic of debate there, too,

Billy decides to see if narrowing his topic to "bilingual education in North Carolina" will help. He types "bilingual education" and "North Carolina" into ERIC. To his surprise, this search only results in sixteen hits—a much more manageable number than 11,000. A similar search in his library's book catalog results in only seven hits. Billy now feels that he has a sufficiently narrowed topic that he can adequately research and write about.

Although Billy may not realize what he has done, he has actually just determined what conversation to enter. With any topic that you focus on, whether it is education or the Revolutionary War or business models, you will quickly discover that there are many different conversations going on about that topic. This is what Billy did when he found so many sources related to bilingual education. No one can understand and take part in all of the conversations related to one topic. There simply is not enough time, particularly when only given a few weeks to complete a project. This is why you need to narrow your topic as much as possible before looking for sources. Once you have narrowed your topic, you can then scan through this research to determine what kinds of conversations about this topic are going on and which one you want to enter. Billy did this when he narrowed his topic to bilingual education, discovered people were discussing this in relation to particular places, and then determined to focus narrowly on North Carolina. He now has a specific conversation that he is entering, and this is the kind of specific conversation that you need to know you are entering before reading research. Scanning titles or abstracts of articles and books is a quick way to find out what conversations are going on without intensely reading many sources that may not be part of the conversation you eventually enter.

Before reading these sources, a tentative thesis would help Billy to think about what he's looking for and further narrow his search for what to use in his essay. He now has a limited number of sources that at least partially focus on a specific conversation he wants to be a part of, but Billy probably will still not want to be part of all the specific conversations going on in these sources. In fact, doing so would likely still require writing a book that Billy doesn't have time to write. So he formulates a tentative thesis for his essay so that he knows what his ideas are and so that he can see what people are saying about these ideas. After some prewriting, he formulates the following thesis: *Bilingual education in North Carolina helps Latino-American students by providing an atmosphere where they can use two languages, Spanish and English, to explore their cultures and to integrate their private and public lives.* Billy reads the sixteen articles, particularly focusing on the areas where the writers discuss how bilingual education affects students' pride in their cultures and how it affects their comfort levels at home and in school. Not all of the chapters in the books pertain specifically to these topics, or these conversations, so Billy skims through the chapters and determines one or two in each to focus on.

This reading takes some time, but by the time Billy is done reading, he feels that he understands the conversations people are having about bilingual education in North Carolina. He also changes some of his ideas about bilingual education. Some of the writers make effective arguments about the negative effects of bilingual education on students, so he thinks through his ideas again, using more prewriting to sort them out, and formulates a new thesis to use as he writes his essay: *Bilingual education in North Carolina allows Latino-American students to explore their Latino and American cultures, but it may negatively impact their abilities to adapt to public life.*

Billy's willingness to change his thesis based on new knowledge about his topic is important. Without this willingness, approaching research as a conversation is not effective. When you are part of a normal conversation, you often will change your ideas based on what other people say or tell you. If you see research in the same way, you know what you think about a topic before entering a conversation, but it is often a good idea, particularly when you don't know what others think about a topic, to listen to what they are saying before you enter the conversation yourself. This way, you know what their ideas are and where they are coming from, and you can take time to understand these ideas and how you would answer them before talking. This is what Billy does when he reads his sources: he listens to what they say and then reformulates his own thesis before beginning to write a draft. His opinions have changed based on the conversation, so he now knows what he will say as a part of the conversation.

"...it is often a good idea, particularly when you don't know what others think about a topic, to listen to what they are saying before you enter the conversation yourself. This way, you know what their ideas are and where they are coming from, and you can take time to understand these ideas and how you would answer them before talking."

Writing a draft of the essay or crafting an outline of a presentation is now Billy's, and your, step into the conversation. It is an opportunity to actually join the conversation and contribute to it in a meaningful way. You can do this because you now know exactly what conversation to enter, what others are saying in this conversation, and what you want to add to it. If all you are doing is joining a conversation in order to agree with someone, to say "I agree" without adding anything else, then your voice becomes unnecessary. When writing or speaking, you never want your voice to be unnecessary. So you should consider how your ideas, your experiences, and even the different people you are talking to through research are adding to the conversation. Are you agreeing but providing new examples or new ways of thinking about something? Are you disagreeing and telling others why? Are you doing a little of both? These are important questions to consider as you look at your new, reformulated thesis and your research to determine what to write and how to enter the conversation.

With Billy's new thesis, he has two clear topics, two clear conversations, within bilingual education in North Carolina that he wants to enter into. The first is that it "allows Latino-American students to explore their Latino and American cultures" and the second is that it "may negatively affect their abilities to adapt to public life." As he read his sources, he took notes on which ones addressed which of these topics. This tells him where these sources will fit into his essay. In addition, he noted which sources agreed with his ideas and which disagreed. Even though he modified his original thesis based on ideas he read, he still doesn't agree with everyone. He knows he can't simply ignore those who disagree with him; just like in a face-to-face conversation, this would negatively affect his ethos by being rude and making him seem ignorant about the topic. Instead, he determines how he will interact with those writers that he agrees with and those he disagrees with. Sometimes he speaks to other writers one at a time, especially if their ideas directly address what he is talking about or if other writers spoke about this writer often, indicating that he or she is a well-respected person in the field who needs to be directly addressed; sometimes he speaks to other writers in groups, especially if they express similar ideas. As his essay takes shape, he occasionally still modifies his ideas as he writes based on the focused reading of his sources he continues to do as he includes their voices in his essay. At the end of the writing process when he turns in his essay, Billy realizes that his essay doesn't say what he thought it would when he first began writing. However, he also realizes that it is an essay that is thoughtful and addresses the ideas that other people have, regardless of their viewpoints.

Billy's choices are unique to his situation, just as your choices will be unique to your situation. Perhaps you will read research, listen to a conversation, and decide that your original ideas haven't changed. Or perhaps you will completely change your mind and have to revise your entire thesis to match these ideas. These are all reasonable approaches as long as you take time to listen to the specific conversation you want to join and as long as you address the ideas that others are raising in this conversation. Your voice then becomes a necessary part of this conversation for others to respond to.

Conducting Academic Research

Jenny Dale

In many of your courses at the university level—including College Writing—you will be expected to integrate research into papers, presentations, and other projects. Research is critical in academic writing and speaking because it places your work in a larger conversation. Research can help you expand on your ideas, discover new ones, and strengthen your argument. When you integrate outside sources into your work, you build your credibility by proving that your argument is supported by existing research. This chapter will provide a brief introduction to research and will cover the basics of finding, accessing, and using outside sources to build and support effective arguments.

» Types of Sources

When you are researching a topic, you are likely to come across a wide variety of sources. Certain assignments may require you to have specific types of sources: primary and/or secondary, or popular and/or scholarly. It is challenging to meet these requirements if you're not sure how to find and identify these different types of sources, so this section will briefly introduce some of the different types of sources you can expect to find in the process of doing research, and how you can distinguish between them.

> "Research is critical in academic writing and speaking because it places your work in a larger conversation."

Primary and Secondary Sources

You may have heard sources referred to as either primary or secondary when you have done research in the past. The University of Maryland provides the following definition of primary sources:

> Primary sources are original materials. They are from the time period involved and have not been filtered through interpretation or evaluation. Primary sources are original materials on which other research is based.

They are usually the first formal appearance of results in physical, print or electronic format. They present original thinking, report a discovery, or share new information. (University of Maryland Libraries)

While this definition is clear and succinct, you might notice that it does not provide any specific examples of primary sources but focuses instead on general guidelines. This is because what constitutes a primary source varies widely depending on the context or academic discipline. For instance, if you are doing historical research on World War II, a primary source might be a letter or diary that provides a firsthand account of a soldier's experience during the war, or a newspaper article from 1944 reporting on U.S. troops in Europe. If you are doing research on a psychology topic like bipolar disorder, a primary source might be an original research article that reports on a study of treatment options for patients with this disorder. If you are doing research on the artist Cindy Sherman, a primary source might be one of her photographs. All of these examples "present original thinking, report a discovery, or share new information."

Secondary sources, on the other hand, are removed in some way from primary sources. Considering the examples in the last paragraph, a secondary source in history might be a book on World War II that relies on numerous primary sources like letters and newspaper articles to provide context. In psychology, secondary sources might be review articles that summarize and evaluate original research articles. In art, secondary sources might include a scholarly journal article or an in-depth review of an exhibition published in a newspaper or magazine. Like primary sources, secondary sources can take many forms. Common types of secondary sources you are likely to come across in the process of doing research for a College Writing class include books, articles, and websites.

Popular vs. Scholarly Sources

Many of your college research assignments will require certain types of secondary sources, like articles or books. When you are doing research, you are likely to find a mix of popular sources, like newspaper and magazine articles, and scholarly sources, like books and journal articles. The following chart from UNCG Libraries provides a quick overview of the differences between these two categories:

Table 1. Characteristics of popular and scholarly sources.

	Popular	Scholarly
Who writes the articles?	Professional journalists	Researchers or scholars in a field
Who is the primary audience?	The general public	Other researchers and scholars
Do the authors cite their sources?	Maybe in passing, but you usually won't find formal references	Always—look for a reference list or footnotes/endnotes
Are there ads?	Always	Rarely
Are current events covered?	Yes	No—the peer-review process is long

Notice in the right column that scholarly sources (also called academic, peer-reviewed, or refereed) are written both *by* and *for* scholars. They are written by experts in their fields, such as professors, graduate students, lawyers, nurses, or other specialists.

It is important to note that scholarly sources are not "better" than popular sources; the two serve different purposes. Scholarly sources are typically going to provide more in-depth analysis of a particular topic. They often cite primary and secondary sources, including other scholarly sources. Popular sources tend to be shorter, written for a more general audience, and rarely cite sources. However, if you are researching a recent event or a topic of current interest, popular articles are your best bet as they are much more likely to cover current events and news. Scholarly sources take significant time to research and write, and then go through a review by other scholars before finally being published, so the timeline to publication is much longer. The benefit of this peer-review process is that scholarly articles have been both written and reviewed by experts in a field, making them extremely authoritative.

» Finding Web Sources

With a general sense of the types of sources you are looking for, you can begin searching for sources that help support your argument. If you are anything like most college students, you probably start any search for information in Google or other similar search engines. There is no shortage of information available on the web, and you can find sources on almost any topic you might be interested in. Let's say you want to do research on standardized testing for an argumentative paper or persuasive speech. Google is a great place to start, but a quick search for standardized testing brings back more than 6.1 million results at the time of writing. While there are always going to be sources that are not credible enough to be cited for academic research, like Wikipedia, you are likely to find quite a few good sources as well as lots of useful information that will help you as you move ahead with your research.

Using the web for research is convenient and is second nature to many of us, but since most of what is available on the web has not been edited or reviewed, it is particularly important to carefully evaluate these sources before deciding to use them. There are many tests that you can use to evaluate sources—a Google search for evaluating web sources brings back more than 2 million results—but librarians at UNCG tend to use the **ABCs:**

A has a double meaning: authority and accuracy. Determining authority requires you to assess the person, people, or organization responsible for the website. Look for "about us" or "contact us" links if the author is not immediately clear. Think about your context—a website on standardized testing by someone with a master's degree in Education has more authority than a site written by a professor of Literature. In any case, it is critical to be able to identify the person, people, or organizations responsible for a website. When authors cannot be identified, authority is significantly compromised. That is one major issue with sources like Wikipedia. Remember that you are using outside sources to build your own ethos as a writer, and sources with authority issues can negatively impact that ethos. The second A, accuracy, can sometimes be difficult to determine if you are new to a topic. Establishing the authority of the source helps with this, and you can also look for clues like citations and for information that you can easily fact-check.

Bias can be tricky to identify, but it relies heavily on establishing authority. Bias in sources is an issue because biases are opinions or tendencies that might affect the information presented. Biased sources are often one-sided or do not provide the full picture on a particular topic or issue. Do the people or organizations responsible for the site have any clear biases about the content? This can be very nuanced—it is often not as easy as finding a site entitled "Standardized Testing is the Worst" (the bias there is fairly clear) or a site written by the Educational Testing Service. Bias is a particularly sticky issue when we are dealing with controversial topics, as strong opinions are likely to be voiced. Just because a site has a clear bias does not mean that you should discard it as a source, but rather that you should seek out additional sources that are more neutral. You can help mitigate bias by seeking out multiple perspectives on a topic so that you have a fuller picture of the information available.

Currency, the last element of the *ABC* test, is relative. Typically in a College Writing course, you are going to be looking for the most recent information on a topic. It is important to remember, though, that the most recent information on standardized testing is likely to be newer than the most recent information about World War II. Staying within five years is usually a good guideline, but for some topics you may need to be more flexible. It's important to read the assignment carefully, and it is always a good idea to check with your instructor to determine how recent your sources should be for a specific assignment.

Even if a site does not pass this *ABC* test, it can still be useful for the research process. Wikipedia, for instance, is a source that consistently fails the *ABC* test and should not be cited as a source in an academic paper or presentation; still, it can be an excellent resource for you as you begin to explore your topic. Using the standardized testing example, it would be impossible to cover all issues related to standardized testing in a single paper or speech. But reading through the Wikipedia entry "Standardized test," I can start to refine my topic a bit more by narrowing it down to college entrance tests in the United States, and then even more specifically to the SAT. Wikipedia does a great job of internally linking to other relevant articles, and the article on the SAT mentions that there have been controversies over how well the SAT actually predicts college success, which sounds like a potentially interesting topic. Though I would not be citing information from Wikipedia in my final Works Cited list, I can use it to help jump-start my research process and narrow my topic down to something more manageable. I can also follow Wikipedia's references to other sources and apply the *ABC* test to those to see if they are credible enough to cite.

» Finding Images and Videos

In addition to the plethora of websites and articles available through Google, you can also find millions of images and videos. My standardized testing search brought back thousands of images, including photographs, charts, graphs, cartoons, and more. Images and videos can add visual interest to a research project and can add richness to your paper or presentation. Many multimedia sources available online are protected by copyright, the legal rights held by any content creator. Copyright is typically not much of a concern for educational projects like papers and presentations, as these are usually protected by fair use standards written into copyright law. Still, if you use an image, you need to cite it as you would any other type of source. This goes back to building your ethos because you are providing a clear map to your research process by citing all of the sources you are using.

Because you will need to find enough information about an image to cite it, you may need to go beyond your basic Google search. The Google Image Advanced Search page allows you to limit your sources to those that have Creative Commons licenses. Creative Commons licenses allow copyright holders to make their content available for free use under certain circumstances. For instance, a photographer might put her images up on a site like Flickr with a Creative Commons license that allows anyone to use them for non-commercial purposes, as long as they attribute the image to her. Creators can also license other multimedia objects, like videos, under Creative Commons. Often, using Creative Commons-licensed media makes citing easier because you can find more information about the creator. For more information about Creative Commons, visit the UNCG Libraries' Creative Commons guide at: http://uncg.libguides.com/creativecommons.

» Using Library Resources

The web is always a great starting point, but when you are doing academic research, you almost always need to go beyond what is freely available. One way to ensure that you are getting the highest quality information available is to use the resources provided by UNCG Libraries. The Libraries have *millions* of books and articles that are at your disposal as a UNCG student. This section will provide a brief overview of a few of those sources, but there are hundreds of resources available through the Libraries' website at http://library.uncg.edu. The Libraries also have specific research guides for College Writing I and II. Click the "Research Guides by Subject" link, select "English" from the alphabetical list, and then choose the course you are in from the "Course Guides" box on the left side of the page, which lists each research guide that has been created for English courses. If you need help with your research, you can always contact your College Writing Librarian or use the **Ask Us!** button on the Libraries' homepage.

As you use library resources, be aware that they do not speak Google. In general, you cannot type in a question or a long phrase and expect to get useful results. The best strategy is to do some brainstorming before you start searching to help you consider the terms you want to use. If you are researching our sample topic of how well the SAT predicts college success, you should make notes of any critical terms related to the topic: *SAT* and *college success* are terms that are obvious from our topic, but you might also want to consider terms that are broader (like *standardized test* or *college admissions test* for *SAT*) and narrower (like *grade point average, retention,* or *graduation* for *college success*). Having a variety of search terms ready helps if you find that your initial search is not as successful as you would like it to be. When you have identified a handful of useful terms, you can use those to search for relevant sources in the library catalog or databases. To make your search as effective as possible, use connectors like AND and OR to help target your search. A search for *SAT* AND *college success* will bring back results that deal with both of these topics, which helps you narrow down your results to those that are likely to be relevant. A search for *SAT* OR *college admissions test* will bring back any results that deal with either of those concepts, so that broadens your results.

Library Catalog

The library catalog is your gateway to the millions of books mentioned earlier. You can access the catalog anytime and from anywhere that you have internet access. Visit http://library.uncg.edu and click on the "Catalog" tab in the large red box. This will search for items that we own, including print and electronic books, DVDs, CDs, and more.

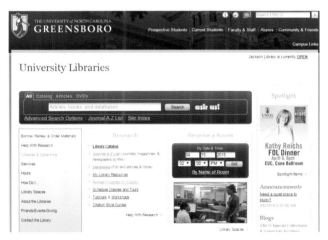

Figure 1. The UNCG Libraries' homepage.

The search depicted above brings back 13 results from UNCG Libraries. These 13 sources may be sufficient, or you may want to make some changes to your search. A search for *standardized testing* AND *college success* brings back 57 results—significantly more than our original search.

To get more information about one of your search results, you can simply click on the title. One result that came back for the second search above was *College Admissions for the 21st Century*. Clicking on the title leads to a page with more information about that book, including basic publication information, a summary, and location information within UNCG Libraries (see Fig. 2).

Figure 2. The catalog page for *College Admissions for the 21st Century*.

Scrolling a bit farther down the page, you can see that this book is divided into chapters (see Fig. 3). In order to use a book as a source, you may not need to read the entire work—focusing on the chapter or chapters that are most useful to you is your best approach. In this case, you might find good information in the chapter entitled "A New Way of Looking at Intelligence and Success."

Figure 3. Table of contents display for *College Admissions in the 21st Century*.

Library Databases

You may have used library databases before, either here at UNCG or in high school. Simply put, a library database is a searchable collection of resources. The UNCG Libraries provide access to hundreds of these databases, and most of the content included is content that cannot be found on the free web. Each database is unique, but they all work on the same basic principles of using good search terms and search connectors like AND and OR. A general database that is an excellent starting point for most research topics is **Academic Search Complete**, which you can find on the Databases page on the Libraries' website. Looking at the Research Guides by Subject linked from the Libraries' homepage is a good way to find out which subject-specific databases are recommended for a particular area. In English, for instance, MLA International Bibliography, JSTOR, and Project Muse are great databases for finding scholarly sources related to literature, language, and rhetoric.

When you use a library database, it is a good idea to have your list of potential search terms handy. Your best bet is to split your terms into separate search boxes, which are connected with the AND search connector. A search for *SAT college success* in Academic Search Complete brings back 14 article results, while splitting the terms into two boxes with *SAT* in one and *college success* in another brings back 52 results. On your search results page in Academic Search Complete, you will find plenty of options to narrow and filter your results, including a box that limits your results to articles from peer-reviewed or scholarly journals.

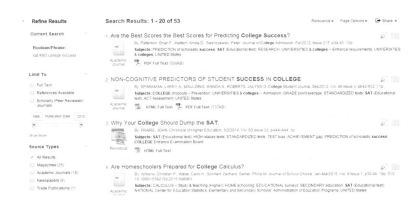

Figure 4. Academic Search Complete results page.

To find more information about a source that looks interesting in Academic Search Complete, click on the title. There, you'll find everything you need to cite the article, subject terms that can help you come up with new search terms, and usually an abstract that will give you a sense of what you can expect from the article. You will also find links to full text if UNCG has access to it, and a toolbar that allows you to email, save, or print the article. Even if UNCG does not have access to an article, you can place a request to have the article sent to you through a service called Interlibrary Loan (ILL). This also works for book sources, but you will want to make sure you leave plenty of time for the source to be sent to you. It can take a few days for an article and a week or more for a book to get to you, so ILL is not a great option if you've waited until the night before your project is due to start researching. Starting early will give you access to even more resources and help.

Figure 5. An article page from Academic Search Complete.

» Citing Sources

Citing sources is a critical part of the research process. Not only does it protect you from plagiarism, which is a violation of UNCG's Academic Integrity Policy, it also builds your credibility by indicating that your ideas are supported by research. In most English classes, you will typically be asked to cite sources in MLA style. Citations are meant to help your audience find the sources you have consulted, which is why they require so much detail; your readers need to have as much information as possible in case they want to find any of your sources. One thing to remember about citations is that they are somewhat like mathematical formulas. You never have to memorize the order of citation elements; you just need to be able to plug the information about your sources into the correct format. There are excellent citation resources online—OWL at Purdue and Citation Fox are two great sites maintained by universities. Citation generators like EasyBib can be very helpful, but it is important to check the generated citation against a source that you trust, like the MLA citation manual, or an online source like OWL at Purdue, just to be sure that the details are correct.

You may already be familiar with citing sources in MLA for written work, like research papers. For a research paper, you provide a Works Cited list at the end of the paper and create parenthetical citations when you refer to a source in-text. Citations in a speech or presentation work in a similar way. Typically, you will turn in a Works Cited list containing all of your sources or create a Works Cited slide at the end of your presentation. During your speech or presentation, you will provide oral citations for your sources as you reference them. For instance, if you are referring to an article by John Smith called "Standardized Testing is Good," you would say something along the lines of "According to John Smith in his article 'Standardized Testing is Good,' standardized testing has positive effects on student academic success." Introducing the statement by indicating the source is a verbal cue to your listening audience that you are pulling in an outside source. You will also need to cite all images or videos used in your presentation. (For more detailed information on citations, see Ben Compton's chapter "Rhetorical Elements of Academic Citation.")

» Getting Help

This chapter only scratches the surface of the resources we have available and the strategies that can help you use them most effectively. If you need help with any part of the research process, from brainstorming search terms to selecting the appropriate library resource to citing your sources, you can always contact the UNCG Libraries. You can contact the Reference Desk in Jackson Library for help in person, by phone, by text, or by chatting with us. Click the **Ask Us!** button on the library homepage for more details.

The Art of Summarizing, Paraphrasing, and Quoting

Brian Ray

From journalists to patrol officers, writers on the job know more than one way to rope some words together and corral them into their prose. They know how to quote, reference, allude, summarize, and paraphrase with an awareness of the effects each method has on readers. This chapter will explore the various aspects of three central techniques—quoting, summarizing, and paraphrasing—as well as their rhetorical dimensions. When done well, effective use of sources may not draw much attention. But when done poorly, it stands out. That's why this chapter will also include some mistakes to illustrate and drive home the rhetorical importance of using sources properly.

Writers use sources for a variety of rhetorical reasons. The use of facts, statistics, historical precedents, reasoning, or examples appeal to a reader's need for logical evidence in support of opinions. By pointing explicitly to supporting evidence, writers and speakers demonstrate that their assertions have grounding in the real world and are shared by other people. Meanwhile, those who make claims without evidence have no support other than the forcefulness of their own views, which is often not enough to persuade audiences. Of course, writers also need to explain specifically *where* they are drawing their evidence from through proper citation. Facts and statistics are persuasive, but audiences also often want to know the source so that they can verify information for themselves. A writer or speaker who fails to provide sources becomes open to charges of fabrication or misuse of sources.

When integrating source material, writers should first ask whether and why they need to quote, paraphrase, or summarize a particular work. Each one has unique effects on audiences and requires special attention and practice. Summary provides the overall context of a particular source; paraphrase enables quick and simple reference to particular parts of a source; and quotation allows writers to weave the exact phrasing of another text into their own while giving that other due credit. Familiarity with these different ways of integrating sources gives writers a degree of versatility when dealing with sources, and they are all necessary in order to effectively support one's arguments. The next section will address the methods of each of the major tools for using sources—summary, paraphrase, and quotation.

» Summarizing

Briefly defined, a summary describes the overall argument or point of a particular text. Many less-experienced writers think of summary as a negative thing, as derivative of the original. In high school, writers are often told to explicitly avoid summarizing books, films, or stories because it doesn't demonstrate original, critical thought. On the contrary, summary is a vital step in building an argument. How can writers explain to readers how they disagree with pro-life or pro-choice advocates, for example, without first summarizing and situating these views in relation to their own? Summaries emphasize the big picture, so it's necessary to include some summary as a way of providing context for specific claims.

The key to an effective summary is brevity and intentionality. When instructors warn their students not to summarize, what they usually mean is to avoid excessive summary that has no purpose other than taking up space. When writers sense the need to summarize a source, it's best to think first about what major point is important to convey to readers and how this helps clarify their own argument. It is most often sufficient to write a sentence or two encapsulating the source's main argument, motivation, or significance for this purpose. A writer who summarizes at length most likely needs to reconsider the original intent of using that particular source.

Summary is different from quotation or paraphrase because it stays at the level of big ideas, and it therefore seldom requires a page citation. After all, what exact page would a writer cite in order to claim that Maxine Hairston's *Successful Writing*, for example, provides a comprehensive tutorial of the basic elements of composition?[1] By contrast, writers paraphrase when they rewrite a part of a text (a paragraph, several sentences) in their own words. Quotations provide a frame into which writers import the exact words of their source. Since paraphrases and quotations focus on specific parts of a text, they require page citations. By contrast, a summary is likely to include only the author and the title of the work.

Effective writing can also use the summary as a form of implicit argument. In fact, one may even say that a summary is always an argument, since the particular words chosen to describe a source are loaded with meaning. Gerald Graff and Cathy Birkenstein make a similar point in the popular but simplistic writing textbook *They Say/I Say*, observing that the use of adjectives and verbs can portray a source positively or negatively without explicitly agreeing or disagreeing with its content.[2]

"Therefore, summaries have more meaning than they get credit for. They are not innocent bystanders to the act of arguing."

Stop a moment and read the last sentence, which effectively summarizes an entire chapter from Graff and Birkenstein's book. I used the adjectives "popular" as well as "simplistic," which implies a kind of antagonism with the book even if I have not stated it directly. The truth is that I don't find the simplicity of Graff and Birkenstein's book a negative aspect, though it could be read that way. Thus I might be better off using a phrase like "elegantly simple" or even just "simple" which is less loaded than a word like "simplistic." Here I'm illustrating the need to choose words carefully, even when "merely" summarizing a work. A single word such as "supposedly" or "apparently" carries subtle meanings, and writers can deploy them when describing works in order to prepare readers for more direct arguments. Therefore, summaries have more meaning than they get credit for. They are not innocent bystanders to the act of arguing.

Summaries are also valuable tools for structuring and arranging a text. For example, in some ways the thesis statement acts as a summary of a paper's main argument. Experienced writers also tend to stop at several points throughout longer works in order to summarize what they've argued up to that point, essentially saying "Here's what I've said, and here's what I plan to say next." Conclusions also serve as summaries, condensing the paper's central arguments again into several sentences that lead to a final, memorable statement about the text's significance for its various audiences. In this sense, writers summarize themselves in order to organize their points and present them coherently.

---

1. Maxine Hairston, *Successful Writing*, 5th ed. (New York: Norton, 2003).
2. Gerald Graff and Cathy Birkenstein, *They Say/I Say* (New York: Norton, 2007).

» Paraphrasing

A paraphrase is a valuable alternative to the quotation. It allows writers to communicate specific parts of an article, book, or other forms of texts and speeches succinctly. An effective paraphrase can save writers and readers time and energy by emphasizing the main point of a particular argument. Additionally, it gives papers a sense of cohesion and voice by transitioning between quoted material, summaries of works, and a writer's own argument. Without paraphrase, research-based writing can seem choppy and become difficult to understand. Writers who rely solely on quotation will run into trouble. As Hairston says, "You don't want your paper to look as if you patched it together from other people's ideas instead of giving your own opinions and interpretation. Each quotation should be used for a definite reason."[3] Writers should only quote in order "To support an important point you are making; to illustrate a particular writer's point of view; to cite examples of experts' contrasting opinions; to illustrate the flavor or force of an author's work; to give an example of the author's style."[4] Furthermore, "Usually you'll do better to summarize [or paraphrase] an opinion or point of view rather than illustrate it with a quotation."[5]

The last portion of the previous paragraph reads a great deal like a patchwork, or what Lynn Troyka and Douglas Hesse refer to as a "cut and paste special," a piece of writing that not only seems derivative but also unorganized and incoherent.[6] Although some of Hairston's writing is quote-worthy, this essay could state the same arguments in its own words more succinctly. Doing so, it only stands to gain. Nonetheless, Hairston has done a good job of defining the major, rhetorical reasons why someone should quote—and this essay should give her credit if it is going to rely on *Successful Writing* in any significant way.

Now consider a more effective and original attempt to incorporate Hairston's ideas, one that uses paraphrase to give her due credit without taking up much space. Essentially, Hairston gives five reasons to quote a text rather than to paraphrase. But some of the reasons overlap and could be collapsed into each other. Hence, it might not be worth the space to quote her at length. Rather, writers might phrase her ideas in their own words, like this: in the composition textbook *Successful Writing*, Maxine Hairston cautions writers against overusing quotations on the grounds that audiences often prefer to hear an author's own voice, punctuated by quotations rather than dominated by

---

3. Hairston, 182.

4. Ibid.

5. Ibid.

6. Lynn Troyka and Douglass Hesse, *Simon & Schuster Handbook* (New York: Simon & Schuster: 2007), 546.

137

them. Hairston identifies a few major reasons to quote directly from a work: to support a crucial point; to sample an author's particular use of language; or to showcase conflicting opinions on an issue with evocative words.[7] This act of paraphrase, as a model, constitutes an opinion or interpretation of the source material. Although this chapter draws heavily from another work, it also brings a fresh perspective to Hairston's ideas.

Unlike a summary, a paraphrase can accommodate indirect citation, in which writers integrate facts and figures from a source without mentioning them specifically. While a direct citation always includes the work and author, an indirect citation requires only a parenthetical reference at the end of the paraphrase. Thus the paraphrase assists the organization and flow of an argument. Imagine if writers had to stop and directly reference the title and author of articles or books any time they wanted to support their claims: the result would be an unreadable mashup. The writer's own views and voice would become lost in the flood of others' names. By paraphrasing and providing indirect citations, writers stay in the spotlight of their own arguments, simultaneously giving credit where necessary and showing readers they have read and thought carefully about their topics.

Paraphrasing is especially useful when dealing with sources that contain a great deal of numerical data and analysis. A writer may want to point to the specific rate of heart disease for a particular age group when writing a scientific paper. However, that information may be buried in an extended analysis of data from a long-term study. In this case, the writer in question wants to reference a particular statistic but sees a quotation as either unnecessary or too cumbersome to work into her argument. Likewise, a summary of the work as a whole doesn't seem especially relevant to the writer's own arguments. As long as the writer in question doesn't blatantly misrepresent or mischaracterize the source, then simply stating the fact with an indirect citation does the job.

» Quoting and Framing

A piece of writing that does nothing but summarize and paraphrase, however, can strike readers as equally dull or incoherent. Such an essay might even come across as overly broad or vague. Writers should thus incorporate quotes into their paper for the reasons that Hairston outlines, especially in order to engage specific parts of sources they use. Of course, doing so requires some artistry. When quoting from a text, effective writers will introduce their quotes first and then connect each quote to their main argument. Effective techniques exist for using direct quotations, as do ineffective ones. "The main problem with

---

7. Hairston, 182.

quotation arises when writers assume that quotations speak for themselves."[8] Consider the last sentence, which goes directly against the advice it cites. In fact, it leaves several questions unanswered by failing to elaborate further on the idea that quotes require something else in order for them to contribute to an argument. What does it mean that quotations do not "speak for themselves"? Why do some writers make this assumption, what problems does it lead to, and how can they address these problems?

Here is a more effective use of the previous quote: As Gerald Graff and Cathy Birkenstein argue in their influential composition textbook *They Say/I Say*, "The main problem with quotation arises when writers assume that quotations speak for themselves."[9] Contrary to what some writers think, it is often *not* self-evident how a piece of information relates to an author's point. Readers have not read the various works that a writer draws on in a given paper. In other words, audiences lack the context that makes cited material relevant or persuasive. Since all writers have a lot on their hands, some forget to tie their quotations to their arguments. A writer's job is to not only provide evidence but to give some of that missing context and to explain the implications of a cited work on the argument at hand.

Not all quotes need an explicit introduction, and it can often grate on read-ers' patience when a writer stops to introduce the same writer over and over again. In some cases, it works better to embed quotes into an essay without directly stating the author's name a second or third time. This method "had incorporated snippets of other writers' texts into his work" by weaving phrases into sentences, using quotation marks to distinguish the source material from the writers' own words.[10] The previous sentence comes close to doing that but fails, in the end, to maintain grammatical structure. Think of embedding as inviting a word or phrase over for dinner. The writer must take care that the borrowed phrases fit into the host sentence. In other words, the word or phrase needs the same style chair, silverware, and cuisine as everyone else—otherwise it looks out of place. Use of brackets and ellipses can help here. Any time a writer wants to preclude the middle of an important passage, or otherwise alter a quote, these tools convey what the author has added for the sake of stylistic congruity. An ellipsis mark, or "three spaced periods… signal[ing] that words, phrases, or whole sentences have been cut from a passage" allow for flexibility when using source material, as does bracketing.[11]

---

8. Graff and Birkenstein, 40.

9. Ibid.

10. Lethem.

11. John Ruszkiewicz, Christina Friend, and Maxine Hairston, *The Scott Foresman Handbook for Writers*, (New Jersey: Prentice Hall, 2007), 574.

Writers also need to ensure that embedded quotes, like all cited material, do justice to the original sources. It is both unethical and ineffective to shoehorn someone else's words into your argument or to quote a work out of context. For example, the quote from Jonathan Lethem comes from his clever essay, "The Ecstasy of Influence," where he describes ways in which William S. Burroughs—a popular experimental novelist—embedded other works of fiction into his own writing *without* using quotation marks. At first, readers of this essay might think Lethem indeed discusses the academic technique of embedding. In truth, he never touches on the subject. If anyone ever looked up Lethem's essay, they would discover the fraudulent use of his words. They would see how they appear in a manner inconsistent with the ideas they express in their original context. Such fraud would weaken this essay's credibility as well as the writer's. Even if the previous paragraph were rewritten so the quote fit grammatically, then it would still violate the principles of citation. Therefore, any research-based writing must represent sources fairly and avoid the temptation to quote someone out of context for the sake of backing up a claim.

The skillful use of material in any piece of writing has a significant rhetorical impact on its reception. Essays that rely heavily on other works, to the point of stringing together several texts, imply that the author has done a fair deal of research but has yet to synthesize that material into an original argument. By contrast, writing that exclusively summarizes or paraphrases will indicate an inability or unwillingness to wrestle with the specific claims or facts used in other texts. It's best to find a balance between your words and those of others, one that requires careful consideration and close reading of each source. The decision to paraphrase or quote, and whether to explicitly introduce material or embed it, always depends on audience, occasion, and intention. At certain times, it's best to show the exact words an author uses. At others, only the information is relevant—and you can save space and time by summarizing.

Of course, whether paraphrasing or quoting, an ethical realm always exists in the use of source material. A quote might be paraphrased, quoted, or embedded with technical proficiency. But that's only half the battle. The other half lies in making sure you do justice to the writers you quote rather than using them for your own ends. Good writing negates the need for misquotes, in fact, since the point of quoting is not only to show authors that support your thesis but also those who disagree. A strong piece of writing consists of many voices and opinions, which coalesce into one.

Situating Evidence through Contextualization

Alison M. Johnson

The Vietnam War was from 1965 to 1973. More than 500 Vietnamese civilians died in My Lai. Many consider Tet Offensive to be an American military victory. Only three sentences into this chapter and my reader may be asking: what does this have to do with anything? The point is this: evidence does not help to support an argument unless it is contextualized by the author who uses it. For example, I could take this discussion of My Lai to explain that the massacre was a horrible atrocity that occurred during the Vietnam War to show how destructive humans can be under duress. The same fact about the My Lai casualties, however, could be used to point out that though it was indeed horrible, it is a relatively small number when compared to the American fatalities, totaling over 58,000. Thus, writers have to explain how the evidence they use supports the claims they make, for if they don't, these pieces of evidence can be interpreted a number of different ways, which can cause readers to become confused and ultimately not persuaded by the writer's argument. This confusion ultimately undermines the purpose of academic writing.

Sure, it's easy to use various pieces of evidence to support a viewpoint. However, it's not so easy to ensure that the audience will interpret this information the same way the author intended. Thus, in order to avoid confusion, which could lead to losing one's audience altogether, a writer needs to contextualize her/his argument and the evidence s/he uses within it. In fact, many beginning writers have already been taught to do this even though they may not be aware of it. Whenever people write an introduction they are supplying background information to their argument; they are orienting their readers into the conversation with which they are engaging. Introductions are places of contextualization and are extremely important, for if a reader has no idea what the author is talking about, then they are less likely to be persuaded by the writer's argument. Similarly, in a smaller way (especially since introductions can be quite lengthy), a writer also needs to contextualize the evidence s/he uses to support her/his argument.

So what precisely is contextualization? Contextualization is situating one's argument in context with what others have said and using the information others have provided in order to support the argument one is proposing in an effort to persuade readers. Basically, it's telling the reader why the information the writer is providing is important and how that information supports one's claims. Without this, as seen earlier, the evidence one incorporates into one's argument is useless. Just imagine what my readers would think of this chapter if I didn't clarify how the information about My Lai could be used to support the arguments provided near the end of the first paragraph and just left that discussion "hanging." In fact, when we don't contextualize our statements, we indeed leave our readers "hanging," unsupported by any sense of logic. Contextualization builds the logos of an argument and creates a coherent whole, which readers are more likely able to follow, which will, in turn, help the reader to adopt, or even fairly consider, the viewpoint the writer has put forth. Further, contextualization not only strengthens the logos of an argument, but also one's ethos as a writer. When writers clarify what they mean by the evidence they supply, readers tend to believe their deductions from said logic.

It must be noted that there are various elements that need contextualization in an argument. Along with contextualizing an argument by providing an introduction to an essay, one should also clarify meaning of any numbers or statistics, charts or graphs, and quotations one uses in one's argument. Sometimes this means that the writer must provide background information about these elements, and at all times, it means that the author must show how these figures and facts contribute to the point the writer is trying to make. Remember, contextualizing evidence should not be lengthy. Most of the time a few words or sentences will do, varying, of course, with how detailed the evidence is. When contextualizing information from a source, the writer will most likely want to introduce the source the information came from (which could include the author's name and/or the title of the work and/or what the author does for a living, when relevant) and provide her/his specific interpretation of that information, so the reader may follow the writer's line of thought.

» Numbers and Statistics

Often, we are so astounded by certain numbers or statistics that we assume that they need no explanation. This is a trap that many beginning writers fall into because the more established writers we read tend to contextualize them so easily that the contextualization they supply goes unnoticed. To use the first piece of evidence given in this chapter about the My Lai massacre, historian George C. Herring writes, "The murder of more than 500 civilians, including women and children, in the village of My Lai by an American company under the command of Lieutenant William Calley in March 1968 starkly revealed the hostility some Americans had come to feel for all Vietnamese" (260). This line ends his paragraph that speaks about the post-Tet increase in Vietnamese–American tensions. Thus, he uses the massacre of My Lai to support his point that racial tensions between white American men and Vietnamese citizens substantially increased post-1968, with fatal effects. If he didn't use the words "hostility" or clarify who precisely the civilians were, we as readers may not understand the implications of the event. But, when we think of over 500 civilians losing their lives unjustly and tragically it begins to bear a much greater significance and allows him to more starkly make his point. Thus, he uses just a few words to clarify his reading of the massacre and persuades the reader that this event exemplifies the increase of hostility between the Vietnamese and Americans after the 1968 Tet Offensive.

Students also would want to be sure that they contextualize any numbers they may use in their arguments and consider *how* to portray those numbers. Just because the writer reads a number in a certain way does not mean that her/his audience will read it as the author originally did. How numbers are phrased carry significance and invite different readings. For example, if one read that 12.6% of African Americans who made up about 9.3% of the armed forces in Vietnam became casualties by the war's end (Westheider *African American Experience* 49; Westheider *Fighting* 13), one may not find that significant, though it would certainly have a negative connotation. To borrow Joanna Wolfe's idea as articulated in her article "Rhetorical Numbers," we can cast this statistic in a number of other ways:

1. 87.4% of African Americans that served in Vietnam survived the war.

2. Over 1 out of every 10 African Americans in Vietnam became a fatality while fighting for their country.

3. Almost 9 out of every 10 African Americans in Vietnam survived to tell their tale of the quagmire.

4. The death rate for African Americans was roughly 30% higher than the rest of the men there.

5. African Americans were about 1 1/3 times more likely to die in combat than their white counterparts in the war.

Each of these different representations of the same number tells a different side to the story. The first one implies that most African Americans survived the war and thus were relatively lucky. At the same time, however, it also begs the question of what the writer means by the word "survive." This word choice implies that they may have returned home physically, but perhaps they were wounded or suffered from mental illness, like post-traumatic stress disorder. The second phrasing connotes the fact in a more negative light, implying that many died as a result of their experience there. It invites the reader to imagine a group of ten people, out of which one dies. The third example implies rarity, but highlights the story the survivor has to tell about his experience in the war. The fourth and last illustration of this statistic implies that though the number (12.6%) may seem low, it is in fact significant, and points to possible racist practices within the military at that time, though the fifth articulation is more confusing that the fourth. Therefore, writers will want to pay attention to how they situate the numbers and statistics they use in their arguments, if they use them at all (they are not always necessary of course). They will want their readers to interpret the data how they read them in the first place. Furthermore, writers should also consider how numbers and statistics are presented to their audiences, for even their presentation speaks volumes about how they can contribute to an argument. Some questions a writer may want to ask oneself and address in one's writing when contextualizing evidence could be: 1) How did the author I read convince me this was important? 2) How does this relate to the point I'm trying to make? 3) Is this enough information to persuade my reader to adopt my viewpoint?

» Charts and Graphs

Just like with numbers and statistics, writers should also be sure to provide an explanation of any charts and/or graphs they may use in their papers. Writers need to tell their readers what these visuals mean and how they contribute to the writer's conclusions. To reiterate, one does not need to include charts or graphs in order to be persuasive. The best rule of thumb when trying to decide whether to include a chart or graph in a paper is to ask: Would I lose my reader if I put this information into words? In other words, is it easier to convey the information, since it is so specific or dense, by incorporating a graph and/or chart than it is to write it all out? If your prose tends to get redundant and the syntax becomes stagnant, then yes, you might want to include a graph or chart to explain what you mean. Keep in mind though, often writers will find these charts or graphs already supplied in the sources they use to back up their claims. Unless you have conducted the research yourself, you should *not* make up a chart to explain what you mean.

Charts and graphs, just like statistics and other numerical data, also need explanation. Imagine I just dropped the following chart into a paper without any background information on the data or any explanation of my interpretation of the data:

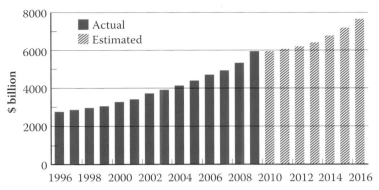

Total Spending
US from FY 1996 to FY 2016

If I just provided a single line before or after the presentation of the graph that read, "This is how the government spends our money," my reader would probably be lost, asking, "So what? What's your point?" That's precisely how readers feel when authors don't contextualize the data they supply. In fact, I could actually use this graph to convey several points. I could say that it is extremely vague and that's why we shouldn't trust websites that are put up by bloggers. Or I could say that our national spending habits are atrocious and they do not look like they'll be getting better any time soon. Or I could question what we are spending our money on and whether that merits how much we are spending. And so on and so forth. These are all several different points I could make based on the information provided in one graph. With that said, it is important to realize that we can often lose our readers if we do not tell them what our evidence means to us. This is why contextualizing charts and graphs, or any evidence you supply, is so essential to a writer's argument.

To borrow even further from the above example, I must confess that this graph was supplied by a blogger and its reliability is questionable at best. If I had just dropped it into my paper and left it "hanging" without contextualizing what it meant for me, my reader would most likely be prompted to look at my Works Cited page to see if the source is credible. If it isn't a reliable source, then not only have I lost the logical progression of my argument, but also my ethos as a writer comes under scrutiny, and my audience would probably not be persuaded to adopt my viewpoint at all. If my intention in using this as an example was to explain that one shouldn't trust bloggers' websites, but I didn't state this interpretation explicitly, my reader would be lost in confusion. Either way, the result is the same: I failed to convince my audience, which is the antithesis of argumentative writing.

» Quotations

Often, writers understand that numerical data, regardless of how it is presented to the reader, should be contextualized to guide the reader to the interpretation the writer wants them to have. However, this concept tends to fall to the wayside when it comes to incorporating other people's words—quotations. Some beginning writers have the tendency to plop and drop quotations into their writing without explaining how it strengthens their own argument. Again, just as with any numerical data, contextualizing words is extremely important, for it allows the reader to see the meaning behind the quotation as the writer does. For example, if I quoted Kurt Vonnegut's *Slaughterhouse-Five* and wrote, "So it goes," I could mean stuff happens, or that it is Billy Pilgrim's rationalization for dealing with death. However, if I don't tell my audience what I mean by the quotation, they'd be lost and so would my point.

Just as style, coherency, and diction are important aspects of writing, so is contextualization, for it guides the reader to see the writer's point more clearly. Here are some questions to help writers ensure that they have contextualized their evidence sufficiently: 1) Can an outside reader understand what I mean by incorporating this quotation, number, statistic, chart, or graph? 2) Does my audience understand how this relates to the point I'm making? 3) Did I say it succinctly enough? and 4) Did I properly cite the source? Citations can be viewed as mini-contextualizations since they name precisely where the information came from. Keep in mind, though, there is a fine line between over- and under-contextualizing. Writers shouldn't bog down their readers with information that doesn't really pertain to their point; this is over-contextualization. Under-contextualization is not supplying enough information to keep one's readers on board with the argument one is making. When one supplies the right amount of information, enough to guide the reader along the writer's thought process so they can consider the conclusions the writer has come to as a logical progression, contextualization is a great tool that can be used to boost a writer's ethos and the logos of one's argument.

» Works Cited

Chantrill, Christopher. "Charts." *US Government Spending*. N.p., n.d. Web. 9 Jan. 2012.

Herring, George C. *America's Longest War: The United States and Vietnam, 1950–1975*. 4th ed. Boston: McGraw-Hill, 2002. Print.

Vonnegut, Kurt. *Slaughterhouse-Five*. New York: Random, 1999. Print.

Westheider, James E. *The African American Experience in Vietnam: Brothers in Arms*. Lanham, MD: Rowman & Littlefield Publishers, Inc., 2008. Print.

- - -. *Fighting on Two Fronts: African Americans and the Vietnam War*. NY: New York University P., 1997. Print.

Wolfe, Joanna. "Rhetorical Numbers: A Case for Quantitative Writing in the Composition Classroom." CCC 61.3 (2010): 452–475. Print.

Organizing Research by Synthesizing Sources

Amanda Bryan

Let's be honest—research can be difficult. Research can be intimidating. It can be hard to know where to start. Luckily, it doesn't have to be. Many students admit that they do not know how to perform research or organize research, or at least they feel inadequate in this area of the academic world. Their experiences consisted of typing in one broad, usually vague, word into a search engine (or perhaps the library's database) and saving the first two or three downloadable articles that popped up. Unfortunately, too often students neglect to consider what their sources say or how they fit together. This neg-ligence results in research papers that either simply do not say anything, repeat the same point over and over again, or state different, interesting points that are not well organized or properly connected. After researching, a student may have found the greatest sources available and still have not organized them in a way to highlight their strengths within his or her argument. Such research results can hurt one's authorial ethos. Synthesizing sources can help with the difficult, and often intimidating, aspects of identifying what research says and recognizing how it strengthens an argument.

> "Synthesizing sources describes how multiple texts or arguments *connect together*."

Students often confuse synthesizing sources with summarizing sources. As Brian Ray points out in "The Art of Summarizing, Paraphrasing, and Quot-ing," summarizing a source broadly describes the overall argument of the text. Synthesizing sources describes how multiple texts or arguments *connect together*. Many writers understand these connections in their minds while compiling sources, but then lose them when they try to write or even after a few hours elapse. Synthesizing sources mentally organizes your research. Being able to articulate how sources relate to each other, and to a larger conversation, contributes to a more coherent written project. When able to synthesis sources, students, and their readers, will have a better sense of the larger argument and its importance. This type of research enhances the logos of an argument because the argument is now organized in a logical, coherent manner.

For example, let's assume that a professor assigns a research paper, and this student chooses the recently publicized topic of domestic violence in sports. Through research, the student finds three sources:

- The first source examines the NFL (National Football League) and the prevalence of domestic violence allegations brought to the commissioner's attention in the last ten years.

- The second source discusses one specific case of a domestic violence charge against a member of the United States' women's national soccer team.

- The third source provides a cultural commentary about how domestic violence seems more prevalent in today's sporting culture, but really isn't, because of the heightened awareness of domestic violence in general and the increased viewership of female fans.

It sounds like this student has a great start. But how do these three texts relate to one another? The first two discuss two different sports, a range of prevalence, and different genders. The third source doesn't specify a sport at all but discusses "sports" in general. In addition, it addresses gender but only in terms of spectators, not athletes. How does this student put these three sources into conversation with each other and with his or her particular stance?

After the initial research is completed, it is a good time to solidify a paper's stance, or argument. On the one hand, if a student wants to argue that gender influences both the reporting of domestic violence cases by the media and the frequency of incidents, then, when introducing research into the paper, one may want to address the gender differences discussed in the three sources first. On the other hand, if a student wants to focus his or her argument on the disparate reporting of domestic violence cases based on the different violence levels in various sports, then he or she may want to first point out how one source examines professional football and another professional soccer.

As mentioned before, writers usually synthesize ideas and authors in their heads. It is, however, important to write down these connections. Whether notes appear in the margins of an article, on a sticky-note, or as an email back to oneself, writing down relationships will make them more concrete in one's mind and will provide something to reference while writing a paper. After all, at some point, everyone will have to decide how to arrange sources in their papers. Framing as a way of synthesizing sources is a helpful next step. Framing is a concise, specific way of stating how sources relate. Surprisingly, many words we already know to describe relationships become beneficial in this activity.

- Are the ideas in source one *similar* to those expressed in source two?

- Are they radically, or only mildly, *dissimilar?*

- Is source three *congruent* with the ideas in source two, or do they *diverge* at some point? (In other words, not only are they similar, but also are they consistent with one another?)

- Is one of these texts *essential* to understanding the nuanced topic or issue being discussed?

- Does source three perhaps *detail* an aspect of the argument not addressed elsewhere?

Once students are able to answer these questions, or others like them, they will better understand their sources. Understanding how sources connect to one another will provide a more decisive and coherent argument.

» Common Synthesis Assignments

I argue that all research papers include synthesizing sources, usually done in the outlining or invention stages; however, many professors will specifically assign activities that mandate a synthesis of sources. These assignments usually take the forms of annotated bibliographies, synthesis papers, literature reviews, and/or historiographies. When writing any form of research, it becomes important to have a broad, but narrowed, topic. For reference, note how in the previous example the student chose to discuss not simply domestic violence, but specifically domestic violence in sports. If, when conducting research, she or he becomes overwhelmed by sources, the topic could be limited even more to a discussion of domestic violence in professional football.

Annotated bibliographies are, in the broadest sense, a list of sources. Different professors will require different things in an annotated bibliography, and students should always check for specific requirements. (For additional information about annotated bibliographies, see Alison M. Johnson's chapter "Genres Other than Essay Writing in Academic Discourse.")

Synthesis papers (also known as argument syntheses), conversely, take more of a formal paper format. Usually two to three pages in length, a synthesis paper specifically focuses on the relationships of sources. One of the main purposes of a synthesis paper assignment is to practice putting authors and texts into conversation with one another. Professors design, and assign, synthesis papers to help students better organize their overall arguments and place sources together in a logical manner. After writing a synthesis paper, students will have a detailed, coherent record of their sources, insightful knowledge about how they connect to one another, and how their papers' claims relate to their sources.

Synthesis papers still have titles, brief introductions, and Works Cited pages. In addition, synthesis papers allow a writer to offer his or her own opinion on the overall conversation, usually in the conclusion. After choosing a suitable topic, some basic steps to writing a synthesis paper include:

+ Read sources carefully.

+ Develop a thesis statement. This should be a student's arguable opinion about the topic and not simply a statement of fact.

+ Re-read these original sources for statements, ideas, quotes, and/or statistics that support or contradict your thesis. Write them down along with a comment of if they support or contradict your argument.

+ Create an outline that includes space for summaries and connections.

+ Make sure to not discuss the sources simply in the order in which they were found. Instead write about them in a logical order, placing similar texts alongside one another.

+ Write a first draft, focusing on transitions. Effective and specific transitions successfully demonstrate how sources support and/or contradict one another.

+ Revise and edit the draft. Pay attention to strengthening arguments, transitions, and word choices in addition to checking for simple grammatical oversights.

+ Create a Works Cited or Reference page, using the correct citation style requested by the professor.

+ Title the essay in a way that reflects the particular point of view taken on the researched topic.

While synthesis papers are common assignments in College Writing I and II, almost all students will be assigned a literature review in the later stages of their college careers. Professors across all disciplines assign literature reviews. In the natural and social sciences, literature reviews function as background information to further substantiate and highlight the importance of current research. In the humanities, they often function to illustrate the gaps in research or critical thought. In all disciplines, writing a literature review demonstrates the extent of students' knowledge on their research topics. Some of the largest differences between a synthesis paper and a literature review include the paper's length and the scope of research. Oftentimes, literature reviews incorporate nearly *all* of the research done about a precise and fairly narrow topic over the span of approximately ten to fifteen pages. Review essays discuss what has been previously written on the topic as well as a critical analysis of the sources discussed. Throughout a review essay, writers discover different variances in research and what could be, or needs to be, done to further the discussion.

Historiographies differ from literature reviews in a few key aspects. A historiography is commonly a research essay about the history of how a particular event is recorded or the methodological choices made by historians. To this end, they force students to consider what sources historians use and how different accounts of the same event or time period connect together. Often historiographies include questions about who writes historical accounts and how authors' agendas influence history. A historiography examines what is considered "factual" or "historical" and how an author's perspective impacts his or her reports, just as gender, age, race, and nationality can affect a person's explanations. As these historical accounts influence the construction of knowledge that all students learn, one can see that historiographies hold importance outside the discipline of history. In English courses, historiographies similarly focus on the body of historical work on a particular subject. Critically questioning how people construct knowledges about a topic informs this type of writing. As one can guess, like literature reviews, historiographical essays are extensive and very detailed. Synthesizing sources is integral to provide clearer connections between different authors and this makes a student's unique perspective sharper. These assignments may complicate one's views on a topic, but with the ability to synthesize historical sources, a greater awareness of the issues that impact different interpretations of events will be gained.

Synthesizing sources organizes research in students' minds. It allows one to make connections between the research one finds and articulate how each piece relates to the others. Additionally, by synthesizing sources, students' stances on topics become solidified. The ways various resources support, or contradict, main arguments are established as well. Some assignments throughout your college career may mandate the synthesis of sources, but even if professors do not assign the above essays, synthesizing sources while compiling research benefits your organization, your understanding, and your overall research project. Research becomes less intimidating and more manageable once it is organized.

"Research becomes less intimidating and more manageable once it is organized."

» Works Consulted

Alfano, Christine L. and Alyssa J. O'Brien. *Envision: Writing and Researching Arguments*. 4th ed. Boston: Pearson, 2014. 177–86. Print.

Lunsford, Andrea A. *EasyWriter*. 5th ed. Boston: Bedford/St. Martin's, 2014. 192–8. Print.

Ruszkiewicz, John J. *A Reader's Guide to College Writing*. Boston: Bedford/ St. Martin's, 2014. 199–202. Print.

Rhetorical Elements of Academic Citation

Ben Compton

» A Brief Overview of Citation

Any time a student writes a research paper, lab report, or presentation during their college careers, they will have to cite their sources. The structure of these citations can feel confusing, rigid, and pointless. Why, for instance, do writers need to cite the names of the authors and page numbers parenthetically by use of in-text citations? Doesn't that just clog up the paper with needless trivia? Isn't putting something in quotes enough?

These are all valid questions that deserve to be answered. This chapter attempts to address these questions and explore how students and writers can see the citation process as a rhetorical act that brings further meaning and illumination to their work. This chapter will also look at a few citation styles, such as the Modern Language Association (MLA) and the American Psychological Association (APA), to see their essential differences and similarities.

» Why Do We Cite?

One of the most important reasons to use accurate citations is that they contribute to the ethos of the writer. For audiences who are familiar with the paper's topic, citations show that the writer has done research and that they know the tone, tenor, and content of the conversation into which they are entering. This is important because it establishes that the writer and his/her arguments are credible, informed, and relevant. This credibility lends weight to the writing and enhances the writer's standing as a voice in the field who has something to offer the ongoing academic discussion. For audiences who are not familiar with the topic, these citations will help to show that there is a larger discussion and that the argument is not simply a series of random assertions.

The seventh edition of the *MLA Handbook for Writers of Research Papers* begins with an important reminder: "Every time you write a research paper, you enter into a community of writers and scholars" (xiii). By considering research and writing as contributions to a larger community, it is easy to see that accurate citations are important because they show that the author is aware of the rules and conventions of the communities for whom they are writing. Writing within these conventions evens the playing field and allows the participants in the community to share a common language and communicate in a standardized way that maximizes clarity and minimizes ambiguity. By entering into the discussion in this way, students can take control of the conversation in the same ways the critics, scholars, and writers to whom they are responding do. In this way, students cease to be outsiders in the academic discourse; rather they are active participants in an ever-widening exploration of the ideas that will fuel the next generation of critical, academic, and scientific thought.

These citations also let the audience know where the writer's ideas come from, an essential element in academic integrity. (See Charles Tedder's chapter "Academic Integrity" for more information.) Of course, it is not the job of the writer to simply parrot back information, rather it is incumbent upon them to synthesize, transform, and further the seemingly disparate threads of the academic conversation into a coherent argument that both engages with the past

> "Audiences should be able to look at a list of sources and follow them back to the original texts."

and shapes the future. These citations can be like breadcrumbs that allow the audience to tag along with the author on the path to discovery. When audiences can follow this process, they gain a clearer and better idea of how the author arrived at his or her innovative and unique new thesis.

Because writers want their audiences to follow their argument and logic as closely as possible, they need to be clear and accurate with their citations. Audiences should be able to look at a list of sources and follow them back to the original texts. The ability of a reader to revisit these original sources allows them to gauge the accuracy of the information and to gain an understanding of the original context of the cited material. Additionally, this data may assist future scholars in their research.

» In-Text Citations vs. Bibliographic Citations

Before going any further, it is useful to delineate between the *in-text citations* and *bibliographic citations* because they contain slightly different types of information and distinct purposes. In-text citations are, as their name implies, citations that appear within the body of the paper. These citations are contained within parentheses and serve to give the reader some basic information about the source and to point them to its bibliographic citation. These bibliographic citations appear at the end of the paper on either the Works

Cited page (MLA) or References page (APA). These types of citations contain significantly more information about when, where, and by whom the original work was published. These citations aid readers and researchers in locating the source in case they want clarification or more information.

Note that a Bibliography is not the same thing as a Works Cited or References page. A Bibliography is a list of all relevant sources that a writer has consulted in their research process, regardless of whether or not they are directly cited in the paper. The Works Cited and References pages list only the works that have been actually cited in the paper.

» Block Quotes

Sometimes, when writing a paper, students will find themselves needing to use longer quotes in order to fully explain and react to an idea. In both MLA and APA, these longer quotes will be set off from the rest of the text to ensure that the reader knows when the quote begins and ends. While both citation styles use block quotations, the rules for them are a little different.

In MLA style, a writer uses a block quote when the cited passage is four lines or longer. The writer will start the quote on a new line indented one inch from the left margin. Because the quote is already set off, there is no need to use quotation marks. Immediately following the final punctuation mark, the writer will add the parenthetical citation.

In APA style, writers will use block quotes when the cited passage is 40 words or longer. Like in MLA, APA block quotes start on their own line, but these are only indented 1/2 an inch. Again, because it is already set off, there is no need to use quotation marks. As in the MLA style, the parenthetical citation should come immediately following the final punctuation mark. All block quotes should be double-spaced.

With these ideas in mind, it may be useful to explore some of the specific similarities and differences between MLA and APA style.

» Modern Language Association (MLA)

Many fields within the humanities, including English, Art, Music, and Comparative Literature, use MLA as a primary citation style. MLA style has a few distinct characteristics, but the most evident is the emphasis on the name of the individual or individuals who created the work. In order to understand why they provide this emphasis on individual author(s), it is helpful to stop and consider the implicit values of some of these fields. First, many of these disciplines are primarily concerned with the texts themselves and, as such, with their creators. To this end, MLA style puts the name of the creator front and center in both in-text citations (those that appear within the body of the paper) and bibliographic (those that appear at the end of the paper in the Works Cited page citations). Consider the following passage from an academic paper on W.B. Yeats:

> In addition to using imagery and language, Yeats also utilizes the dramatic and poetic structure of the poem to meditate on the futile, but necessary search for perfection in a fallen world. When *The Monthly Review* first published the poem in December of 1902, Yeats was embarking on more formal experimentations of the limits of both poetry and theatre. It was a time when many were questioning how the theatre of Ireland would develop. Thomas Sturge Moore, writing in *The Monthly Review* in the same year, opined that Ireland's theatre was in a critical phase of growth and that care needed to be taken in what types of plays to develop (103). Although Yeats had been interested in theatre since his youth, actively working on theatrical projects through the 1890s, it was at the beginning of the twentieth century that he began to commit himself to more readily exploring the boundaries of the theatre. His dramatic poem, *The Shadowy Waters*, first published in *The North American Review* in 1900 and first performed at the Irish National Theatre Society in 1904 is evidence of this transformation. (Ross 370)

In the above passage, there are two different ways of citing an author's work. First, there are direct references to an opinion piece that Thomas Sturge Moore wrote in *The Monthly Review*. Because these citations have a "lead-in" statement that introduces the author of the work, all the writer needs in the parenthetical citation is the page number(s). The second citation in the paragraph has no introductory "lead-in" and, as such, requires us to add the name of the author in the parenthetical citation.

If a work has more than three authors, a writer would cite all the authors' last names in the first in-text citation [for example: (Zelda, Ender, Turtle, Jonah 42)], and then use only the first author's last name and the phrase "et al." (this is a Latin phrase that means "and others") for all subsequent citations [for example: (Zelda, et al. 42)].

Some sources, especially those found online, may not list page numbers. If this is the case, simply put the author's last name into the parentheses. If you do not have the name of the author, list the article's title in quotes in the parentheses.

Let's also look at the way that a writer would cite these bibliographic entries on his or her Works Cited page:

Works Cited

Moore, Thomas Sturge. "The Renovation of the Theatre." *The Monthly Review.* Vol. 7. (April–June 1902): 102–116. Googlebooks. Web. 6 Oct. 2014.

Ross, David. *The Critical Companion to William Butler Yeats: A Literary Reference to His Life and Work.* New York: Facts On File, 2009. eBook Collection (EBSCOhost). Web. 11 Oct. 2014.

As is evident, the Works Cited page requires more information than the in-text citation. In addition to the name of the author, also required are the name of the text, where it was published, the name of the publisher, its year of publication, and whether it was a print, electronic, or web source. These entries are arranged in alphabetical order with hanging indentations (the second line of the bibliographic entry is indented).

Additionally, because publishers will sometimes put out new editions or versions of a text, it may be necessary to list the original date of publication and the date of republication. Look, for example, at the citation below:

Caldwell, Erskine, and Margaret Bourke-White. *You Have Seen Their Faces.* 1937. Athens, GA: University of Georgia Press. 1995. Print

The first date is the original date of publication and the second is the date of republication. It is important to note this because there are often subtle organizational differences between editions of a book. Providing both dates lets the reader know both when the original text was published and when the specific version the writer is using was printed. Knowing the specific edition of the book helps readers, writers, and scholars to stay on the same page and see how texts change throughout time.

» American Psychological Association (APA)

Many disciplines, including the majority of sciences, social sciences, and psychology, use APA as their primary citation style. APA citation style differs from MLA in many ways, but the most obvious is that the year of publication features prominently in both in-text citations and bibliographic citations on the reference page. In order to understand why, it is helpful to consider the goals of writing in the disciplines that use APA as their primary citation method.

In these fields, more often than not, the most current information is considered the most relevant to the discussion. For example, research on quantum physics from 1985 may be illuminating, but may not reflect the most recent advancements in the field. For this reason, listing the year of publication serves to show the audience both the timeliness and relevance of the writer's work and the work they are referencing. Consider the following two paragraphs from the literature review of research study on the use of theatre in special needs classrooms:

Studies (Corbett et al., 2011; Trowsdale & Hayhow, 2013) have shown that activities that involve modeling and mirroring are effective intervention tools for self-awareness and social awareness because "most of human learning occurs by watching and imitating others. Children with autism who possess fundamental imitation ability are able to learn from observation, imitation, and modeling" (Corbett et al., 2011, p. 506).

or

Gessaroli, Andreini, Pellegri, and Frassinetti (2013) have noted, that "a number of studies suggest that the mental aspects of self-awareness are diminished and/or atypical in autism spectrum disorder (ASD). For instance, individuals with ASD have difficulty identifying and reflecting on their own mental states" (p.794). But, while many individuals with autism may have difficulty with certain elements of self-awareness, Gessaroli et al. contend, "not all aspects of self-awareness are impaired in ASD. Indeed, children with ASD are able to compare the currently perceived mirror or specular self-image with the mental representation of their bodily self-image" (p.794).

In both of these paragraphs, it is possible to see citations that privilege the year of publication along with the names of the authors, something that MLA citation style does not do. By referencing recent studies, the author of this work enhances their own credibility and the legitimacy of their research. Notice too that after the first reference to Gessaroli, Andreini, Pellegri and Frassinetti is made, the source is then simply referred to as "Gessaroli et al." In APA, writers can add the "et al." after the primary author's name when there are three or more authors of one text. This abbreviation helps to save space and increase clarity.

Let us also look at the bibliographic information for these sources as presented on the References page (the APA version of the Works Cited page).

References

Corbett, B. A., Gunther, J. R., Comins, D., Price, J., Ryan, N., Simon, D., ... Rios, T. (2011). Brief report: Theatre as therapy for children with autism spectrum disorder. *Journal of Autism & Developmental Disorders, 41*(4), 505–511. doi:10.1007/s10803-010-1064-1

Gessaroli, E., Andreini, V., Pellegri, E., & Frassinetti, F. (2013). Self-face and self-body recognition in autism. *Research In Autism Spectrum Disorders, 7*(6), 793–800. doi: 10.1016/j.rasd.2013.02.014

Trowsdale, J., & Hayhow, R. (2013). Can mimetics, a theatre-based practice, open possibilities for young people with learning disabilities? A capability approach. *British Journal of Special Education, 40*(2), 72–79. doi:10.1111/1467-8578.12019

Notice that the year of publication is still featured prominently in these citations. This points to the fact that the timely relevance of the work is vital to understanding whether the research is still current. Note, too, that unlike MLA citations that list the author's full first and last names, APA citations only use the last names and first initials. One of the reasons for this is that work in fields done in the sciences, social sciences, and psychology are often done in groups, as opposed to many of the humanities where research can be more of a solo endeavor. Including only the last names and first initials both saves space and underscores the importance of collaboration over individual research.

» Some Practical Advice

While MLA and APA are two of the most common citation styles, there are many others that students may run into as they become familiar with their fields of study. Chicago, Turabian, and AMA (American Medical Association) styles are also used in academic disciplines such as philosophy, history, and medicine. It is important that students become familiar with conventions and expectations for work in their field, but how can one person possibly keep all of these rules in their head at once? It can be frustrating to try to remember the exact difference between how to cite a podcast and how to cite a lecture. Because there is so much information, rather than trying to remember *everything*, it is more useful to just remember where to look. With that in mind, here are four quick pieces of advice:

- Students should purchase an up-to-date style guide for the citation method of their particular field or discipline. These manuals are invaluable resources that students can always throw in their backpacks or keep beside their desks as a quick reference.

- Students should also familiarize themselves with online resources. There are many places to go online to get useful information about how and when to make citations. Two of the best of these resources are the OWL website at Purdue University and Diana Hacker's website on research and documentation. These websites provide users advice on how to do a variety of different types of citations (multiple authors, songs, photographs, and so on).

- Be wary of "citation machine" websites that claim to do citation formatting. While these websites may simplify the citation process, they often provide inaccurate or poorly formatted results. One of the main reasons for this is that these websites often require the students to input the bibliographic information. Students who are not aware of what to look for in a bibliographic reference may forget to include specific pieces of information. So, even though these websites can offer shortcuts, students still need to know how the citation process works and how to check and make sure that their entries are accurate.

- Do not be shy about asking for help with questions or for clarification about citation and documentation. Your instructor may be able to help, but the library and the Writing Center are also great places to get assistance. The library has specific staff members who specialize in different fields and areas of research. These staff members are familiar with the accepted stylistic citation requirements for their fields and will be happy to provide assistance with research and accurate documentation. Along with the library, the Writing Center is an excellent resource for any questions that may come up about citations. The staff and consultants at the Writing Center are trained to work with students in one-on-one sessions to help them at all stages of the writing process, including citation.

Because this process can be confusing, it might be helpful to look at some sample bibliographic citations from common sources in both MLA and APA style. These lists are by no means exhaustive, but they should be enough to begin to demonstrate how these citations look.

» Sample Bibliographic Citations: MLA

The following is a list of sample citations for a Works Cited page in an MLA-style paper. Notice that all entries are double-spaced and alphabetized with hanging indentations.

Book by a Single Author

Last name of author, First name. *Title of Book*. Place of Publication: Publisher Name, Year of Publication. Print.

Napier, Mick. *Improvise: Scene from the Inside Out*. Portsmouth, NH: Heinemann, 2004. Print.

Book by Two Authors

Last name of first listed author, First name of first listed author, and First and Last name of second author. *Title of Book*. Place of Publication: Publisher Name, Year of Publication. Print.

Gaiman, Neil, and Terry Pratchett. *Good Omens: The Nice and Accurate Prophecies of Agnes Nutter, Witch*. New York: HarperTorch, 2006. Print.

Book by More than Three Authors

MLA style lists two ways to cite books with more than three authors. First, by simply listing the names of the authors:

Last name of first listed author, First name of first listed author, First and Last name of second author, First and Last name of third author, and First and Last name of fourth author. *Title of Book*. Place of Publication: Publisher Name, Year of Publication. Print.

Tate, Gary, Amy Rupiper Taggart, Kurt Schick, and H. Brooke Hessley, eds. *A Guide to Composition Pedagogies*. New York: Oxford UP, 2014. Print.

The other way that the MLA suggests to do this is to simply list the last name and first name of the book's first listed author and then add the phrase "et al." instead of listing the rest of the authors. This may be useful when the list of authors is becoming too long or difficult to manage. For example:

Last name of first listed author, First name of first listed author, et al. *Title of Book.* Place of Publication: Publisher Name, Year of Publication. Print.

Tate, Gary, et al., eds. *A Guide to Composition Pedagogies.* New York: Oxford UP, 2014. Print.

Shorter Work within a Collection

Last name of author, First name. "Title of Work." *Title of Book.* Ed. Name of Editor. Place of Publication: Publisher Name, Year of Publication. Page Numbers. Medium of Publication (i.e., Print or Web).

Watson, Jay. "The Rhetoric of Exhaustion and the Exhaustion of Rhetoric: Erskine Caldwell in the Thirties." *The Critical Response to Erskine Caldwell.* Ed. Robert L. McDonald. Westport, CT: Greenwood Press, 1997. 285–297. Print.

Journal Article—Print

Last name of author, First name. "Title of Article." *Title of Journal.* Volume. Issue (Year of Publication): page numbers. Medium of publication (i.e., Print or Web).

Harkins, William. "Karl Čapek's R.U.R, and A.N. Tolstoy's Revolt of the Machines." *The Slavic and East European Journal.* 4.4 (1960): 312–318. Print.

Journal Article—Web (Accessed from a Database)

Last name of author, First name. "Title of Article." *Title of Journal*. Volume. Issue (Year of Publication): Page Numbers. *Name of Database Used to Access Journal*. Web. Date Accessed.

Natividad, Annie C. "Movie Review: Precious: Based On The Novel Push By Sapphire." *Journal Of Creativity In Mental Health*. 5.3 (2010): 339–342. *Academic Search Complete*. Web. 22 Feb. 2015.

Wenthe, William. "'It Will be a Hard Toil': Yeats's Theory of Versification, 1899–1919." *Journal of Modern Literature*. 21.1 (1997): 29–48. *JSTOR*. Web. 16 Nov. 2014.

Website

Name of editor, author, or compiler (if available). "Name of webpage." *Name of Website*. Version number (if available). Name of the Publisher or Sponsor of the Site (if available), Date of creation or last update (if available). Medium of Publication (Web). Date of Access.

The Purdue OWL Family of Sites. The Writing Lab and OWL at Purdue and Purdue U, 2008. Web. 15 Apr. 2014.

Sometimes specific information about a website may not be available. There are often pieces of information that may be missing from a website such as the name of the author, the publisher, the page numbers, and the date the website was created or last updated. If this information is not available, use the abbreviation "N.p." to indicate that the name of the publisher is not provided and the abbreviation "n.d." to show that there is no accessible date for the entry. For example:

"Confederacy of Dunces (Toole)—Author Bio." *Litlovers.com*. N.p., n.d. Web. 13 Jan. 2015.

An Image

Last name of artist, First name. *Title of Image*. Year of original creation. The institution and city where the work is housed. *Title of Website*. Web. Date of Access.

Lange, Dorothea. *The Migrant Mother*. 1936. Prints and Photographs Div., Library of Congress. *Dorothea Lange's "Migrant Mother" Photographs in the Farm Security Administration Collection: An Overview*. Web. 25 Feb. 2015.

A Video

Last name of artist, First name. "Title of Video." Media type. *Name of Website*. Name of Website's Publisher, date of publishing. Web. Date of Access.

Astley, Rick. "Never Going to Give You Up." Online video clip. *YouTube*. YouTube, 24 Oct. 2009. Web. 25 Feb. 2015.

» Sample Bibliographic Citations: APA

The following is a list of sample citations that would be listed on a References page in an APA-style paper. All entries are double-spaced and alphabetized with hanging indentations.

Book by a Single Author

Last Name of Author, First and Middle Initials (if given). (Year of Publication). *Title of book*. Place of Publication: Name of Publisher.

Dewey, J. (1910). *How we think*. New York, NY: D.C. Heath and Company.

Book by Multiple Authors

Last Name of Author, First and Middle Initials (if given), & Last Name of
Second Author, First and Middle Initials (if given). (Year of Publication).
Title of book. Place of Publication: Name of Publisher.

Valle, J., & Conner, D. (2010). *Rethinking disability: A disability studies approach
to inclusive practices*. New York, NY: McGraw-Hill.

Journal Article

Last Name of Author, First and Middle Initials (if given). (Year of Publication).
Title of article. *Title of Journal/Periodical, volume number*(issue number),
page numbers.

Grandin, T. (2006). Perspectives on education from a person on the autism
spectrum. *Educational Horizons, 84*(4), 229–234.

Online Journal Article

Many online and electronic sources have something called a **Digital Object
Identifier (DOI)**. These numbers are meant to provide stable and standardized addresses for digital content. If the article has one, then the citation
would look like this:

Last Name of Author, First and Middle Initials (if given). (Year of Publication). Title of article. *Title of Journal, volume number*(issue number), page
numbers. doi: DOI number.

Trowsdale, J., & Hayhow, R. (2013). Can mimetics, a theatre-based practice, open possibilities for young people with learning disabilities? A
capability approach. *British Journal of Special Education, 40*(2), 72–79.
doi:10.1111/1467-8578.12019

If the article has between two and seven authors, list the last names and initials of all of the authors:

Joronen, K., Rankin, S. H., & Astedt-Kurki, P. (2008). School-based drama interventions in health promotion for children and adolescents: Systematic review. *Journal of Advanced Nursing, 63*(2), 116–131. doi:10.111 1/j.1365-2648.2008.04634.

If the article has eight or more authors, list just the first six authors, and then use an ellipsis (three periods separated by spaces) to separate the sixth and last author:

Corbett, B. A., Gunther, J. R., Comins, D., Price, J., Ryan, N., Simon, D.,… Rios, T. (2011). Brief report: Theatre as therapy for children with autism spectrum disorder. *Journal of Autism & Developmental Disorders, 41*(4), 505–511. doi:10.1007/s10803-010-1064-1

If the article does not have a DOI, then the citation would look like this:

Last Name of Author, First and Middle Initials (if given). (Year of Publication). Title of article. *Title of Journal, volume number*(issue number), page numbers. Retrieved from (URL of website).

Garrett, T. D., & O'Connor, D. (2010). Readers' theater: "Hold on, let's read it again." *Teaching Exceptional Children, 43*(1), 6–13. Retrieved from http:// eric.ed.gov/?id=EJ898482.

An Image

Author last name, First initial. (Role of Author). (Year image was created). *Title of work* [Type of work], Retrieved Month Day, Year, from: URL (URL of website).

Lange, D. (Photographer). 1936. *The Migrant Mother* [Photograph], Retrieved Feb. 25, 2015, from: http://www.loc.gov/rr/print/list/128_migm.html.

A Video

Author last name, first initial. [Screen name of person who posted, if available]. (year, month day of posting). Title of video [Video file]. Retrieved from (URL of Website).

Astley, R. [rickastleyvevo]. (2009, 24 October). Never going to give you up. [Video file]. Retrieved from https://www.youtube.com/watch?v=dQw4w9WgXcQ.

General Tips for Bibliographic Entries

♦ In MLA, the collection of bibliographic entries at the end of the paper is referred to as a "Works Cited" page; in APA it is referred to as "References."

♦ All entries are alphabetized by last name of author. Entries without an author are alphabetized by title.

♦ All entries have hanging indentations (first line is not indented, all subsequent lines are).

♦ All entries are double-spaced.

» Works Cited

Hacker, Diana, and Barbara Fister. *Research and Documentation Online.* 5th ed. Bedford/St. Martin's. n.d. Web. 4 Dec. 2014.

Modern Language Association. *The MLA Handbook for Writers of Research Papers.* 7th ed. NY: Modern Language Association, 2009. Print.

Rhetorical
Situations

Reading an Assignment Sheet

Summar Sparks

Assignment sheets can be overwhelming. Frequently, they are an odd combination of the specific and the vague: "analyze the nonfiction book *Zeitoun* in 321 words," "reflect on your revision practices using 12-point Times New Roman font," or "write a Blackboard post in which you critically respond to the assigned reading, and then comment on the posts of two other students in no fewer than 73 characters." While most of us are familiar with the language of word counts, fonts, and Blackboard, fewer of us are comfortable with terms such as "analyze," "reflect," and "critically respond." Since the format requirements are fairly exact and understandable and the content requirements seem less precise and detailed, it can seem easier to focus on the logistical aspects of the project and avoid thinking through the substantive parts of the assignment sheet.

While assignments can often cause feelings of anxiety or panic, thinking about the assignment sheet as presenting a rhetorical situation can provide a more productive way of approaching your work.

» Purpose

The first step to understanding an assignment sheet is to think through the purpose of the assignment. What does the instructor want you to learn through this particular project? What skills is the project designed to help you develop? What skills do you have the opportunity to demonstrate? As you think through these questions, remember to closely examine the syllabus. Often, the syllabus for a course will include a section listing the learning objectives. Read these objectives and consider how the specific assignment speaks to the general goals of the course. Additionally, the syllabus will often include a schedule, and frequently this schedule is divided into units. Look closely at the units and think about how a specific writing assignment fits into a particular unit; consider how the writing assignment relates to the readings and other course materials. The approach you take to an assignment is often the key to your success.

Generally, the goals of the writing assignment will correspond to the course readings or class work. For example, if the class readings have involved a substantial number of literacy narratives (which are focused personal narratives that describe how the author learned to read and/or write) and the assignment sheet asks for you to "reflect on your own writing practices," then you might think about reading through your class notes to determine what literacy narratives accomplish. You also might think about treating the readings as models and skimming through previous readings to get a sense of approaches to this particular type of writing. Thumbing through the assigned readings will help you discover practical ways of fulfilling the objectives of the assignment.

> "Most of the time, instructors will be evaluating your work based on how well you accomplish the objectives of the assignment."

Occasionally, instructors will include a purpose section on the assignment sheet itself. If this is the case, read it very carefully. Consider creating your own rubric or checklist based on the information presented in this section. Most of the time, instructors will be evaluating your work based on how well you accomplish the objectives of the assignment.

» Audience

The next aspect of the rhetorical situation to consider is the audience. Who will be reading your writing? Most often, the answer to this question is your instructor. But, for some assignments, the audience might be a bit more complicated or diverse than just your instructor. For example, an assignment might ask you to imagine that you are writing a memo to the president of a certain corporation. If this is the case, while your instructor will be reading your work, he or she will expect it to appeal to a particular person in a particular situation. The particular entity is the direct audience while your instructor is the indirect audience. To demonstrate your ability to appeal to both audiences, you need to consider the discourse conventions of the communities that you are addressing as well as the knowledge of the specific people who will be reading your work. The audience of your text should influence both the content and the form of your writing.

In general, to effectively appeal to your instructor, you will need to use academic discourse conventions. But be aware that the expectations of your instructor may change. If you are writing an informal essay, your instructor may expect a more conversational tone and a more exploratory thesis. If you are writing a more formal essay, your instructor may expect a more academic tone and a more developed thesis. To return to our previous example, to appeal to the president of a particular corporation, you will want to use the discourse conventions of the business world. Looking at models will help you determine the format of memos, and this, in turn, will help you develop a convincing ethos.

You also need to consider the background knowledge of your audience(s). If you are writing about a book assigned by your instructor, you will probably need to include less summary than if you are writing about a work with which your instructor may be less familiar. If you are writing to that imaginary corporate president, you likely do not need to include a very thorough description of the corporation itself.

» Text

Next, you need to consider the text itself. At this point, it may be useful to look at some of the technical requirements included in the assignment sheet. The length of time provided for you to complete an assignment may suggest the extent to which you should revise your work. If you have an entire semester to complete a project, you will most likely need to revise your work multiple times. However, if your instructor asks you to write something for the next class period, you probably need to only revise your work once or twice.

The suggested length of the assignment also provides insight into the scope of the project. If you are asked to write a one-page analysis of a text, then you will need to pick a very specific aspect of the text to examine. In one page, you simply do not have room to develop an argument about a broad topic. However, if you are given a five-page assignment, then you may choose to tackle a topic with a wider scope. With five pages, you have the space you need to adequately develop such an argument.

» Author

Finally, you need to think about how a particular assignment relates to your interests and other classes. Often, it is tempting to think of assignments as something that simply must be done in order to pass a class and earn a certain credential. While such a mindset might help you earn a degree, it does not help you gain an education. Instead of thinking about assignments as something to cross off a to-do list, consider writing occasions as potential vehicles for gaining a greater understanding of yourself and your surrounding communities.

The College Writing class provides an opportunity for you to think about yourself and your world in a different light. While your instructor develops the parameters of an assignment, you have the responsibility to make the assignment relevant to your personal goals and objectives. When you are thinking through a writing project, consider the questions that you have about the world and think about ways that you could use a particular assignment to further examine those issues. For example, imagine that you are primarily interested in approaching class or socioeconomic issues from a sociological perspective and are asked to write a literacy narrative. The composition assignment, the literacy narrative, provides you with the opportunity to examine how class issues impacted or affected your own learning processes. As you begin a project, think about how the project might present an opportunity for you to further explore your interests. In addition to asking yourself how a project relates to your own interests, carefully consider how an assignment might allow you to further pursue a topic that you are learning about in another course.

The College Writing classroom often provides a unique opportunity for interdisciplinary work. While it is unethical and against the academic integrity policy to submit a paper for credit in more than one class, you can choose to investigate one topic from multiple perspectives by writing multiple papers about that topic. By focusing on one subject, you may gain the opportunity to delve deeply into that topic and more thoroughly explore it. For example, imagine that you have been asked to complete a rhetorical analysis on a text of your choice. And pretend that you have been learning about ethnography in your anthropology class. By choosing to analyze an ethnography, you will provide yourself with the opportunity to think about a topic that interests you from a variety of disciplinary perspectives and you will gain a greater understanding of both the strengths and weaknesses of ethnography as a research method. Think about what you want to gain from completing an assignment and approach your work with those objectives in mind.

While assignment sheets can be daunting, considering them as presenting a rhetorical situation can help you develop a greater appreciation and understanding of them. In turn, this will help you both earn more satisfactory grades and, more importantly, make the most of each learning opportunity. As you read your next assignment sheet, consider the purpose, audience, text, and author. After all, you can't get it done if you don't know what "it" is.

Writing a Rhetorical Analysis

Lauren Shook

A popular writing assignment in a College Writing class is a rhetorical analysis of a text, which is an essay that identifies and explains the text's rhetorical choices (rhetorical triangle, rhetorical context, and rhetorical appeals) in order to clarify how the author persuades his/her audience of his/her message. A written rhetorical analysis is a foundational assignment that allows you to demonstrate your understanding of rhetoric; will prepare you for future informal and formal writing assignments, such as an annotated bibliography or a research paper; and most importantly, helps you comprehend your own persuasive arguments. For instance, in a research paper, you will be required to find, read, and evaluate sources, skills that a writer also uses in composing a rhetorical analysis.

You have been reading about rhetoric for several weeks and discussing at length the rhetorical appeals, canons, triangle, and context of a singular text. Sure, maybe you can look at a TV commercial about weight loss and identify ethos or logos, or understand fully that pathos oozes from Sarah McLachlan and SPCA's heart-wrenching, tear-producing, "change-the-channel-now" advertisement on animal cruelty. But for a rhetorical analysis essay, your instructor is not only asking you to *identify* rhetorical appeals or canons, they are asking you to write an essay that *analyzes* a text's rhetorical components.

Maybe you freeze, paralyzed by non-stop questions zooming through your head: Where do I begin? What is an appropriate thesis statement for a rhetorical analysis? Will I have enough to write about? Do I have to talk about ethos, pathos, and logos in addition to the rhetorical canons in one four-page essay? How will I organize my paper? Do I have to write a full introduction and full conclusion? These are just some questions that students often ask when faced with a rhetorical analysis writing assignment. So, let's answer these questions, one by one.

As we work through each of these questions, keep in mind the following. One, this chapter does not illustrate how to read for rhetorical appeals, but how to *write* about rhetoric and construct a cohesive, coherent rhetorical analysis. Before you begin your analysis, you might find it helpful to review other chapters in the text that discuss and explain rhetorical analysis. (For more information about rhetorical analysis, see the following chapters: Jacob Babb's "An Introduction to Rhetoric and the Rhetorical Triangle," Amy Berrier's "Rhetorical Context Is (Almost) Everything," Christina Romanelli's "Writing with the Rhetorical Appeals," Lauren Shook's "Reading for the Rhetorical Appeals," and Will Dodson and Chelsea Skelley's "The Canons of Rhetoric as Phases of Composition.")

Two, this essay primarily discusses how to compose a rhetorical analysis on a written text rather than other genres and mediums, such as a TV commercial, print advertisement, or even an architectural space (like a classroom). Three, keep in mind that this essay does not intend to be a "one-stop shop" for writing a rhetorical analysis; instead, this essay is merely a guide to help you begin the process. Each writer has a different method, and each writing instructor has different guidelines. Some instructors will give you very direct instructions for writing a rhetorical analysis, telling you to organize your paper in particular ways. Other instructors may have specific directions on how to write an introduction for a rhetorical analysis. Still other instructors may want you to define the rhetorical appeals, triangle, and canons in explicit details while others want you to concentrate more on analysis. This essay cannot possibly address all instructors' particulars; thus, you should always consult with your writing instructor and the assignment sheet as you draft your rhetorical analysis. Finally, I provide an example rhetorical analysis of Sojourner Truth's "Ain't I a Woman?" which you will find in this book's Appendix. In order to help you understand how one drafts a rhetorical analysis essay, I will refer to the sample rhetorical analysis periodically throughout this chapter. You may wish to read through the rhetorical analysis sample before reading the rest of this guide.

» Where Do I Begin?

To answer that question, you must ask two main questions regarding the text at hand:

1. **What** is the rhetor's argument?

2. **How** does the rhetor make his/her argument?

Asking and answering these two essential questions will give you a starting point for your analysis. You will need to review the text at hand, which means that you will read, watch, or look at it multiple times, according to the text's genre. Second, in order to answer the two previous questions, you will need to annotate the text and take detailed notes. (For additional help, see Sonya Blades's chapter "Reading Critically" and a sample annotated version of Sojourner Truth's speech "Ain't I a Woman?" located in the Appendix.) While you take notes, other questions will inevitably pop into your head. Take, for example, inquiries about the rhetor. Who is the rhetor of the text? A twenty-five-year-old male basketball star, a child star from the 1980s, an NRA card-holding grandmother, a male-to-female transgender person? How does the rhetor use his/her identity to connect to and persuade the audience? Why does it matter that the rhetor is who they are? There are a multitude of questions that you can ask about the text because that is precisely the point of this assignment: to ask questions about the persuasiveness of an argument.

> "Essentially, a rhetorical analysis should contain a thesis statement that provides an argumentative interpretation of how a rhetor persuades her/his audience."

Notice that the above questions have a pattern. The first question is often "what"-based, while follow-up questions are often "how"-based. After you have asked "what" and "how," the most crucial part of the analysis is to explain "why." Imagine your reader is a two-year-old child who asks "Why?" after everything you tell her. In a rhetorical analysis, you juggle identifying rhetorical choices, explaining how they work, and linking those rhetorical choices back to the rhetor's argument. In a rhetorical analysis, addressing the *what, how,* and *why* could look something like this:

> Truth proves herself a woman [**what**] by revealing herself to be a mother [**how**], which is what nineteenth-century America would primarily regard women as. In nineteenth-century America, a woman's main goal in life was to be a mother, and by claiming motherhood, Truth claims the highest regard of nineteenth-century womanhood in order to argue for African-American women's rights [**why**].

Asking questions will yield a more in-depth investigation of the text that will give you the information needed to build a thesis statement and solid body paragraphs. In asking questions about a text, you can answer those questions and write down your answers, then later concentrate on shaping them into coherent sentences and paragraphs.

» What Is an Appropriate Thesis for a Rhetorical Analysis?

Thesis statements are argumentative, which means that someone else should be able to disagree or create a sound counterargument against your thesis statement. This is a concrete rule for any type of written essay, including a rhetorical analysis. Essentially, a rhetorical analysis should contain a thesis statement that provides an argumentative interpretation of how a rhetor persuades her/his audience. Invention via pre-writing questions will enable you to draft an effective thesis statement: What is the rhetor's argument, and how does s/he persuade her/his audience? Answer each of those questions separately. Then, combine and style them. (For more information on pre-writing strategies, see Kristine Lee's chapter "Pre-Writing Strategies: Ways to Get Started Successfully.")

ARGUMENT: Truth effectively argues that African-American women should be treated equally as white women and freed African-American men.

HOW: Truth emphasizes her own womanhood by using rhetorical questions, drawing attention to her own body, and appealing to Christianity.

COMBINED: In "Ain't I a Woman?" Sojourner Truth argues that African-American women should be treated as equally as white women and freed African-American men. Truth emphasizes her own womanhood by using rhetorical questions, drawing attention to her own body, and appealing to Christianity.

STYLED: In "Ain't I a Woman?," Sojourner Truth emphasizes her womanhood by using rhetorical questions, drawing attention to her body, and appealing to Christianity in order to argue for African-American women's equal rights.

Thesis statements need not (and probably cannot) outline every little detail of your analysis; rather, the thesis should highlight the important parts of your analysis.

One note before moving on: A generic thesis statement that some students fall back on is "Sojourner Truth uses ethos, pathos, and logos to persuade her audience that African-American women deserve equal rights." While this thesis statement seems like a safe and sure bet, this statement is not actually a thesis statement. Simply listing that someone uses ethos, pathos, and logos is not arguable; it is a fact. Remember, every text contains ethos, pathos, and logos, and most rhetors are aware of how to use each of these appeals in their texts. Granted, some rhetors use one appeal more than another or one appeal more effectively than others (say, pathos rather than logos), but rest assured that each and every text we read, hear, or see contains all three appeals. It is a given. Second, that type of statement is vague and tells the reader nothing about the specific ways the rhetor persuades his/her audience; furthermore, such a statement fails to demonstrate your interpretation of the text. Bottom line: when drafting a thesis statement for a rhetorical analysis, you want to address how the rhetor makes her/his argument and the specific ways in which s/he does so.

» Will I Have Enough to Write About?

The above question has many variations: How many body paragraphs do I need to have? How long do my body paragraphs need to be? What if I only have one thing to say about ethos, but I need a whole paragraph on it? What if I need to write multiple paragraphs on ethos? Answering these questions lies within finding numerous examples in the text you are analyzing. In the sample rhetorical analysis of Sojourner Truth's speech (located in the Appendix), I argue that Truth's main purpose is to persuade her audience that she is a woman, who happens to be African-American, and therefore, she demands equal rights. To support my thesis, I needed to find multiple ways that Truth makes her argument. Each way that I found—"using rhetorical questions, drawing attention to her body, and appealing to Christianity"—became a topic sentence for each body paragraph. Topic sentences in a rhetorical analysis should identify one way that the rhetor makes his/her argument. For example:

Topic Sentence 1: Despite Truth's brevity, her speech is full of logos, or logical evidence, to prove Truth's womanhood.

Topic Sentence 2: Truth's use of the rhetorical question also helps Truth draw attention to her own female body.

Topic Sentence 3: In Truth's last statement of womanhood, she invokes Jesus and Christianity in order to prove that women, universally, not just African-American or white women, can fix the problem of social injustice.

Follow each topic sentence with an example. Here is the perfect place to quote from the text, and in fact, rhetorical analyses should always quote from the text. Then, analyze that example and link the example back to your thesis statement. What I have just described is the **MEAL** plan paragraph format: Main idea, Example, Analysis, and Linking sentence. (See Appendix for a sample outline following the MEAL plan format.)

Now you might decide that one example is good enough in each body paragraph, but just to be on the safe side, I encourage you to gather at least two relevant examples per paragraph. Gathering multiple examples does a number of things for your writing: 1) examples strengthen your analysis; 2) examples help build your argument's credibility as well as your own ethos as an interpreter of texts; and 3) examples add to your page length. Strong, relevant examples are your best friend in a rhetorical analysis (or in any essay for that matter).

» Do I Have to Talk about *All* of Rhetoric in a Four-page Paper?

While this is on an instructor-to-instructor basis, the answer is typically, "No." In fact, in a three- or four-page rhetorical analysis, you would do best to hone in on one or two appeals at the most, such as ethos and pathos, while mentioning a few other rhetorical techniques. Remember, the rhetorical appeals are never isolated from one another, so if you include an entire paragraph on the rhetor's ethos, it is very likely that you could also speak to the rhetor's use of logos or pathos. Focusing on ethos in one paragraph while pointing to the rhetor's use of logos or pathos demonstrates two things to your instructor: 1) that you understand that the rhetorical appeals are intimately linked together, and 2) that you are a focused, organized writer.

Furthermore, you will notice in the example rhetorical analysis provided in the Appendix that my body paragraphs do not revolve around appeals but that I incorporate the rhetorical vocabulary into the paragraphs. For instance, the second body paragraph integrates logos and pathos within one paragraph but the controlling focus of the paragraph is on how Truth uses her female body as a way to prove her womanhood and demand equal rights. Check with your instructor on how s/he would like you to address the appeals, canons, or rhetorical triangle in your rhetorical analysis.

» How Will I Organize My Paper?

Unless your instructor gives you specific directions on organization, then you should organize your rhetorical analysis according to what seems most logical. To begin organization, think about how each of your body paragraphs ties together. While drafting the sample rhetorical analysis, I structured the essay by thinking about how the rhetorical questions used by Truth are also rhetorical questions that ask the audience to look directly at her female body, which became my second body paragraph. Then, it felt logical to conclude with the last body paragraph on Christianity because my last example in the second body paragraph mentioned Jesus.

You can reflect the overarching organization of your rhetorical analysis in your topic sentences. As you draft your rhetorical analysis, write out your topic sentences and take five to ten minutes to consider how they fit together. Just as with all other essays, there is no one-size-fits-all organization scheme for a rhetorical analysis (unless your instructor gives you a particular organization scheme to follow).

In order to highlight the connections for your reader, you will do best to work on transitioning from one body paragraph to another. Transitions take many forms. Sometimes, you can use one-word transitions ("first," "second," "next," "another," etc.) while other times you may use longer phrases or even implied transitions. Transitions should be a GPS for the reader—you are giving directions for how the audience is to read your analysis. Look again at the sample rhetorical analysis. When I move from body paragraph 1 to body paragraph 2, I use a combination of transitional strategies.

> **TRANSITION EXAMPLE:** Truth's use of the rhetorical question also helps Truth draw attention to her own female body. After asking, "Ain't I a woman?" Truth immediately demands that the audience look directly at her…

My first body paragraph discusses how Truth employs rhetorical questions to make her argument, whereas my second body paragraph changes to how Truth directs attention to her own female body. My task is to show readers the connection between these two paragraphs. Therefore, I do a couple of things: 1) I repeat the topic of my first body paragraph: "use of the rhetorical question," and 2) demonstrate that the rhetorical questions aid Truth's attention to her body. I use the transition "also" to indicate that I am keeping with one aspect of Truth's rhetoric but am moving in an *additional* direction. "After asking" is a transitional phrase that directs the reader to a specific example in the text that will clarify my point. Not comfortable with transitions or unsure of how to use them? You might search online for a list of transitions, or if your instructor has assigned the textbook *They Say/I Say*, you will find a very helpful list of transitions there. You can also find additional help with organization in Chelsea Skelley's chapter "Arrangement as Rhetorical Composing."

» Do I Have to Write a Full Introduction and a Full Conclusion?

Yes and yes. Like any other academic essay, a rhetorical analysis requires an introduction that properly contextualizes the essay for the reader and a conclusion that demonstrates the significance of your essay.

Writers use many approaches for drafting an introduction, and you should apply what you already know about how to write introductions. However, you might also consider providing the rhetorical context for the text at hand. (For more information about rhetorical context, see Amy Berrier's chapter "Rhetorical Context Is (Almost) Everything.") Most of the time, this will require research, but the extra work will be worthwhile because it will show your instructor that your knowledge of rhetoric expands beyond the appeals, canons, and triangle. For the sample rhetorical analysis on Sojourner Truth's speech, I researched who Truth was, when she delivered the speech, and what other historical moments were happening at the same time that she delivered her speech. This context allowed me to think about *why* Truth is making her argument and furthermore, gave me a perfect entry into my own interpretation of her argument.

As for a conclusion, obviously you want to restate your interpretation and how you arrived at it (without repeating that word-for-word), but you could also point to the significance of your interpretation, speculate on what significance the analyzed text holds, or address why it is important to perform a rhetorical analysis of that particular text. For the conclusion in the sample rhetorical analysis, I thought about what we could gain from reading an 1851 speech or how that speech could be applied to our contemporary, twenty-first century moment.

» But I Don't Agree with the Text that I Have to Analyze! How Can I Analyze It without Bias?

Here's the thing. We all have biases, but how we deal with those biases in our writing affects our audience's perception of our ethos. A rhetorical analysis of a text is actually the perfect opportunity for you to practice writing without your biases getting in the way. For instance, I might not agree with aspects of Sojourner Truth's speech, but I was still able to speak objectively about Truth's argument and how she makes it. The same can be said even when you find yourself agreeing wholeheartedly with the text at hand, which was true as I read Truth's speech. In either case of disagreement or agreement (or even ambivalence), strive to approach the rhetorical analysis assignment with objectivity. When writing a rhetorical analysis, your focus is on what the text means and how it convinces its audience of its meaning.

In a rhetorical analysis, avoid making statements such as "Truth is correct for stating X" or "Truth is at fault when she believes that Y." You may critique or praise the argument but only if it is in service of *how* the rhetor makes his/her argument. Remember, the point of a rhetorical analysis is to understand *how* a rhetor makes his/her argument; a rhetorical analysis is not the place for you to respond to the rhetor's argument. Save your response for other assignments in your College Writing course. Furthermore, a rhetorical analysis should not serve as only a summary of the text's argument; rather than focusing on what the text says or if you agree with the text, ask yourself *how* the text works and if it does so effectively or ineffectively.

» So What? Why Do I *Need* to Write a Rhetorical Analysis?

Rhetorical analyses serve numerous purposes in College Writing courses. The most obvious purpose for writing a rhetorical analysis is so you can demonstrate your understanding of rhetoric. Perhaps the least obvious purpose, but the one that is actually the most important, is that writing a rhetorical analysis can help you understand the rhetorical choices that you make in your own writing. Learning how to analyze another's rhetorical choices can and should be a self-reflexive process for you, a space that allows you to be more aware of your rhetorical context, rhetorical triangle, and the rhetorical appeals and canons that you will use throughout your College Writing course. For example, if I understand how Sojourner Truth's organization supports her argument (an example of logos), then I can think about how my own organization will aid my written arguments. Writing a rhetorical analysis can be a daunting task, but it need not be. It only takes understanding what a written rhetorical analysis requires of you.

Viewing Peer Review as a Rhetorical Process

Lavina Ensor

In different types of writing contexts both inside and outside of the university, peer review is often used to help writers improve their writing. Stephen King, one of the most prolific writers of our time, has often remarked that his wife, Tabitha King, is an invaluable peer reviewer for all of his novels; apparently, she will read and provide feedback on a novel before he even sends it to his editor. Before this chapter on peer review appeared in *Rhetorical Approaches to College Writing*, many of my own peers reviewed it and offered suggestions about adding or removing information, organizing the essay more effectively, and rethinking my rhetorical approach. Moreover, the rhetorical act of peer review mirrors most academic conventions of college-level writing—which are the same academic conventions that govern the creation, review, and publication of various scholarly articles you'll probably read throughout your college career.

Although peer review can take many different forms, it is generally not to be confused with editing or proofreading, where the focus is mainly in removing mechanical and usage errors from the text. Peer review can include editing, but more importantly it immerses writers and readers in a rhetorical scenario where they can "see" the close interaction of different points of the rhetorical triangle: the audience, the writer, and the text/subject. Writers of all proficiencies and experiences practice peer review, seeking responses from reviewers who will give feedback on ways in which to clarify both the content and the structure of a piece of writing.

During peer review workshops in College Writing classes, instructors will usually provide some sort of guiding rubric for you to follow. Still, the act of reviewing your classmates' essays may seem a bit daunting. For example, you might wonder if you are qualified enough to make suggestions about another piece of writing. You may not exactly understand what to look for. You may feel that some aspect of the essay needs to be addressed but feel confused about how to articulate suggestions for improvement. You may also shy away from criticizing the essay at all for fear of being perceived as an obnoxious "know-it-all," which is understandable; after all, no one (or mostly no one) wants to be a know-it-all. Remember, though, that peer review workshops are supposed to be helpful. Through helping your classmates address the specific strengths and weaknesses of their own writing, you may come into a better understanding of your own.

One of the most important things that peer review can accomplish—for writers of all levels of experience and proficiencies—is to alert a writer to how her or his ideas will be received by an audience. As you respond as the "audience" for your peers' essays, remember that doing so is not merely a passive act but an active one. You need to read with the express purpose of figuring out what the writer is trying to say and whether she is saying it in a clear and effective way. Here are a few things that both the reviewers *and* writers want to pay attention to during a peer review session:

> "One of the most important things that peer review can accomplish—for writers of all levels of experience and proficiencies—is to alert a writer to how her or his ideas will be received by an audience."

» The Thesis Statement

As a reader, can you figure out the main point or argument that the writer is making? Tell the writer what you think her thesis is. In doing so, you show the writer the effect her main idea has on an audience, which can begin to help her know if she conveyed her ideas clearly on the page. Look for the placement of the thesis statement as well—wherever it is, does its placement seem logical? Drawing from your understanding of the rhetorical appeals, particularly logos and ethos, see if you can make connections between the thesis statement and the content of the body paragraphs. Also pay attention to the ways in which the writer goes about proving her thesis, looking carefully at both the points she is making *as well as* the analytical relationships between the points. Does she use signposts to continually reorient the reader to the "beat" of her essay? Does the writer explain how the examples she uses are connected to the main idea of the paper?

When your own paper is being reviewed, remember that when writing, thoughts often seem much clearer in our own minds than they do when we try to transfer them to the page. You may have lots of good ideas that seem very clear and obvious in your own mind and think you've written them out plainly. However, remember that your audience has no way of knowing the complexity or the different trains of thought it took to construct your thesis.

As such, you should pay close attention to their feedback about your main idea because they are responding to what's actually *on the page*. If your classmates confuse or misunderstand your thesis, consider that you may not actually have included all the information a reader needs to know in order to understand your central point or argument.

» Evidence and Source Material

This is a large, complex area to respond to as a reader. For all the claims that you make, you must remember to maintain your ethos as a writer and provide evidence from valid sources in support of your claims. As such, it's very important to pay close attention to the way your peers use evidence to corroborate their claims. If a writer makes a broad claim (for instance, "most women like to wear makeup"), ask yourself if she has provided some sort of evidence in support of this claim. As a reader, you can alert the writer to places in the essay where she has made a claim but has not backed it up.

Also pay attention to how the writer integrates her sources. Help the writer develop her use of logos by assessing the logical connection between the claim made and the source provided. Make sure that the source material directly speaks to the claim and helps to explain it, makes it clearer, or increases its relevance to the main idea of the essay. For example, a statistic about the amount of money spent on cosmetics in Italy during 2010, while perhaps related to the claim, does not support or clarify the purpose of the claim. Of course, check to make sure that in-text citations follow correct style guidelines here as well.

» Arrangement

Arrangement, or the manner in which an essay is organized and information is presented, can greatly affect an essay's intelligibility. Because it can be difficult to know exactly how to make suggestions in this area, try to keep track of the essay's main sections. Make notes in the margins next to each paragraph where you briefly describe the content of that paragraph. Ask questions or make suggestions about the writer's organization, such as:

+ "Why did you decide to discuss point X before point Y?"

+ "What is the relationship between this paragraph and that paragraph?"

+ "Your argument might be clearer in the essay if you moved paragraphs 4 and 5 before paragraphs 2 and 3. It seems like the reader might need to know the ideas in 4 and 5 in order to fully understand the things you are saying in 2 and 3."

When reading, watch for places in the essay that make you feel confused, jolted, unsettled, or unable to keep up with the writer's train of thought. Show the place to the writer by marking it or underlining it, then talk with her about why you feel confused (something like, "I felt like you switched subjects really quickly, and I wasn't sure how they were related"). You should also pay attention to the way your classmate has connected invention and arrangement. Look at *what* she has chosen to say and then look for *where* in the essay she has provided source material to support or explain her statement. Has she made claims and then provided evidence later, without making clear connections between the two? If so, mark these areas as places where she might want to think about how she is arranging the information in the essay.

When receiving feedback from your peers, ask them to address your organization. Let them know that you *want* their feedback and are interested in hearing what they say. Don't get me wrong—I'm not necessarily suggesting that you come right out and say, "Say something, now!" Still, asking specific questions of your peer reviewers, such as "What do you think of this transition right here?" or "Does the arrangement of information in this paragraph help make my point clear?" or "Does this paragraph seem too off-topic?" can let your peer reviewers know that you want them to thoughtfully examine your paper and that you are open to their feedback.

» Tone

Stay aware of your tone when making comments as well. Obviously, it would be very bad form to make malicious or mean comments about someone else's writing. Refrain from making overly humorous comments as well. I once had a student tell his classmate, "Dude, that sentence is waaay too long." Phrasing your feedback in this manner can create a tone that is flippant and disrespectful. You want your paper to be taken seriously, so you need to make sure that you engage with and talk to your peers in a thoughtful, respectful, and interested tone that lets them know you are taking their papers seriously as well.

On the other hand, do not restrict your remarks to simply "good!" because this does not help the writer either. "No tone" does not equal "good tone." If you don't make comments or remarks about your classmate's essay, your disengagement will probably be interpreted as disrespectful—both by your classmates and the instructor. Instead, you want to be thoughtful and considerate in your feedback. It doesn't hurt to "hedge" your language a bit. If you look at some of the sample questions I've provided, you'll notice that I use phrases like "This seems as if…" or "You might want to…." This kind of phrasing tends to yield more productive feedback.

Asking questions also helps both readers and writers in the session to understand that they are having a rhetorical conversation about writing; peer review is not a heavy-handed critique of everything each of you has done "wrong" in your essays. To this end, you might want to begin the discussion by asking the writer questions about the piece, i.e., "Why did you decide to begin your intro paragraph with information X and Y?" or "Could you explain what you mean by idea X in this paragraph?" Also, remember to give your classmates positive feedback, too. Not only will it help your classmates relax when hearing your suggestions for improvement, but it helps build confidence, which is an extremely important part of writing.

» Some Final Thoughts

Peer review is helpful for more reasons than simply breaking down and responding to the specific components of an essay; you are reviewing and being reviewed by people who are sharing your writing experience. Together, you have worked with this particular instructor, written the same essays and research papers, and participated in the same classroom atmosphere. Working with your peers in this scenario will help you clarify misunderstandings about the assignment itself, confusion about citations, or even something as simple as which titles to italicize and which to put in quotes. These questions and confusions are common, and peer review will help you gain answers to them before turning the essay in to your instructor.

Finally, know that peer review is *not* just about being able to tell the writer exactly how to "fix" something or about pointing out her usage or mechanical errors (editing/proofreading). You are reading each other's essays rhetorically with an eye for how the rhetorical appeals and the canons are working to increase the essay's persuasiveness and coherence. Take yourself and your peers seriously during peer review, and take care to respond thoughtfully to the writing and your classmates' questions. Peer review allows you the chance to give and receive feedback from people who care about the assignment you are working on—because they are working on it, too.

Instructor Feedback as Part of the Rhetorical Conversation

Kristine Lee

The feelings you have when you get a paper back from an instructor can sometimes be overwhelming. You may have a million thoughts cross your mind: What does that comment mean? Why did she ask me that question? How can I develop my analysis to support my point? It's really easy to skip over comments and just look for the grade, but this commentary has created a beneficial rhetorical exchange that includes you *and* your instructor.

One of the most important tools writers can possess is agency—the power to act, create, invent, and revise rhetoric. While writing, writers make choices to produce a convincing argument, for example, thinking about how an essay is arranged, if the evidence is credible and supported by strong analysis, and if the thesis is clear. These rhetorical considerations are what make writing unique, and instructors have similar considerations when crafting feedback. Ultimately, the goal of instructor feedback is to start a conversation—one that is interactive and productive, as well as thought-provoking. Interpreting this commentary is the key to developing your work; you have the agency to create and revise while implementing points from this rhetorical conversation. The goal of instructor feedback is not simply to fix errors, but to involve you more deeply in critically engaging your ideas with the perspectives of others. This rhetorical conversation progresses as you revise your work, the results of which can be seen in the final portfolio as well as future essays. You will respond to feedback with your own development of ideas, voice, and questions. The way you integrate feedback into essays as you progress through the course will reflect the ongoing rhetorical conversation you are engaged in as you continue to revise.

When instructors craft rhetorical commentary for students, there are several questions that come into play: Who is the audience? What may be most helpful for this writer? What kinds of examples can provide direction? What resources can assist this writer? What kinds of questions can I pose to help this writer develop ideas further? How can this writer think about and address the other sides of this argument? Instructors want commentary to be thorough and clear, and they have a specific aim: to make sure their rhetorical commentary is effective. This commentary can frequently be viewed as one-sided, but it's not—much like the ebb and flow of a natural spoken conversation, the commentary instructors provide is meant to make you think of the responses you may have, and how you can navigate your writing for continued development.

The first step instructors take when creating feedback is thinking of their audience and how they can help students achieve their writing goals. Much like the first day of class, this process is about getting to know you. Whether instructors use rubrics, examples, websites, or questioning, the aim is to have a sustained conversation with you throughout the term, to challenge you to think in ways that may be unfamiliar, and finally, to help you grow as a writer. The conversation instructors have started is meant to be continued, not only by your response as a writer, but through progressive interactions during the writing and revising process. It's always a good idea to have a separate pair of eyes looking over your work, and the aim of instructors is to provide you with valuable feedback from a different perspective. Just as class discussions become more productive and insightful with layered perspectives, so does your writing with the feedback you have received.

Here are some guidelines that can assist you in interpreting instructor feedback: First, keep an open mind. Often, instructors will intentionally ask questions in comments that will make you think—sometimes in ways you haven't before. You may feel uncomfortable during this process, but this exchange can be very fruitful and can ultimately shape your argument. Instructors may also invite you to think about your argument or point from a different angle, which may be difficult to do at first. Give yourself some time to work through these suggestions. The goal of these questions is to guide you in critically thinking about your topic, point, argument, or some other aspect of your writing. For example, if I were writing an essay for my College Writing class on why students should seek out a college education, this could be my basic argument: "Students should pursue higher education to become better citizens." When I get my paper back from my instructor, I notice that she placed this feedback in the margins:

How exactly does the pursuit of higher education make students better citizens? In what ways will this experience continue to be valuable after the degree is completed? What actions could students take to be better citizens as they obtain a degree? Contemplate these questions to make your thesis more specific. See the link below for additional information on thesis statements. This site also includes examples of effective thesis statements.

The second step of interpreting instructor feedback is to explore and brainstorm. After reading this comment, I would first go to the website to see examples and information on thesis statements. While the examples may be on entirely different topics, I will examine how they are structured, and take note of what makes them effective and convincing for readers. Next, I will brainstorm answers to the questions my instructor posed. Looking at each question individually is helpful:

How exactly does the pursuit of higher education make students better citizens?

1. *There is access to more service opportunities while in college. These can be performed through the Empty Bowls project, sorority or fraternity service projects, or campus-wide days of service.*

2. *Students are exposed to diverse perspectives in the college environment. This exposure will help students learn from the voices of others.*

In what ways will this experience continue to be valuable after the degree is completed?

1. *Following completion of the degree, students will continue to use the skill of having open dialogue with others.*

2. *Students will continue to remember how their service is invaluable to the community. They could start their own community service outreach project.*

What actions could students take to be better citizens as they obtain a degree?

1. *Take every opportunity to help others—in the UNCG community and beyond.*

2. *Work hard to appreciate and value the perspectives of others as they learn.*

After this brainstorming process, I now have the tools I need to construct a much more effective thesis:

"Higher education molds students into better citizens by instilling the values of service, appreciating and interacting with diverse perspectives, and participating in an open dialogue with others. Long after completing the degree, students can continue to put these values into practice to enrich their communities."

The dialogue that takes place between instructor feedback and revision makes it possible to consider shaping an argument or thesis in ways that may not have been previously considered.

While this is only one example of instructor feedback, you may get several other kinds of comments that can be just as helpful. An instructor may decide to provide an example of their own creation to help guide your writing, or they may give you additional resources to assist with developing knowledge or understanding. The aim is always the same: to spark your agency to create and respond to the comments available.

Thankfully, feedback doesn't have to end with only one set of comments. In fact, peer reviewers, instructors, Multiliteracy Center staff, and other reviewers may emphasize different areas to develop and point out a variety of strengths in your writing. Revision should include multiple rhetorical conversations, and these perspectives will continue to fortify your writing by setting up guidelines to deepen your analysis and develop your ideas.

Yet another structure instructors put in place are rubrics, which show writers the instructor's expectations from the very beginning of the writing process. While it may appear that this rubric is only there to show you how you got the grade you did, be sure to really study the categories of the rubric, how it is marked, and the additional comments written. Once again, this sets up a rhetorical conversation between the instructor and the writer. They have provided a visual chart of expectations, but these categories are there for a mutual benefit and conversation; you can ask your instructor for examples of these categories and have a conversation about your writing.

Every writer has individual agency and the opportunity to make rhetorical choices. The comments provided by instructors can assist in polishing an argument, developing points, and strengthening texts. This agency makes it possible to actively revise as well as implement new ideas and development. Ultimately, the writer must take the next step in continuing the conversation by taking action, responding with agency. By incorporating feedback from others while revising, writers develop their ethos as writers as well as their arguments. The act of writing and revising includes a multitude of voices and should address other perspectives, and the writer guides the process of integrating this feedback with rhetorical power.

Conferencing Rhetorically

Rae Ann Meriwether

While many composition instructors emphasize the fact that rhetoric is everywhere—in pictures, websites, songs, comics, music, and everyday conversation—students unaccustomed to thinking rhetorically often forget the importance of their rhetoric when interacting with instructors outside of the classroom. Since many instructors hold student conferences throughout the semester, it is important to remember that these individual meetings are indeed rhetorical situations. As such, they demand conscious forethought on the student's part to present herself most effectively in this specific context and to this particular audience (i.e., the instructor).

As a College Writing student, you might be unfamiliar with the practices of student/instructor conferencing and perhaps find the concept overwhelming. In this technological age, when much interpersonal communication takes place via e-mail and text messaging, you might not be used to face-to-face conversation with an instructor. Conferences require intense, focused conversation, and it is easy to feel as if you have no idea what to say or how to say it. On the other hand, you might look forward to these meetings, knowing exactly what you want to discuss and how to maximize your conference time. Regardless of your experience or level of comfort with student/instructor conferences, remember that usually an instructor holds conferences with one broad objective in mind—to help *you* succeed in her class.

While your success is the underlying goal of most student/instructor conferences, instructors usually inform students of additional, more specific goals for each conference. For example, they might schedule conferences in order to get to know their students on an individual basis, help revise an essay draft, discuss learning needs and strategies, go over a specific assignment, review a portfolio, or for various other reasons. Other instructors may require that you come to the meeting with an agenda of your own, ready to ask questions and lead the discussion. The instructor's specific intentions will provide clues as to how you should approach the conference rhetorically.

If you recognize the student/instructor conference as a rhetorical situation, then it follows that such a meeting should have a purpose and that your rhetoric must take into account the subject, audience, context, and methods of appeal in working toward that purpose. Quite often, students make the mistake of approaching a conference as if they were the audience and the instructor the writer/speaker. Students walk into a conference with the expectation that they will listen and respond to the instructor's comments and questions without having to do much else. Of course, the instructor will thoroughly consider and employ her most effective rhetorical strategies; she will ponder how best to respond to student needs, what questions will be most helpful as they revise papers, what to say to inspire them to think critically about the subject at hand, and so on. Yet, the instructor's efforts do not preclude the student's. As in any successful conversation, there must be give-and-take between the parties. Both the student and the instructor must express their desires and needs, and both must listen to each other respectfully and respond accordingly. In short, both must alternate the roles of audience and speaker.

Since the student's role requires speaking as well as listening, you should go into the conference with something to speak *about*. The best way for you to maximize the student/instructor conference experience is to come prepared with specific questions about the assignment or the course. Students who are struggling to incorporate quotations seamlessly into a research essay should bring a draft of the paper and a copy of one or two research sources. Students who feel proud of a polished paragraph or two in an argumentative essay might wish to read aloud in the hope of gaining confirmation that those paragraphs work well in the overall argument. Students confused about how point of view affects narrative might ask whether first- or third-person works best and then choose a specific section to discuss and go over in detail with the instructor. No matter the task at hand, you should always come prepared with questions or issues to discuss.

"Since the student's role requires speaking as well as listening, you should go into the conference with something to speak *about*."

In addition to being prepared, consider your ethos during the conference. Many composition instructors are friendly and personable, so it may seem appropriate to address them as friends rather than instructors. However, friendly or not, instructors want students to take their classwork seriously, to work hard to improve no matter what quality of work they begin with, and to show that they have put some thought and reflection into the meeting at hand. If a student spends the first ten minutes of a twenty-minute conference talking about last night's football game or what she did for the holidays, the instructor will probably assume that the student cares little for academic work. If the student responds in monosyllables to the instructor's questions or barely speaks at all, the instructor will probably infer that she has not put any thought or effort into this meeting and thus is wasting both of their time. While most instructors do not grade students on conference work *per se*, the impressions they receive of students in conferences can hold some weight when it comes time to grade individual assignments, portfolios, or even the overall grade for the course. Rhetorically savvy students will present an academically serious ethos to their instructors.

While preparing for your role as a speaker in the student/instructor conference probably seems like quite a bit of work on its own, playing the audience role may be even more difficult for some. Students should listen to instructors with an open mind but temper this openness with a healthy dose of independent, critical thinking. As most of us know, balancing these two stances can be extremely difficult. Students usually trust their instructors and with good reason; becoming college instructors requires striving through many years of higher education and hard work. However, trusting the instructor does not mean mindlessly following the instructor's suggestions; a student who does so indicates either a lack of critical thought or downright laziness. Instead, listen with respect and discernment, carefully considering everything that she says, but also maintaining ownership over your work. In the end, *you* are responsible for the essay, presentation, project, or portfolio.

Participating in a conversation, as both speaker and listener, demands attention, effort, and activity—it does not work if the speaker talks without regard for her audience or if the listener sits quietly without hearing or questioning the speaker. For student/instructor conferences to succeed, students must accept responsibility for speaking *and* listening well—utilizing all of their rhetorical skills to make the conference the most productive meeting possible.

Genres Other than Essay Writing in Academic Discourse

Alison M. Johnson

At certain times in a college student's academic career, one may be asked to complete assignments that seem very unfamiliar. Students are often familiar with the genre of essay writing—and the various generic forms that kind of writing may take—but other forms may not have been approached and/or explained in your academic career. You may find yourself asking: What is an annotated bibliography? I've seen abstracts, but how do I write one? Or even, what is a prospectus? Students may tend to see these assignments as "busy work," but they are not. In fact, these different kinds of assignments help students further appreciate what academic conversations are all about—engaging with critical conversations and making sure that you have something new to add to that conversation. The goal of this chapter is three-fold: to help students navigate their way through these unfamiliar generic forms of academic writing, to explain why these types of writing are important, and finally, to address why instructors might assign these types of writing assignments. Specifically, we will look at three different genres of writing: the annotated bibliography, the prospectus, and the abstract.

» The Annotated Bibliography

Annotated bibliographies may seem daunting at first, but they are actually a great way to help students synthesize their sources. (For more information on the importance and value of synthesizing sources, please refer to Amanda Bryan's chapter "Organizing Research by Synthesizing Sources.") So what is an annotated bibliography? An annotated bibliography is a collection of primary and secondary sources where each bibliographic citation is accompanied by a brief summary of the source and an explanation of how the writer plans to use that source in his or her research and argument. These assignments tell the writer's audience two things at once: what the sources the writer has researched say and how the writer plans to use them in his/her research project. How one may write them varies according to individual instructors, so one would want to be sure to read the assignment sheet closely and thoroughly.

Some instructors may want two paragraphs per bibliographic entry, whereas others may only require one paragraph. Either way, writers are essentially performing the same task for each source they include in their annotated bibliographies. The first part is providing the bibliographic entry for the source. In English classes, this will follow MLA format. The second task to complete is to accurately summarize that source. (For a more thorough investigation of how to fairly and accurately summarize a source, see Brian Ray's chapter "The Art of Summarizing, Paraphrasing, and Quoting.") Finally, in the last portion of an annotated bibliographic entry you will explain to your audience how you anticipate you will use that source in your project. Questions writers of annotated bibliographies may want to consider include: How does this source speak to or diverge from other sources I have consulted? What are some criticisms of the source that I can offer? Does this source lend credence to what I am advocating in my paper? If so, how so? If not, why not? In other words, how does this source fit with or contest my thesis statement? Why is this source needed in my project? Students may even want to pose questions that they anticipate they will answer later in their papers.

A sample annotated bibliographic entry may look like this:

> Fielding, Maureen Denise. "Karma and Trauma: Le Ly Hayslip's Healing Vision." *From Madwomen to Vietnam Veterans: Trauma, Testimony, and Recovery in Post-Colonial Women's Writing*. Diss. U of Massachusetts Amherst, 2000. 211–67. Print.
>
> Fielding contends that Le Ly Hayslip suffers from Post-traumatic Stress Disorder and Hayslip's texts, *When Heaven and Earth Changed Places* and *Child of War, Woman of Peace* elucidate her attempt to heal herself. Along with trying to heal herself from the traumas she experienced during the war, she also tries to reconcile American-Vietnamese relations through the publication of her autobiographies. This reconciliation is particularly evident in her enterprise The East Meets West Foundation. However, capitalistic influence brought to Vietnam during America's occupation there has resulted in further exploitation of women, children, and workers, via child and adult prostitution, the establishment of American company factories, and drug distribution and abuse. Fielding maintains that while "Hayslip's narratives begin the healing process… unfettered capitalism may reverse the process" (267).
>
> I plan to argue that Hayslip's text reinstills the notion that "peace," "freedom," and the ability to express one's rights can only reside in the West, since the East has been represented as a space of voicelessness. Fielding's

could be beneficial to my argument for it shows how human rights violations, concerning the right to work in a safe environment and in a safe occupation, continue in post-war Vietnam, ideologically understood as the East. More interesting to my line of inquiry, however, Fielding notes that when Le Ly attempts to make a better life for herself in war-torn Vietnam by moving to Danang and Saigon, she finds that"[h]er world continues to be unsafe, and she cannot speak, cannot testify about her trauma" (241). There are two possible reasons for Le Ly's inability to speak. Fielding argues that she cannot testify because her traumatic experiences render her mute. Another possible reason for her inexpressibility, however, lies within Vietnamese cultural dictates. Quoting Hayslip, Fielding states that "[h]er mother admonishes her never to talk about her employer's assault: 'What do you want people to think…that you are a husband tease and a tattle? No. Never anger the people who feed you'" (241). Given this, one can see that her culture will not allow her to speak. In light of this explanation, how can human rights legislation reconcile the traumatic symptom of inexpressibility with advocating one's voice before a court of law? If the traumatized victim is silenced, then a court cannot hear his/her testimony. Further, what if one's cultural life, that one has a right to participate in, dictates voicelessness in these matters? How is one to reconcile the right to be heard with the right to observe and adhere to cultural norms? These exemplify further inherent paradoxes written into human rights legislation.

While this particular example is professional and quite long, it still shows you how each component of the annotated bibliographic entry is met. This is an example from my own writing, in which I was preparing a paper to deliver at a professional conference. Above, you can see how the first paragraph summarizes the source. I have purposefully left out any critique of the source at this point, so that I may represent the author's (Fielding's) argument clearly and fairly. In the second paragraph, I have explained how I plan to use the source, noting what can be of particular value in my research. This is seen when I write phrases such as, X "could be beneficial to my argument." What's more is that in the first two sentences of the second paragraph I note the express connections between Fielding's work and my own. However, throughout the remainder of the paragraph, I trouble Fielding's assessment of Hayslip's work by postulating other possible readings of Hayslip's text (e.g., "Another possible reason for her inexpressibility, however…") and by posing questions that are pertinent to my line of study.

Some instructors, however, may not want their students to write something this long and detailed. Instead, they may find that it would be more beneficial for students to practice economizing their language, which, indeed, is a valuable skill. In this case, they may ask that you only write one-paragraph entries for each source. In that case, a sample entry may read as follows:

> Grossman, Lt. Col. Dave. *On Killing: The Psychological Cost of Learning to Kill in War and Society*. 1995. New York: Back Bay Books, 2009. Print.
>
> Grossman explores the various psychological costs of killing in war, which often results in Posttraumatic Stress Disorder or at least a sense of overwhelming guilt. Of particular importance to his study, he differentiates the Vietnam soldier from the soldiers of wars past. Shockingly, the nonfiring rate in Vietnam among soldiers "was close to 5 percent," whereas in World War II and wars prior to WWII was anywhere from 80–85% (252). Thus, these men in Vietnam had more exposure to traumatic events, and often found themselves having to pull the trigger. I could use these statistics and testimonials to show how psychologically costly this war was in comparison to the ones before it.

Here we can see how I have shortened the overall thesis statement of Grossman's work to a mere two sentences. The third sentence picks out something that I think could be of value to my overall project and the last two sentences explicitly explain how I plan to use this source in my project. Remember, though, if you are asked to write in this one-paragraph style for an annotated bibliography, your entries should be free from vague and/or unclear language. Rather, they should fairly represent your source as descriptively as possible, point to what is of value in that source, and explain succinctly and clearly how you plan to use that source in your writing. In other words, students will want to be sure they pointedly, yet quickly, explain how this information will further their thesis statement.

Finally, once you write each of your entries, you will arrange them in alphabetical order, just like you would in a Works Cited page. Overall, the assignment should look like this:

> Full Bibliographic entry (e.g., Fielding, Maureen Denise)
>
> One paragraph or two in which you summarize the source and explain how you will use the source in your project.
>
> Full Bibliographic entry (e.g., Grossman, Lt. Col. Dave)
>
> One paragraph or two in which you summarize the source and explain how you will use the source in your project.
>
> and so on, and so forth, for all of your entries.

Okay, so there's the schematics of how to write an annotated bibliography. But, why do students need to write these? Why might they be assigned? First, as mentioned previously, they are an excellent way to help students synthesize their sources. Annotated bibliographies allow writers to see how their sources speak to each other and how the writer, then, fits into that conversation. Not only do they show writers what has been said about their topic, but they also demonstrate how what the writer has to say is meaningful, new, unique, and inventive. This kind of writing is normally assigned before a student turns in his/her final project, for obvious reasons. This allows instructors to give students constructive feedback before they ever turn in their drafts or final papers. Instructors want to make sure that their students have something to *add to* the conversation, rather than just merely repeating what others have said.

> "Annotated bibliographies allow writers to see how their sources speak to each other and how the writer, then, fits into that conversation."

Annotated bibliographies are a great way to make sure that you have direction in your writing. They ensure that you have a focused topic and that you are contributing to that conversation in some meaningful way. Further, they help you, the scholar, see how the field has progressed over time. For this reason, you may want to pay particular attention to more recent scholarship on your topic. What qualifies as "recent" as opposed to "dated" scholarship depends on your field of study. Some fields progress much more quickly than others, like software programming as compared to gender studies, for instance, so you will want to be sure to read the assignment prompt carefully and/or ask your instructor how recent your scholarship needs to be. By examining the progression of one's field of inquiry, you will be able to see gaps in the scholarship or problems with what currently exists. These are gaps that you can attempt to fill or problems and possible solutions you can outline for your audience. Doing such work contributes more agency to your project overall, demonstrating how you are investing yourself and intervening in the scholarly conversation at hand, which is exciting work. (A sample annotated bibliography can be found in the Appendix.)

» The Prospectus

Many students may not have even heard of this word before. So, what *is* a prospectus? In essence, a prospectus is a project plan. Another name for this kind of writing is the academic proposal. These are normally assigned at the beginning stages of a student's writing. In this kind of assignment, often you will be asked to *briefly* outline what the current conversation on your topic is, explain how you plan to intervene in that conversation, and then elucidate how you plan to make your claims. In other words, students will first state what others have said about their topic (I'm sure you can see how an annotated bibliography could be useful here). Next, the writer will explain what he/she is adding to that conversation by posing a tentative thesis statement. Finally, the author will point to other scholars that will help him/her make that claim. These other scholars in the final portion of the prospectus are often ones who practice theory. Prospectuses are typically one to two pages in length, but can vary with one's individual instructor. (See Appendix for a sample prospectus.)

Instructors assign prospectuses for a variety of reasons. First, this kind of assignment allows instructors to check if their students have an original argument. They want to be sure that their students are adding something of value to the conversation at hand. In "Finding a Conversation to Find Research," Courtney Adams Wooten advocates, "If all you are doing is joining a conversation in order to agree with someone, to say 'I agree' without adding anything else, then your voice becomes unnecessary" (121). Instructors want to make sure that your voice is never unnecessary. Undoubtedly, you wouldn't want that either. Second, much like annotated bibliographies, assignments like the prospectus stave off procrastination, forcing the student to do some preliminary research and thinking about one's topic. Third, they allow you to see how your thinking fits in with others in the field, allowing you to find and exercise your intellectual autonomy, which can be empowering and even enjoyable. Finally, prospectuses also expose gaps in the scholarship that the writer may not have considered. This allows instructors to respond productively to students' work. They can help point to other sources that may help the student make one's case or challenge one's presumptions. Overall, prospectuses are an invaluable tool in academic writing, for they allow students to see how *their* ideas fit into the larger academic conversation of the topic they research.

» The Abstract

Some of you may be familiar with abstracts, whereas some of you may not have come across this particular genre. Either way, not to worry; here is a brief overview of what an abstract is, how to write one, how they are used, and how they are helpful in producing scholarship on a topic. An abstract is a brief overview of what the writer's research paper is about and they typically range anywhere from 250 to 500 words. The goal in writing an abstract is to explain "what the paper achieves," as Anne Sigismund Huff describes in *Writing for Scholarly Publication* (68). Students should aim to address which main subjects are explored in the paper, how the author contributes to those subjects, and why the author's contribution to the topic is important (Huff 71–2). In regards to this third rhetorical move that authors make in their abstracts, students will want to be sure that they answer the "so what?" question that Gerald Graff, Cathy Birkenstein, and Russel Durst pose in their popular text *They Say/I Say* (92–101).

In order to achieve all this work in such little space, students will want to economize their language as much as possible; this means that students will have to work on saying a lot in very little space. When writing abstracts, one should strive for using present tense, active voice, short yet information-packed sentences, and variation of word choice. If a student is given a specific word count for the assignment, which will most likely happen, there is one pretty hard-fast and standard rule: do not go over the word limit. When scholars distribute calls for papers (CFPs), a term I will address later, they often get many abstracts in response to their call. Sticking to the word limit demonstrates respect for that person's time, the conference, and the field. Ultimately, being mindful of the word limit exhibits how you have a sense of your own writerly ethos. However, at the same time, the writer will be expected to use the space meaningfully. In other words, instructors will expect students to write very close to the word count they have given their students, but not to exceed beyond that limit. The following is an example of an abstract. The word count allotted for this call for papers was 350 words:

Sam Hughes as a Second Generation Trauma Victim in Bobbie Ann Mason's *In Country*

Bobbie Ann Mason demonstrates how the trauma of war can be transferred onto those who did not take part in the war itself in her novel *In Country*. Sam Hughes, the protagonist, is the daughter of a Vietnam War soldier who died in country. This traumatic legacy of the war conflicts with her identity construction. Mostly, Sam constructs her identity by engaging in her family's history, that of her deceased father and her uncle Emmett with whom she lives. Sam illustrates how war's trauma transverses boundaries of gender, experience, and generations.

Sandra Bonilla Durham argues that Sam realizes that "all Americans are war casualties and are, in that way, united" (52), by the time she reaches the Vietnam Veterans Memorial. For Durham, this realization prepares Sam for a "promising future" (52). Lisa Hinrichsen, on the other hand, argues that the novel shows how trauma begins with the individual and then extends to larger—national and global—implications. In a related mode of inquiry— investigating the impact of trauma, but looking at Sam differently—I look at how trauma has transferred to the second-generation individual, Sam, for even Sam admits that the war "had *everything* to do with me" (71, emphasis original). In other words, in Mason's novel trauma works in the opposite way that Hinrichsen suggests—the national traumatic legacy of the Vietnam War affects the individual.

In order to prove how Sam is a second-generation trauma victim, I will rely on Marita Grimwood's definition of "second generation" and Dori Laub's theory of bearing witness in "Truth and Testimony: The Process and the Struggle." Further, to demonstrate how Sam must masculinize herself to fit into the gendered rhetoric of the Vietnam War, I will rely on Susan Jeffords' *The Remasculinization of America: Gender and the Vietnam War*. By associating herself with masculine behaviors and experiencing "unfeminine" streams-of-consciousness, Sam incorporates herself into the largely male-dominated history that claimed her father's life and bears that trauma as a result. (326 words)

Note here how I have addressed the subjects of the conversation (Bobbie Ann Mason's novel, trauma, and writing about the Vietnam War), my contribution to that topic (how gender and generational experience function in the novel), some other scholars in the conversation (Durham and Hinrichsen), how I plan to execute my argument (with the help of Grimwood and Laub), and why my contribution to the subject is important (I'm arguing the opposite of another scholar and therefore joining the conversation in a new way). You can use this breakdown and insert your own parenthetical explanations to help guide you in writing your own abstracts if you wish.

Now that we have covered the mechanics of how to write an abstract, one may ask how they are used. Abstracts are used in a variety of ways. One of such ways is to gauge an author's work quickly. When scholars put together a conference, often they will issue a call for papers (CFP) that asks for abstracts that pertain to the topic. For example, the above abstract was submitted to the American Literature Association's Symposium "War and American Literature." Submitting abstracts to CFPs, with the hopes of being invited to speak at the conference, gives students and more senior scholars alike the opportunity to come together and share ideas. Conferences are a great way to share your work with people who are often just as excited about your work as you are, which is a very rewarding experience and a wonderful feeling.

Abstracts are also often found at the beginning of journal articles. These tend to be much shorter than those asked for with CFPs. Readers use these abstracts to gauge if reading the article could be of value to them. The audience of the article may want to know if this piece engages their topic explicitly and/or directly. Readers may further ask what kind of information this author is presenting and whether it could be valuable to them in their own specific research areas. Essentially, in this way, abstracts give readers a very quick and easy way to evaluate the piece.

So far we have covered how to write abstracts and how they are used, but why might an instructor assign writing one? What's the payoff for the student? Abstracts require students to be decisive about the language they use. They allow instructors to see how specific students can be when asked to whittle down what they have taken pages to articulate to a mere paragraph or two. Abstracts also help students examine their range in diction; their efficacy in writing short, clear, cogent sentences; and their ability to write in present tense. Most importantly, writing an abstract is a great way for you to gauge whether

"Abstracts require students to be decisive about the language they use."

or not you have something to *contribute* to the conversation you are entering and whether or not you can articulate that contribution's importance to an audience. If you find that you are not making a contribution to the scholarship at hand, then it is time to reevaluate your paper overall and make sure that you are saying something new and intriguing, which ultimately gives your audience a reason to read or listen to your argument.

Hopefully, students should now feel at least a *little* more comfortable with writing in these three genres: the annotated bibliography, the prospectus, and the abstract. However, before we bring this chapter to a close, I would like to offer one brief, but very important, caveat. If your instructor assigns one of these kinds of writings and asks you to complete it differently than how I have outlined it here, by all means *follow your individual instructor's directions* first and foremost. Be sure to read the assignment sheet the instructor has given the class and follow it rigidly. Remember, not all writing is the same. I am sure that your lab report and write-up from your Biology class looks very different than the argumentative essay for your English course. The same principle applies to these other kinds of academic writing. However, being able to write in these different genres not only provides you with opportunities to showcase how you can adapt your rhetorical skills to different modes, but they also allow you to work through your writing process in ways that could be rhetorically promising, since these kinds of assignments tend to build upon each other to help ease you into the process of writing a strong, effective argument. With that said, I sincerely hope that these forms of writing have become a little more familiar to you and, in that way, more approachable and helpful to your writing and researching processes.

» Works Cited

Graff, Gerald, Cathy Birkenstein, and Russel Durst. *"They Say/I Say": The Moves that Matter in Academic Writing: With Readings*. 2 ed. New York: W. W. Norton & Co., 2012. Print.

Huff, Anne Sigismund. *Writing for Scholarly Publication*. Thousand Oaks, CA: Sage Publications, 1999. Print.

Rhetorical Analysis and Visual Media

Zach Laminack

Visual rhetorical analysis, though it might sound complicated, is related to the kinds of visual interpretations we make daily, whether negotiating road signs, seeing an advertisement, or reading someone's facial expressions. We negotiate, interpret, and make sense of images almost constantly. One of the primary ways we make sense of images is through our interpretations of advertising. The difference between quickly associating an advertisement with the brand it advertises and performing an in-depth visual rhetorical analysis is, at the outset, a matter of time and attention to detail. Visual rhetorical analysis asks us to reorient our perspectives from the speed and rapidity we're accustomed to in order to see a visual text as we might see a written text—that the sense of the "whole idea" is actually a function of the cohesion and confusion of the individual elements that comprise the whole.

Visual texts, however, assemble their components in much less obvious ways, made more subtle or covert by the speed of their presentation. TV commercials are a good example. Usually lasting no more than thirty seconds, TV commercials are designed to communicate lots of information in a limited time. Commercials are often layered with references to other images and ideas, but in ways that need no overt explanation. They rely on your ability as a "reader" to rapidly decode the images constituting the message. However, the speed and the goes-without-saying nature of advertising references are invitations for rhetorical inquiry. The essential starting points of visual rhetorical analysis are slowing down and reviewing, whether watching a thirty-second commercial a few more times or carefully considering visual elements, perhaps of a magazine ad that you might just flip through otherwise. Performing visual rhetorical analysis requires attention to detail, asking some key questions (and asking more questions about those questions), and steadily unpacking the layers of references most viewers of advertisements and visual media take for granted. Before considering an example, in this case a World War II-era U.S. Government poster, one key question needs to be addressed. If we think of images as texts, how can we "read" images in the same way that we read traditional textual media?

» Reading the Image as a Text

Images, like texts, depend on a process of visual decoding in order to understand or make a meaning of the elements that compose the whole. Reading is just such an act of visual decoding, but one so familiar that we rarely stop to think about it.[1] Something familiar is also something that goes without saying, and one of the purposes of rhetorical analysis is to reorient our perspectives on the familiar, or to "defamiliarize" our assumptions about what it is that goes without saying. The new perspective on the familiar that we gain from the questions of rhetorical inquiry forms the basis of rhetorical analysis, whether we perform that analysis on traditional textual media or on images and visual media. From this perspective, we can read advertisements, photographs,

---

1. Several theorists and rhetoricians have argued this point. Some, like Jonathan Silverman and Dean Rader, have written entire textbooks around this point. See their *The World Is a Text: Writing, Reading, and Thinking About Visual and Popular Culture*, 3rd ed. (Upper Saddle River N.J.: Pearson/Prentice Hall, 2009).

television, film, digital media, art, or architecture as kinds of texts, working systematically at the combination of the elements that compose them.

Briefly, let's look at an example of how to defamiliarize architecture so we can read it from a new perspective. Buildings may seem a particularly abstract example, but they also communicate a message. The U.S. Capitol Building (pictured on page 206), for example, stands for more than its form and communicates ideas of government, the nation, and America in several and simultaneous ways. The grand scale of the building, its material, its prominent location on a hill top, its position at one end of the National Mall in line with the Washington Monument in the center and the Lincoln Memorial at the other end all work together to communicate a message of unity and coherence on one level, the importance of the federal government on another, and an image of the nation itself on yet another. By considering the elements of the structure and its location among other structures, we come to see the Capitol as something more than itself, as something perhaps less familiar than we first thought. The techniques of defamiliarizing we can apply to the Capitol are a part of the answer to the second question of how we "read" visual media and images as a kind of text. Now we need to clarify another important point of visual rhetorical analysis: the interplay of image and text.

» The Image and the Text

Apart from text, images communicate with viewers through a system of interactions between reference and referent, or the image and the object. To further clarify the distinction between written and visual text, consider the following international pictograms as examples.[2]

These symbols need no direct textual support in order to communicate their meaning. The image of the telephone handset is recognizable without a caption. In an airport, for instance, a traveler may see the telephone icon accompanied by "telephone, teléfono, téléphone, telefon"; if he doesn't speak English, Spanish,

---

2. These icons were designed through a collaboration between the American Institute for Graphic Arts and the U.S. Department of Transportation. The goal of the collaboration was to produce universally recognizable icons for use throughout the United States transportation network in order to ease communication barriers and institute a standardized system. The first set of thirty-nine symbols was designed and commissioned in 1974, and sixteen more were added in 1979. For more information about these DOT pictograms, see the AIGA website, at http://www.aiga.org/.

French, or German, however, the icon is likely enough information in itself. Likewise the shape of a jet airliner, or the knife and fork, are images that need little explanation. If our traveler finds himself nervously watching a taxi meter counting up on the way to the Stockholm airport and passes a sign reading "Flygplats 4 km," he might continue sweating out his long journey, if he doesn't understand Swedish. But if the word he might not recognize is accompanied by the pictogram of the airplane, our traveler might learn a bit of Swedish and relax about the fate of his rapidly dwindling travel money. These pictograms are important examples of images as a kind of text because we can so easily recognize them. In other words, the reference (the image of the airplane, for instance) corresponds directly to its intended referent (the airplane itself) and thus communicates its intended meaning (airport) without need for the accompanying text as an explanation.

The distinction between the image itself and the text surrounding or accompanying the image is a useful starting point for visual rhetorical analysis. In popular media, images are often accompanied by words, and the words often work with the image to produce the total rhetorical effect. Yet as in the simplified case of the pictograms above, images do not rely absolutely on text to transmit their meaning. Photographs are some of the best examples of this distinction. The photograph on the front page of a national newspaper, for example, is designed to communicate elements of the story to the passerby, while also enticing the pedestrian to buy a copy of the paper. News photos, though, are often arguments in themselves and can be read independent of the article to which they correspond. The interplay between the text and the image, as in the example of a news photograph, can be considered through Jack Selzer's useful distinction between "textual" and "contextual" modes of rhetorical analysis. "Textual" analysis of a news photograph would focus in on the elements of the image independent of the "contextual" information of the article it accompanies. Think of the earlier analysis of the U.S. Capitol: a textual analysis would focus on its specific formal architectural details, whereas a contextual analysis would combine that information with a reading of its location along the National Mall. In the case of our example image, the World War II poster, "contextual" analysis would consider the myriad factors of the historical information necessary to "read" the image, while a "textual" analysis would consider its formal elements, or to use a photographic metaphor, what is within the frame. A thorough visual rhetorical analysis considers both elements simultaneously and asks questions about the interplay between the two modes. For example: How do the formal elements of the image speak to its context? How does our knowledge of context cause us to re-imagine the meaning of the formal elements?

To perform a visual rhetorical analysis, then, we need to slow down and carefully consider the image, both as a complete text and as the total effect of a number of formal elements. From this textual angle, we can proceed to the contextual, raising questions about the total effect of the elements as they work with and against the information surrounding the image, whether directly as in the case of a news article or indirectly in the case of historical, cultural, and economic references the image may either evoke or suppress. In addition to these questions, basic questions of rhetorical analysis are in play as well. As with more traditional modes of rhetorical inquiry, questions about the author, audience, and purpose are equally involved in visual rhetorical analysis as well, as are questions about the degree to which the rhetorical appeals (ethos, pathos, and logos) interact and act persuasively on the viewer. So, in addition to asking questions of "text" and "context," writers of visual rhetorical analyses also ask questions about the author's relationship to her audience or how the author's imagined audience influences her purpose for arranging and delivering a given text in a specific way. Additionally, you might ask what kinds of feelings or reactions the image is eliciting or how it plays to your sense of things or reasons with you. You might think about how it establishes its authority, or to what degree the image relies on you as the viewer to recognize the contextual references it makes. Your answers to these questions, when grounded directly in the textual elements of the image, form the basis of your visual rhetorical analysis.

» Analyzing the Image

As an example, we'll consider a World War II-era poster. The image presents us immediately with the elements we've discussed so far in general terms. Text is printed on the image, and the image accompanies the text. The communicative effectiveness of this piece seems, on first glance, to rely directly on the interplay of the text and the image. Other formal elements, however, set the tone for the way we interpret the text—either the words printed on the image of the book or the words at the bottom of the image that form the caption.

The background of the image is a dark and cloudy red. Its hue rises in intensity nearer to the top of the image, and darkens at the horizon, where storm clouds and lightning bolts add to an ominous mood. In the foreground, several Nazi soldiers, signified prominently by their red armbands (a stark contrast to the grey-white ground and book in the background) and tall jackboots, are tossing books onto a raging fire, which climbs above the heads of the soldiers, as their commander, to the left of the foreground, looks on. The figures in the background, however, help establish the scale of the perspective, both in terms

Books cannot be killed by fire.

People die, but books never die. No man and no force can put thought in a concentration camp forever. No man and no force can take from the world the books that embody man's eternal fight against tyranny. In this war, we know, books are weapons. *Franklin D. Roosevelt*

BOOKS ARE WEAPONS IN THE WAR OF IDEAS

of their distance from the foreground and most importantly against the scale and immensity of the book that rises high above the soldiers and looms over the book-burning party. The tiny figures are attempting to chip away at the stone façade of the book and are setting small fires around its base.

The book forms an important formal contrast to the scene. Its immensity suggests its indestructibility while also suggesting the futility of the soldiers' efforts. Its stone façade reinforces this interpretation and suggests its invulnerability to the fires set at its base. The book here, constituted by these elements, stands in as a signifier for the container of ideas which, like books, cannot be killed by fire. In this sense, the book becomes a fortress, well fortified with the weapons of "the war of ideas." U.S. President Franklin D. Roosevelt's words are literally written in stone on the façade of the book, a formal element that reinforces the strength of the message the words convey. The words "never," "forever," and "eternal" are made doubly significant by the image.

Immediately we are confronted with a rhetorically forceful message derived from the constituent elements of the image: despite their efforts, the Nazis' attempts to destroy knowledge are futile and worthless. The resilience of the book, and the ideas it houses and defends, is underscored by the monumental presence of the book literally rising from the ground and standing between the viewer and the blood-lit sky. The visual elements of the text argue that regardless of political climate, authoritarian regimes, or direct assaults, "man's eternal fight against tyranny" will continue and will prevail.

The triumphal rhetoric of this image is made richer with a look into its contextual elements. In 1933, groups of students and soldiers in Germany participated in large-scale book-burnings in an attempt to destroy and eradicate information deemed "un-German." President Roosevelt's quotation is a direct reaction against the totalitarianism and cultural control implicated in the destruction of books and knowledge. Roosevelt's quotation, along with the powerful image of the monumental book rising against the efforts of the soldiers, also highlights the difference constructed between the democratic and free U.S. and the totalitarian and fascist state of Germany under Nazi leadership. This rhetoric of the image, in light of the context of the image, becomes politically and culturally charged, both as a response to the actions of the Nazis in 1933 and as an explicit reaction to the ideology of control and manipulation. The image also operates on the viewer by eliciting reactions of fear, anger, and dark humor. The Nazis pictured in the image, despite the blood-colored sky and stormy atmosphere, are disfigured and depicted in slapstick poses in order to further underscore the intended message meant to deny the Nazis' political and cultural efficacy, either at burning books and killing ideas or at waging war.

An extended analysis of this image would undoubtedly consider the history of the book burnings further and juxtapose the message of the image and text against the U.S.'s own participation in a propaganda war, which though more benign also contributed to a form of cultural control and political persuasion. This brief analysis of the image, however, demonstrates the principle methods of visual rhetorical analysis and opens questions about the complicated relationship between the image and text. Careful attention to the details and formal elements of the image offer an interpretation of the whole, which, alongside an interpretation of the text, generates the rhetorical effect of the poster. Reading the text in this way illuminates its immediate message and sets it against its historical and cultural background in ways that draw out important questions about the purpose of the text, its creators, and its audience.

The questions applied to propaganda posters from the 1940s are the same questions applied to advertisements from the 2010s. As images become more complicated and disseminate more rapidly, the need to read them as texts becomes more pressing. Cultural persuasion happens on the level of the image, whether through advertisements, films, television, digital media, or photography. If one of our goals is to understand something about the methods and avenues of cultural change, reading into the images of culture offers a glimpse into the process of persuasion and a way to reread the familiar.

Analyzing Film Rhetoric

Dan Burns

Earlier in this collection, Lauren Shook demonstrates the powerful reading strategy of rhetorical analysis through a detailed interpretation of Sojourner Truth's classic speech, "Ain't I a Woman?" Rhetorical analysis invites readers to interpret a writer's rhetorical strategies, including each rhetorical appeal— logos, ethos, and pathos—in order to understand how various elements of the writer's language construct her purpose and message. Typically divided into five parts, these elements include diction (specific word choices), syntax (word order and "sentence sense"), structure (writing genre and organizational patterns), persona (continuity of voice and tone), and examples (particular illustrations of ideas). A writer's careful application of these elements helps to ensure that the audience receives the communicator's message with clarity, efficiency and force.

Speaking and writing are, of course, not the only ways to communicate a message; *films* also use rhetorical appeals to visually persuade and even manipulate their audiences. In fact, to think about "the available means of persuasion" in a given *cinematic* communication situation is to reject the default mode in which audiences, who often think of movies as mere entertainment, uncritically accept a suggested message. Rather than passively digesting the film as one might a gallon soda and jumbo popcorn from the cineplex concession stand, we, as a critical audience, question the film's rhetorical strategies which are aimed at producing certain persuasive effects. When determining a film's rhetorical appeals, our central goal is to identify how the particular *textual* elements that make up what we actually see and hear in the film's storyworld (characters, plot, setting, dialogue, etc.) interact with the general *contextual* details surrounding it. Starting with the film's context, we should first consider the dominant cultural conditions at the time when the film was made; this "big picture" helps us recognize the film's social, cultural, historical, political, and/or generic (genre-related) levels of meaning. In considering this contextual framework, we might keep the following questions in mind: How does the film speak to its specific era? What worldview does its content honor and defend, or mock and reject? Does the director's approach to storytelling align with a generic tradition (romance, thriller, science fiction, etc.) or depart from those conventions, and, if so, how? What larger social, historical, or political concerns might motivate these alignments or departures?

» The Elements of Film Form

In order to more precisely understand and argue with a film's rhetoric, a few basic terms are helpful in adapting rhetorical analysis from a print medium to a visual one. These textual elements simplify to four basic elements of film form: *mise-en-scène*, *cinematography*, *editing*, and *sound*. For example, *mise-en-scène* [pronounced meez-ahn-sen] which translates literally to "putting or placing in the scene," includes *setting*, *art direction*, *lighting*, *costumes*, and *performance* as part of the scene's staging, and each component can reinforce or undercut the director's vision for the film. For example, are the actors' performances stylized or realistic? Does the makeup and costuming enhance or undercut the actor's chosen aesthetic, and, again, do these choices meet genre expectations? How might the scene's set design and lighting also reinforce those expectations? The director organizes these elements in an attempt to deliver a clear message to the viewing audience.

Cinematography or camerawork, often abbreviated as simply "the shot," defines the camera's behavior toward the staged scene. What is the *scale* or distance between the camera and the object it captures? How does the range of camera *movement* toward or away from that object sharpen our understanding of the scene? What camera *angle* or perspective frames the scene and why? Shots are divided into four types according to how much of the human form is visible, a measurement of scale that includes the *long shot, medium shot, close-up,* and *extreme close-up.* The camera's position in relation to the subject being photographed is its angle: *high, eye-level,* and *low.* And last, but certainly not least, common camera movements can include *tilting, panning, tracking, zooming, handheld, crane,* and *aerial shots.* These elements define a film's visual vocabulary, the palette of potential images the director and cinematographer must map out before the film begins shooting. The choices they make have a huge impact on the range and reach of the director's appeals.

Editing organizes these formal elements "in time" as discrete shots are built into a coherent sequence of events. The most widely used expression in film editing is "the cut," another catch-all term connoting the entire editing process while denoting an actual practice. Cutting refers specifically to splicing the closing frame of one shot onto the beginning of another shot, a linkage that occurs so rapidly, given the speed at which a series of film frames pass before the human eye (24 frames per second), as to be nearly imperceptible. Like a print narrative, the manner in which a film organizes time centers on a tension between progression and digression, resolution and suspense. Following this logic, film editing operates on principles of continuity and discontinuity, cohesion and instability. Developed over time into artistic approaches, these editing choices also carry a rhetorical dimension; that is, the director's message is staged, shot, and cut together in order to create harmonious or dissonant effects for the audience. *Continuity editing,* for example, privileges clarity, concision, symmetry, and smoothness of transition: famously a hallmark of the classical "Hollywood" style. In contrast, *disjunctive editing* heightens or distorts the film's representation of the "real world," an approach that suggests the director's goal may be to alienate or upset the audience's expectations for a specific rhetorical purpose.

> "Developed over time into artistic approaches, these editing choices also carry a rhetorical dimension; that is, the director's message is staged, shot, and cut together in order to create harmonious or dissonant effects for the audience."

Sound enables viewers to hear the film's storyworld. The first type of sound is *diegetic;* these are sounds we expect to hear based on visual cues (mouths move and dialogue issues from the soundtrack, a trip through the park reveals chirping birds and wind rustling through the trees). The second type of sound is *nondiegetic;* these sounds are only audible to the audience and not to the characters within the film (a character's thoughts come up on the soundtrack in *voiceover narration*, a descending cello refrain from the *score* sparks our emotions, etc.). Both types of sound can be used to create a variety of effects, to persuade or affect an audience. For example, as a part of the diegesis, *ambient* or *natural sound* can be accounted for onscreen, but like any other element in the film, it is also capable of being manipulated for emphasis. How loudly were those birds chirping? Was the wind "gale force" or light and breezy? How distinct were the voices of the couple reclining on that picnic blanket under the tree? Did they hear the gloved assassin moving through the surrounding foliage as clearly as we could? Similarly, the musical score, a type of *non-diegetic sound*, is a highly effective tool for shaping our attitude toward a scene. Music tends to guide our opinions and feelings about the film's characters, setting, and plot; as these aural cues are not available to those inhabiting the film, they are clearly intended for the audience.

» Sample Analysis: *The Dark Knight*

For our analysis, let's explore a contemporary movie with which everyone is likely to be familiar: Christopher Nolan's hugely successful Batman film *The Dark Knight*.[1] We begin by examining the context of the film; in turn, that context enables us to see rhetorical strategies at work in the film that shape our sense of the director's purpose and message. An enormously popular character with a long history in narrative comic art, television, and film, Batman has become part of America's pop culture DNA. In fact, aside from the huge profit to be made, one wonders what could possibly motivate this highly original director to venture into an overly-familiar, even shopworn superhero narrative franchise. In order to answer that question, we start with the big picture to make some obvious points. One could argue that *The Dark Knight* (like its predecessor, *Batman Begins*, also directed by Nolan) is a pessimistic and deeply critical contribution to the superhero genre as it challenges one of our most cherished cultural values: the ability to distinguish heroism from villainy. The ethical appeal of the superhero typically offers audiences an idealistic vision of "justice for all" in action-packed clashes between absolute virtue and unrepentant vice. However, *The Dark Knight* gives this ethical appeal an unexpected spin in Nolan's apocalyptic re-boot. Indeed, although Batman fulfills the law enforcement needs of a community besieged by colorful criminals and often ineffectual police personnel, our analysis will show that Nolan's vision of the iconic title character is quite different from earlier models, dissolving hard and fast distinctions between good and evil to decidedly unsettling effect.

---

1. *The Dark Knight*, DVD, directed by Christopher Nolan (Burbank, CA: Warner Home Video, 2008).

To begin writing about the film, we first discuss the context or framework from which the film emerges, and then we build to our specific argument about this film's relationship to that framework:

> *Famously an ambivalent hero who must stand slightly apart from the law in order to defend it, Batman in* The Dark Knight *is often portrayed as more pathological than heroic, especially by the series of savagely eloquent arguments delivered by Joker.*

This statement propels our investigation and generates a set of questions:

> What happens when the hero's need to take matters into his own hands undermines the values of the society that depends upon such independent actions for its survival? To what extent should Batman be held accountable to the rules of a system that depends upon him occasionally breaking them?

We follow up quickly with a position and reasons to support it, creating a tentative thesis:

> *Through inventive choices of mise-en-scène, cinematography, editing, and sound, Nolan undermines the classic ethos of the traditional Batman superhero narrative.* The Dark Knight *collapses the distinction between hero and villain and comments particularly on the hero's ethically ambiguous social role. At the same time, the film pushes the theater audience to reconsider their opinions about the distinction between hero and villain.*

Again, when designing the thesis of your rhetorical analysis, be sure to state what the director seems to be doing contextually and what argument the director is making—here "undermines the classic ethos of the traditional Batman superhero." Then, be sure to follow that statement with an explanation of how the film demonstrates this argument—in our essay, "collapses the distinction between hero and villain and comments particularly on the hero's ethically ambiguous social role." The textual analysis that follows will illustrate how the director's argument is expressed visually through a pattern of examples.

As with the rhetorical analysis of a print text, one's *visual* rhetorical analysis should be limited to a manageable rather than comprehensive account of the film. The best way to narrow your approach is to consider an exemplary passage (in cinematic terms, "scene" or "sequence") that best illustrates the director's overall message. In our example, in order to demonstrate the revision of superhero narrative that Nolan is attempting, we would identify and analyze the film's most pointed illustration of that revision: an interrogation of the film's villain that quickly turns its focus on the hero. Because Batman ostensibly serves a community meant to mirror our own, the viewing audience—both in the film and in the theaters—is clearly invoked. Nolan's scene presents a series of conversational exchanges between its protagonist and antagonist that reflect on the morality of Gotham's citizens, remarks that are also intended to address our own ethical convictions in the "real world." The director's awareness of his viewers' values suggests just how far the film pushes against fantasy to reveal actual concerns. In other words, the film provokes the audience to reflect on the thin line that separates law and order from criminality and chaos, but perhaps nowhere so sharply as in the interrogation sequence.

» Mise-en-scène

We have already established that Nolan is working with an established genre, the superhero narrative, but are the conventions or popular expectations of that genre being fulfilled? Do the director's decisions challenge those expectations in some unusual way? If the director and his crew make the counterintuitive choice suggested by these questions, viewers should be sure to consider *why* against the film or genre's larger context. *The Dark Knight* may look like standard superhero fare at first glance, but before deciding that the film presents superhero's business as usual, we should first examine the elements of *misè-en-scene*, such as *lighting*, *decor*, and *performance*. On closer inspection, we find that Nolan's film deploys two oppositional strategies in order to critique the classic conventions of superhero films. The first approach, familiar to most mainstream audiences, is the action spectacle: a sweeping, grand-scale entertainment often called "franchise" film-making for its emphasis on sequels, high profit margins, and visual bombast. By contrast, the second approach Nolan incorporates is a more intimate, character-driven style (familiar to aficionados of his earlier, lower-budgeted films like *Following*, *Memento*, and *Insomnia*). This subtler dynamic is perfect for more detailed studies of human conflict, using a reduced, even claustrophobic, scale to display emotionally-charged encounters.

To support my thesis, I suggest that the best example of this latter strategy is a police interrogation of the Joker that occurs a little over midway through the film. It begins with the renowned villain (played by Heath Ledger) observing Commissioner Gordon (Gary Oldman) as he enters the holding cell the Joker occupies. As the scene opens, the most prominent feature is the *lighting* composition (designed by Nolan and cinematographer Wally Pfister). In a room otherwise bathed in darkness, one fluorescent grid over the cell's steel door entrance illuminates the shot's background. A desk lamp exposes the foreground to Joker's right, casting a cold glow within the inky black over his

shoulder. The play of light on the characters' faces is especially important, given the way its low-key effects add menace and uncertainty to the encounter. Nolan's composition is here both cartoonish—the desk lamp's reflection off the table's surface like a slumber party flashlight under the Joker's ghoulish face—and complex. For example, as Gordon descends to sit opposite the villain, he moves out of the strong "institutional" glare of the room's threshold and becomes enveloped in the Joker's murkier territory. This movement causes at least half of the officer's face to go into shadow. Though an authority figure, Gordon here subtly yields control by shifting from a standing position of power in full light—holding the "keys," as it were, to Joker's freedom—to a seated one in darkness that "levels" their playing field.

Nolan's *dialogue* (he also co-wrote the film with his brother Jonathan) is both terse and tongue-in-cheek as Gordon presses a noncompliant Joker about the whereabouts of crusading District Attorney Harvey Dent. As the film's obvious moral center, Dent polices the line between heroism and villainy enacted by Batman and Joker's characters. Because Dent initially stands for unquestionable morality as a crusader to eradicate crime, his presence is very much felt in the interrogation scene. Indeed, Dent's mission throughout the movie is to simultaneously rid Gotham of criminals like the Joker while also eliminating the need for "freelance" crimefighters like Batman. He is talked about directly in this scene, of course, as Joker is being questioned so that Gordon can physically locate the D.A., whom Joker has kidnapped. But Dent's strict moral code is also evoked because of the brutal, probably illegal manner in which this questioning is conducted. Ironically, the turn of events that follows this interrogation will result in Dent's harrowing transformation into alter-ego villain "Two-Face"—a murderously psychotic "shadow" of his former self.

In short, the manner in which both Gordon and Joker's faces are shaded anticipates Dent's later mutilation and reinforces the film's preoccupation with moral ambivalence. From previous scenes, we know that Gordon's ethos is on increasingly shaky ground because of his superiors' concerns about the amount of power he has allowed Batman. Once Gordon enters Joker's darkened terrain, he makes vulnerable his own position as a moral man who follows the letter of the law. Actor Gary Oldman interprets Commissioner Gordon—a character usually depicted as a well-meaning but ineffective bureaucrat—as a good man ensnared in a flawed system. His hands folded, a wedding ring glinting in the reflection from the desk lamp, Oldman's Gordon engages Joker with an earnestness otherwise lacking in the film's other performances. The actor's strategy of nervously playing with his hands as he talks to Joker, clasping and folding them as if in prayer, calls attention to the ring and foreshadows the danger in which his family will be placed at the film's conclusion.

Performance, as an interpretive art, is clearly reflected in some of Gary Oldman's acting choices, and it joins other elements of the mise-en-scène (like lighting) to help us make important connections with other parts of the film. Heath

Ledger's occluded features during the interrogation scene anticipate his later appearance at Dent's hospital bedside when, in a striking use of computer-generated imagery (CGI), nearly half of the District Attorney's face is revealed to be missing. A justifiably celebrated performance, Heath Ledger's habit of cocking his head a bit when he talks—replete with involuntarily twitches and spasms—communicates every line with a kind of off-kilter contempt. Rather than the grandstanding of earlier Jokers (from Cesar Romero's cackling television personality in the 1960s to Jack Nicholson's campy clown in Tim Burton's 1989 adaptation), Ledger comes across as an edgy cannibal, constantly licking his lips as if to eat off the make-up caked around his ravaged lips. More akin to edgier psychopathic performances (including Malcolm McDowell's teen hoodlum from *A Clockwork Orange* or Andy Robinson's counterculture serial killer from *Dirty Harry*), Ledger's work has been acclaimed as almost too real and punctures our expectations for what a Joker performance should be. With his piercing black eyes and seaweed hair, the actor's skittish range of motion and ecstatic reactions to violence (especially against his own body) adds an unsettling masochistic layer to the character. Ledger's performance only deepens our sense of fascination and disgust with Nolan's grotesque reimagining of Gotham's criminal underworld.

» Cinematography

The way the camera is positioned relative to Gordon's movements—from *high* and *low angles*—can reflect variances of power. A figure shot from above suggests that character's vulnerability and weakness, while a towering subject captured from a low angle implies that character's force, dominance and strength. Similarly, *close-up* and *extreme close-up* shots are often considered a director's most powerful tools for creating empathy, with their capacity to reveal human emotions on a simultaneously intimate and grand scale. *Forward*, *backward* and *lateral* movement complicates the potential meanings suggested by angle and scale as the camera's mobility can yield important information for the audience. Taking note of these movements helps us determine the rhetorical effects of the scene by answering questions like "What is our location?", "Who is involved?", "Why are we situated from this particular vantage point?" and most importantly for this scene, "*Where's Batman?*"

The brilliance of Nolan's use of *camera angle*, *position*, and *scale* is not apparent until Gordon leaves the interrogation room. Then, we finally understand that the camera's position from over the Joker's shoulder is actually Batman's, who has been standing in the darkness directly behind the villain throughout his interaction with Gordon. Though the camera does not usually represent the view of individual characters in Nolan's film, here, significantly, it is "occupied" *by the hero*. Why, we should ask, does the director frame the villain's interrogation from the perspective of the film's hero? Batman's sudden appearance in the room implies subterfuge and unfair advantage. In this shot, Nolan clearly intends to call Batman's ethos into question. As mentioned earlier, this film makes Harvey Dent into Gotham's new champion of individual liberty and public safety, and his legally justified defense of the rights of the common citizen is sharply at odds with Batman's unorthodox actions, whose "crime-fighting" strategies begin to look much more like "vigilantism." Even if Batman is capable of delivering results, he is still outside the law. The interrogation scene—which, on the surface, is intended to question the villain for his role in harming Gotham's "new knight" (Dent)—actually prosecutes an argument against the city's former guardian: Batman.

After Gordon exits, the room's lights flicker on in bright and jarring fluorescence, revealing Batman's presence directly behind Joker. Batman's "surprise" mimics Nolan's trick with perspective—and the hero capitalizes on the director's "cheat" by cheaply pounding the Joker's head into the table with a concussive slam. As violence escalates throughout the scene, Batman's interrogation methods grow increasingly ferocious and illegal, and this *shot*—as a microcosm of what is arguably the whole film's message—equates Batman's ethos with the Joker's. The action of this scene is not the spectacle we have grown accustomed to in the film's earlier aerial ballets (in which trucks soundlessly jackknife at top speed and characters defy gravity through assorted technological marvels). Instead, in this scene, Nolan moves to *handheld* camera, a "grubbier" dynamic that places viewers at the center of messy reality. Handheld provides the best technology for *verisimilitude*—a view that seems or appears real—with the audience occupying a virtual spot alongside the characters onscreen. Here, the effect contributes to the interrogation's increasingly harrowing, even queasy efficiency.

» Editing and Sound

Having already violated our trust by placing Batman behind Joker and then "surprising" us with his presence, Nolan edits their encounter by *cross-* and *intercutting* the action with shots of the anxious reactions from officers watching through the one-way surveillance glass bordering the cell. These cutting techniques disorient the viewer and contribute to a feeling of helplessness while aligning us with the prevailing law and order ethos, despite the urgency of Batman's goals. After an unnerving monologue from the villain that relentlessly unmasks the hypocrisy of the social institutions Batman defends, our "hero" lifts Joker across the table and throws him against a wall. Again, Nolan intercuts this physical movement to show it from the perspectives of the observing police officers. Nearly every action Batman takes is mediated by the reactions of observing police officers in the scene. Capturing Batman's increasingly illegal methods from the vantage point of Gordon and the other police personnel, Nolan tacitly acknowledges Joker's thesis: the standards for conduct upon which society depends and that law enforcement supposedly upholds are easily fractured. Calling our sense of right and wrong into question is precisely what Nolan hopes to do in these exchanges; his camera emphasizes this point, as it careens wildly over the space, following an increasingly unhinged hero as he mops the proverbial floor with the Joker's constitutional rights in full view of Gotham's finest. That Batman performs this service in order to save a man (Dent) who would likely try him and the witnessing officers for police brutality is one of the scene's many dramatic ironies.

Finally, we isolate the element of *sound* as the last contributing factor in shaping the interrogation scene's mood. Certainly easy to overlook, *ambient* (diegetic) *sound* is used to powerful effect in the sequence: consider the noisy creaking of the metal chair that Batman drags to bar the door as Gordon rushes to prevent the villain's assault; the sickening thud of Batman's rubberized fistplates pounding Joker's face; or, more generally, the way these sounds reverberate throughout the sterile and expansive room. All of these carefully controlled sounds contribute to our concern that this interrogation may exceed certain acceptable limits. *Non-diegetic sound* also plays an important role in the exchange, blending with and providing emphasis to the dialogue. When Joker threatens Batman with the warning "You're going to have to play my game if you want to save them," a faint music cue rises on the soundtrack, more curious than dramatic. Attempting to pummel the truth out of his nemesis, Batman discovers that Joker has also kidnapped Rachel Dawes, alter-ego Bruce Wayne's former romantic interest. Unsurprisingly, this news causes the hero's temper to flare and with it the score's volume, swelling until it almost matches the actors' voices. As the scene climaxes, Batman's blows to Joker's body gain in savagery until the villain's triumphant laugh explodes off the room's walls. The Joker's clear victory, etched in the broad slash of smile across his face, is reinforced through a music cue that slides from warning bell to a siren at full-wail. Though Batman learns the whereabouts of both Dent and Dawes, he has compromised his (and Gordon's) integrity in full view of the law enforcement community.

With Batman's ethos tarnished and Joker as Gotham's new amoral authority, viewers will be asked to inhabit the villain's nihilistic perspective for the remaining hour of the film, as a series of psychological "stress-tests" connects its onscreen audience—the citizens of Gotham—with its off-screen one. *The Dark Knight* manages to thrill viewers with the bells and whistles of the contemporary action spectacle while pushing audience expectations beyond those of a traditional superhero narrative. Nolan's considerable challenges to film form and genre conventions are made in order to advance the Joker's bleak message about humanity. Uttered in a chilling rasp to Batman in the middle of their encounter, this message is unequivocal: "Their morals—their code—is a bad joke…dropped at the first sign of trouble. They are only as good as the world allows them to be. I'll show you that when the chips are down—these *civilized* people—they'll eat each other. See, I'm not a monster. I'm just ahead of the curve." Completing the revisionist work introduced by *Batman Begins* in 2005, Nolan's skill as a visual stylist suggests that he, too, is ahead of the curve, breaking new ground by uncovering new depths in a formerly exhausted series.

As you conclude the rhetorical analysis of your chosen film, try to reiterate your thesis in a way that provides closure, or at least a temporary resolution, to the analysis. Have you answered the questions motivating that original position? Have the reasons that support it been given a detailed analytical treatment? If the director has innovated within a familiar genre, account generally for the film's originality. Addressing these issues in your conclusion will challenge your audience to review the film and join—albeit in a much more *civil* context—the "interrogation" in progress!

The Multiliteracy Centers:
Empowering Writers, Speakers, and Designers to Communicate Effectively

Stacy W. Rice

As a college student, you'll be asked to communicate information in various ways—through participating in class discussions, answering exam questions, and engaging in online class forums, to name only a few. In fact, you're probably in the process of composing at least one type of communication right now—an essay—by dint of being enrolled in a college writing course. You may be required in one or more courses to present a speech to your classmates, or to create some type of visual, such as a PowerPoint presentation, to go along with the speech, to produce a video, or even to create a podcast.

All of these situations ask you to communicate through writing, speaking, or some other form of multimedia. These other forms of communication may include websites, slideshows, videos, audio files, and digital photography—among others. For all of these, you will have to think about what makes each communication rhetorically effective. As you sit down to create and compose, it helps to think through such questions as: What is my message? Who is my audience? What is my position regarding my message? What is the most appropriate way to communicate my message? How should I organize and present my message? Are there alternative organizational and presentation styles that could be equally, or more, effective?

In a college writing course, many of the communicative texts students create will be written products such as essays or reports, though instructors may also incorporate oral speeches and multimedia components as well. To help students think through their composing processes for college writing, instructors will often set aside days in particular for students to participate in reviewing and workshopping drafts with peers, or they may set aside office hours during which they conference with students concerning their essays, speeches, and multimedia presentations. Sometimes, though, students might want help beyond in-class workshops or conferences with an instructor. Students may feel more comfortable talking about their work with peers, and in an environment where they can meet, possibly in an ongoing series of sessions, to think through and discuss their communications.

UNCG offers just such a resource for students seeking this type of assistance: the Multiliteracy Centers, the umbrella organization that comprises the Writing Center, Speaking Center, and Digital ACT Studio. Because communication takes multiple forms, there are multiple ways to be a literate communicator. Each of the three Centers focuses on a branch of communication in which their peer consultants specialize.

These centers use the name "Multiliteracy" to convey the multiple modes of literacy that result from the way communication is always inherently multi-modal (Kress 70). When we write, we combine written, visual, and spatial modes to format words in a particular way on the page. When we speak, we use words, gestures, and voice to convey a message in a certain manner. When we design digitally, we can make use of all of these ways of communicating. UNCG offers students the resources of the Multiliteracy Centers to help them become well-rounded rhetors who can effectively communicate in a multiplicity of situations, genres, and media. While none of these centers will tell students one set way to go about accomplishing their communication goals, or simply tell them what to write, speak, or click, they will do something of much more value: they will engage students in conversation about their work, will explore with them the available means of persuasion and effective rhetorical strategies, and will help them develop the critical thinking skills rhetors need in order to critique, revise, and assess their own work.

Together, these three sibling centers offer students one-on-one and group consultations to help them as they brainstorm, draft, organize, revise, and contemplate or practice delivering written, spoken, and multimodal communications—communication combining modes such as the visual, auditory, gestural, and so forth. To make the most of these campus resources, here's an overview of what each center does, what you can expect during a consultation, and where you can access these services.

» The Writing Center

The mission of the Writing Center (WC) is to help students become more thoughtful and confident writers, and to meet this goal, the WC is staffed by knowledgeable and trained peer consultants—undergraduate and graduate students alike—representing a range of majors and minors. Just as the consultants come from varied academic backgrounds, so do the writers they work with. The WC offers their services to writers in all courses, not just writing-centered ones. Writers can meet with one of these consultants for up to an hour to discuss any part of the writing process, even when revising after receiving instructor feedback. A limited number of appointments are available, but writers may drop in—whether online or in-person—for walk-in sessions. Writers can meet with consultants for up to an hour, although depending on the volume of writers present in the WC, sessions may run for only 30 minutes. But what does a consultation look like, exactly?

When visiting the WC, writers can choose to work with a peer consultant on a host of concerns: reading through the assignment prompt to better understand what an assignment is asking for, brainstorming and outlining an essay, revising a draft, checking citations to ensure they follow the guidelines of a certain citation style, and developing counterarguments, just to name a few. Because WC consultants can help writers work through so many concerns, writers can turn to them for help inventing ideas, elaborating on those ideas, and organizing those ideas in a way that effectively reaches their audience. Basically, the WC assists writers throughout any phase of their writing process—from the moment they first learn about the assignment, up until they're polishing it and preparing to turn it in for its initial submission or as a revision.

Some first-time visitors to the WC believe a session will only be about fixing mechanics or grammar issues, items called **lower-order concerns**. While the consultant will not simply "fix" spelling and grammar errors *for* the writer, they will do something much more valuable: they will walk through the assignment *with* the writer. While lower-order concerns like grammar and spelling are important for academic writing, consultants can help writers consider the outline and organization of their writing, style and tone, inclusion of research and sources, and clarity, concepts called **higher-order concerns**. These concerns are elements in a composition beyond grammar and spelling that convey the message and ideas of the writer.

WC consultants can work with writers by helping them spot patterns of both higher-order and lower-order concerns that consistently show up in the writing so that writers can start identifying their own strengths and weaknesses. What is especially valuable about this style of consulting is that writers learn strategies they can practice *beyond* that particular Writing Center session. In other words, writers receive immediate help during the session, as well as long-term guidance they can implement in future writing situations.

Moreover, consultants provide immediate feedback that is unavailable to writers working alone. Consultants can act as a test audience in the sense that they can point out to writers those moments in the essay when their ideas might not be conveyed clearly. Consultants will tell writers how they, as the audience, understood the ideas and concepts in an essay to be working together, what stood out to them or what they took particular notice of, and what questions they may still have after the writer or consultant has read the paper aloud. Consultants engage writers in a conversation about the writing—maybe they'll ask for clarification on some point, or maybe they'll suggest different strategies to organize a paragraph. The strategies consultants discuss with writers can be applied to any writing situation. When consultants dialogue with writers, they're not simply thinking about how to make the specific composition at hand better. Rather, they're seeking to help students develop into better writers (North 438).

For more information on the Writing Center, including its location and resources for writers, visit its official website at writingcenter.uncg.edu.

» The Speaking Center

The Speaking Center (SC) operates on a similar peer-to-peer consultation model as the Writing Center. Like the WC, the SC is staffed by trained students who engage speakers in a conversation about their speeches and oral presentation assignments. In the SC, speakers can work with peer consultants to choose talking points, explore organizational strategies, and even practice delivering the speech in front of a consultant so as to receive feedback from an informed, engaged, and interested audience. Like the WC, the SC will meet students at any phase of the speaking process—whether they have just learned that they will be delivering a speech, to practicing it one final time before delivering it in class for a grade.

The SC also offers speakers the opportunity to record themselves presenting their speeches. This service is helpful because it allows speakers to see themselves as their audience will see them, and can help speakers identify what they did well in the delivery of their speech, as well as what they would still like to work on. This service gives you the opportunity to do a practice run of your presentation, as well as a way to reflect on your presenting and discuss it with a trained peer. Such recordings may provide students with a digital component to add to online compositions.

Not all speakers are comfortable with the idea of presenting to their instructors and classmates. The SC understands that many students have anxiety when it comes to public speaking. They have several resources they can offer, including tips and strategies, to help speakers write and practice their speeches. Additional services and materials offered by the Speaking Center include information on how to manage and combat speaking anxiety, workshops covering a variety of speaking-related aspects, and practice conversing in English for speakers whose first language is not English.

For more information on the Speaking Center, including its location and resources for speakers, visit its website at speakingcenter.uncg.edu.

» The Digital ACT Studio

The third component of the Multiliteracy Centers is the Digital ACT (Action, Consultation, and Training) Studio (DACTS). This center is also staffed by knowledgeable and trained peer consultants who will work with individual or groups of designers for up to an hour on multimedia assignments. The typical types of projects the Studio sees are PowerPoints, Prezis, websites and blogs, e-portfolios, videos/documentaries, and posters, as well as essays that incorporate images. However, this list is not exhaustive; if students are composing and designing a text digitally, they can discuss it with consultants at DACTS.

Similar to the WC and SC, DACTS engages designers in a conversation regarding their assignment and their goals for the session. Consultants involve designers in a dialogue about what message they want to convey, and then together they explore a range of ways to go about delivering that message. While there are many possibilities when creating multimodal designs, consultants will help designers choose which of those possibilities are most rhetorically effective for reaching their audience and meeting the designer's goals for the session. This could include inventing material for the design, organizing that material, or even working on the visual display of that material. For example, when designers are creating a PowerPoint, there are a range of visual designs available to choose from. DACTS consultants will engage designers in a conversation about which of those choices is most appropriate for the given project, and why a particular design choice is more rhetorically effective than another. They will also discuss with designers different options for organizing the slides of the PowerPoint, as well as the rhetorical decisions that go into deciding what information gets included on each slide.

Also similar to the WC and SC, the DACTS works with designers wherever they are in the design process—whether they are just learning that they'll need a PowerPoint for their end-of-semester presentation, or whether they've been running a blog for years and just want a pair of fresh eyes to offer some helpful suggestions for how to organize posts or make the appearance more aesthetically effective. Consultants at the Studio help designers develop the message they want to communicate, plan out—or storyboard—the way they will present that message, evaluate the rhetorical effectiveness of the design, and discuss how the student's design and composition meets his or her own goals, as well as that of the assignment.

For more information on the Digital ACT Studio, including its location and resources for designers, visit its website at digitalactstudio.uncg.edu.

» The Multiliteracy Centers in Review

For your convenience, this chart summarizes the most common types of projects with which each of the Multiliteracy Centers works with students:

The Multiliteracy Centers		
Writing Center	Speaking Center	Digital ACT Studio
Essays	Speech/Presentation outlines	PowerPoints and Prezis
Reflections		Websites and blogs
Creative pieces	Speeches	E-portfolios
Proposals	Presentations	Videos/ documentaries
Abstracts	Speaking anxiety	
Application/Cover letters	Speaking practice for speakers whose first language is not English	Podcasts
Bibliographies		Posters and brochures
Print portfolios		Digital photography

In sum, visiting each of these centers will help you as you grow into a more advanced writer, speaker, and designer. Whether you are writing for an English course or a Biology course, the WC can help you think through your ideas, organize them, and expand on them. Whether you are giving a presentation in front of your class or at a conference, the SC can help you outline your speaking points and practice delivering them. Whether you are designing a multimodal text for your Sociology course or for a social organization you are a part of, DACTS can help you storyboard and decide on how to present your information in your chosen medium. Regardless of how much experience you have writing, speaking, or designing, these services can offer you thoughtful and productive feedback. These sibling centers known as the Multiliteracy Centers exist here at UNCG to help you become a successful and effective communicator, whatever shape that communication might take.

» Works Cited

Kress, Gunther. "'English' at the Crossroads: Rethinking Curricula of Communication in the Context of the Turn to the Visual." *Passions, Pedagogies, and 21st Century Technologies*. Eds. Gail E. Hawisher and Cynthia L. Selfe. Logan: Utah State UP, 1999. 66–88. Print.

North, Stephen M. "The Idea of a Writing Center." *College English* 46.5 (1984): 433–46. Print.

Appendix

Appendix

» Sample Pre-Writing Webbing Exercise

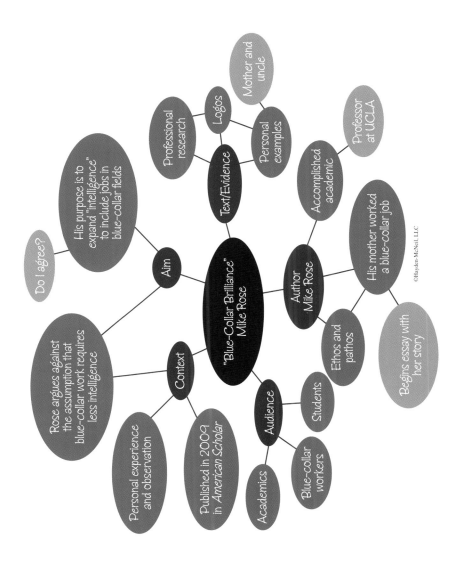

©Hayden-McNeil, LLC

» Sample Annotated Text

Ain't I A Woman?
Sojourner Truth

casual diction

Well, children, where there is so much <u>racket</u> there must be something <u>out of kilter</u>. I think that 'twixt the negroes of the South and the women at the North, all talking about rights, *audience?* the white men will be in a fix pretty soon. But what's all this here talking about?

lots of exclamation points/ pathos

That man over there says that women need to be helped into carriages, and lifted over ditches, and to have the best place everywhere. Nobody ever helps me into carriages, or over mud-puddles, or gives me any best place! And ain't I a woman? *Very powerful!* Look at me! Look at my arm! I have ploughed and planted, *Presents* and gathered into barns, and no man could head me! And *herself as* ain't I a woman? I could work as much and eat as much as a *a mother/ ethos* man—when I could get it—and bear the lash as well! And *Connects* ain't I a woman? I have borne thirteen children, and seen most *with other* all sold off to slavery, and when I cried out with my mother's *mothers/* grief, none but Jesus heard me! And ain't I a woman? *pathos*

Does this strengthen her argument? Could it damage her ethos?

Then they talk about this thing in the head; what's this they *Use of* call it? [member of audience whispers, "intellect"] That's it, *repetition* <u>honey</u>. What's that got to do with women's rights or negroes' *adds* rights? If my cup won't hold but a pint, and yours holds a *emphasis* quart, wouldn't you be mean not to let me have my little half *and* measure full? *urgency*

Is this a preacher?

Then that <u>little man</u> (in black there), he says women can't *"little* have as much rights as men, 'cause Christ wasn't a woman! *man"=* Where did your Christ come from? Where did your Christ *tone* come from? From God and a woman! Man had nothing to do with Him. *responds to the naysayer*

If the first woman God ever made was strong enough to turn the world upside down all alone, these women together ought *call* to be able to turn it back, and get it right side up again! And *to* now they is asking to do it, the men better let them. *action*

Obliged to you for hearing me, and now old Sojourner ain't got nothing more to say.

» Sample Prompt for a Rhetorical Analysis Essay

Paper 1: Rhetorical Analysis

Due Dates

+ Thursday, Sept. 8—Peer Review
+ Thursday, Sept. 15—Revised Draft for Grade
+ Thursday, Dec. 1—Revised for Portfolio (with both peer-reviewed and graded draft)

Assignment

For this assignment, you can choose to expand on your short rhetorical analysis of Jefferson or Stanton, *or* choose another essay (see below) and write an extensive, 3–4-page rhetorical analysis of it. You need to think about the message of the essay and show **how** the author communicates the message to the audience.

Purpose

This assignment specifically corresponds with the following SLOs:

1. Analyze the content and structure of complex texts (written, oral, and/or visual in nature);

2. Compose cogent, evidence-based, argumentative texts;

3. Identify and employ the rhetorical triangle, the canons, and the appeals in both formal and informal discourse;

4. Summarize, quote, paraphrase, and synthesize source material in support of an argument.

Essay Choices

(all found in *50 Essays*)

+ Stanton, "Declaration of Sentiments and Resolutions" (379–382)
+ Jefferson, "The Declaration of Independence" (191–195)
+ Sojourner Truth, "Ain't I a Woman?" (410–411)
+ Audre Lorde, "The Fourth of July" (239–242)
+ Martin Luther King, Jr., "Letter from Birmingham Jail" (203–219)

Writing the Paper

1. Provide a brief context for the essay you are analyzing.

2. What message is the author delivering to the audience and how is this accomplished (Thesis)?

3. Identify and analyze the rhetorical triangle, the appeals, and the canons.

4. For the sake of cohesion, you should consider how you will organize your paper—by the appeals, by rhetorical triangle, etc.

5. Include examples and quotes from your selected essay.

Requirements**

+ Title; example: "Ethos in American Spirit Tobacco Ad" not "Paper 1-Ad Analysis"

+ Length: 3–4 pages (this means at least three **full** pages)

+ MLA format

+ Attach grading rubric

+ Staple or paperclip your paper

**I will not accept papers that do not meet these requirements.

» Sample Outlines

Student Name

Instructor Name

Course

DD Month YYYY

Outline

Rhetorical Analysis of Sojourner Truth's "Ain't I a Woman?"

I.   INTRODUCTION

    A.   Establish rhetorical context of Truth's speech

    B.   Truth uses rhetorical questions, draws attention to her own body, and employs Christian allusions to persuade her audience to see her as a woman deserving the same rights as white women.

II. BODY PARAGRAPH: Truth's Use of Logos

    A.   "Ain't I a woman?" Answer is "yes"

    B.   Draws attention to stereotypes, differences in ways women are treated, but argues they're still women

III. BODY PARAGRAPH: Truth's Body as Evidence in Logical Argument, Pathos

    A.   Repeats "Ain't I a woman?" (Logos)

    B.   Draws attention to physical body: "Look at me! Look at my arm! I have ploughed and planted, and gathered into barns, and no man could head me!" (Logos)

    C.   Whipped by a slave-master

        a.   Logos: Implicit argument that she's even more deserving of rights because of what her body has endured

        b.   Pathos: audience sympathy

    D.   Claims motherhood: children sold to slavery (Pathos)

IV. BODY PARAGRAPH: Truth's Use of Pathos

    A. Religious allusions

    B. "these women together"

    C. Uses humor: "out of kilter"

V. CONCLUSION

    A. Persuasiveness of Truth's speech in her context

    B. How Truth's speech is still relevant

Student Name

Instructor Name

Course

DD Month YYYY

MEAL Plan Outline

Rhetorical Analysis of Sojourner Truth's "Ain't I a Woman?"

I.   INTRODUCTION

    A.   Establish rhetorical context of Truth's speech

    B.   Working Thesis: Truth uses rhetorical questions, draws attention to her own body, and employs Christian allusions to persuade her audience to see her as a woman deserving the same rights as white women.

II. BODY PARAGRAPH: Truth's Use of Logos

Main Point: Truth effectively uses logos as a persuasive tool to argue for African-American women's rights.

Evidence:

1) Truth's repetition of the rhetorical question "Ain't I a woman?" as a logical device: Answer is "yes" because she looks like a woman

2) She points out that man "says that women need to be helped into carriages, and lifted over ditches, and to have the best place everywhere. Nobody ever helps me into carriages, or over mud-puddles, or gives me any best place!" then asks, "Ain't I a woman?"

Analysis/Linking: Her examples argue that African-American women are women and, like white women, should be treated with proper respect, helped into carriages, and lifted over mud puddles.

III. BODY PARAGRAPH: Truth's Use of Body for Logos and Pathos

Main Point: Truth uses her body as part of her argument for African-American women's rights.

Evidence:

1) "Look at me! Look at my arm! I have ploughed and planted, and gathered into barns, and no man could head me!"

2) "and bear the lash as well! And ain't I a woman?"

3) "I have borne thirteen children, and seen them most all sold off to slavery, and when I cried out with my mother's grief, none but Jesus heard me! And ain't I a woman?"

Analysis/Linking: African-American women are emotionally fortified and can endure emotional trauma, making them worthy of the same civil rights as white women.

IV. BODY PARAGRAPH: Truth's Use of Pathos

Main Point: Truth makes effective use of pathos through her religious allusions and humor.

Evidence:

1) Cries out to Jesus with her mother's grief

2) It was Mary that birthed Christ: Christ comes from "God and a woman! Man had nothing to do with Him."

3) If men do not give all women their rights, then women, black and white, will cause more trouble and the state of America will go "out of kilter."

Analysis/Linking: Truth invokes a range of different emotions, effectively using pathos to have her audience relate to her emotionally.

V. CONCLUSION

A. Effectiveness of Truth's persuasion in her time

B. How Truth's speech is still relevant

» Sample Rhetorical Analysis Essay

Student Name

Professor Name

Course

DD Month YYYY

Proving Herself a Woman: Sojourner Truth's Argument for African-American
Women's Rights in "Ain't I a Woman?"

When Sojourner Truth delivered her now famous speech, "Ain't I a Woman?"
in 1851 at the Women's Convention in Akron, Ohio, she was protesting not only
for women's rights but specifically for African-American's women's rights. In
1851, Truth found herself a spokesperson for two emerging and often ancillary
movements: abolitionism and first wave feminism. For one, Truth escaped slavery
in 1826 and became a female pastor. In the audience at the Women's Convention,
according to Truth's speech, was a mixture of preachers, white women fighting
for women's rights, and those opposed to both abolition and women's rights.
Truth was up against two prejudices of nineteenth-century America that believed
that both African-Americans and women were inferior to white men. Therefore,
many in nineteenth-century America doubly discriminated against Truth and
other African-American women because of their gender and skin color. Truth's
speech, then, speaks to both types of discrimination. In her speech, Truth argues
that African-American women should be treated equally as white women and
worthy of respect by proving her womanhood. Truth uses rhetorical questions,
draws attention to her own body, and employs Christian rhetoric to persuade her
audience to see her as a woman and, therefore, as a woman who deserves the same
rights that are afforded her white counterparts.

Despite Truth's brevity, her speech is full of logos, or logical evidence, to
prove Truth's womanhood and subtly argue for equality and respect. Most notable
is Truth's repetition of the rhetorical question, "Ain't I a woman?" The audience
members who stand looking at Truth obviously know the answer to this question
is a simple "yes" because she looks like a woman. Truth, however, challenges
the audience's definition of "woman" by asserting that African-American women

Context

243

are not seen as women in terms of the law or societal norms at the time. She sets the tone for what a woman is and how society treats her and then juxtaposes it to how she has been treated, with the ending sentiment being, "Ain't I a woman?" For instance, Truth directly addresses a man in the room who, according to Truth, "says that women need to be helped into carriages, and lifted over ditches, and to have the best place everywhere. Nobody ever helps me into carriages, or over mud-puddles, or gives me any best place! And ain't I a woman?" (410). Whether or not the identified man actually says what Truth reports is beside the question. Truth's point is to address the audience's stereotypes that define the difference between white and black women and show them to be false. Her rhetorical question, "Ain't I a woman?" serves to dismantle the stereotypes held against African-American women. They, like white women, are women and should be treated with proper respect—helped into carriages and lifted over mud puddles.

Truth's use of the rhetorical question also helps her draw attention to her own female body. After asking, "Ain't I a woman?" Truth immediately demands that the audience look directly at her: "Look at me! Look at my arm! I have ploughed and planted, and gathered into barns, and no man could head me! And ain't I a woman? I could work as much and eat as much as a man…and bear the lash as well! And ain't I a woman?" (410). Truth uses her body as further logos; her body is factual evidence proving her womanhood, and her female body and womanhood actually allows her to do equal the work, if not more, than a man. Moreover, Truth, unlike white women, is a woman who can withstand being whipped by a slave-master. Thus, the implied argument is that African-American women maybe deserve *more* rights than white women. Truth perhaps mentions the lash to conjure not only awe from the audience but emotional sympathy as well. In fact, immediately following her statement about being whipped, Truth laments, "I have borne thirteen children, and seen them most all sold off to slavery, and when I cried out with my mother's grief, none but Jesus heard me! And ain't I a woman?" (410). Here, Truth proves herself a woman by revealing herself to be a mother, which is what nineteenth-century America would primarily regard women as. By claiming motherhood, Truth claims the highest regard of nineteenth-century womanhood. Again, Truth takes one step further to argue for African-American rights. She witnesses her children being "sold off to slavery," which might be worse than the slave-master's whip. African-American women are emotionally fortified and can endure emotional trauma, making them worthy of their civil rights.

In Truth's last statement of womanhood, she mentions crying out to Jesus, which is an effective use of pathos. She references Jesus and later in her speech Christianity in order to prove that women, universally, not just African-American or white women, can fix the problem of social injustice. Truth smartly points out the logical flaws of a male preacher's denouncement of women preachers: "Then that little man in black there he says women can't have as much rights as men, 'cause Christ wasn't a woman!" (411). By making men the barrier of women's rights, Truth can appeal to white women for help in fighting for African-American women's rights. For Truth, women are the reason that humankind has salvation since it was Mary that birthed Christ, boldly declaring that Christ comes from "God and a woman! Man had nothing to do with Him" (411). Furthermore, Truth alludes to Eve, "the first woman God ever made," and her original sin "turn[ed] the world upside down alone," to prove that women are where social justice begins: "these women together ought to be able to turn it back, and get it right side up again! And now they is asking to do it, the men better let them" (411). Truth demonstrates collective strength among women by using the phrase "these women together." Finally, Truth ends on a comical note, implying that if men do not give all women their rights, then women, black and white, will cause more trouble and the state of America will be further "out of kilter" like Truth mentions at the beginning of her speech (410). Truth invokes a range of different emotions, effectively using pathos to have her audience relate to her emotionally.

Truth's 1851 speech became a famous text for the feminist movement of the late 1800s and early 1900s; in fact, Elizabeth Cady Stanton befriended Truth due to this speech. However, we must not forget that Truth was specifically arguing for African-American women's rights. Truth recognized that in the abolitionist movement and the white women's movement that African-American women were falling into the cracks, so she uses herself—a free black woman—to argue for equal rights. Truth's speech still holds value today as many women of color participate in an emerging transnational feminism that demands equal treatment for women no matter race, ethnicity, class, or religion.

Conclu

Work Cited

Truth, Sojourner. "Ain't I a Woman?" *50 Essays: A Portable Anthology*. Ed.

Samuel Cohen. 3rd ed. Boston and New York: Bedford/St. Martin's, 2011.

410–411. Print.

» Sample Annotated Bibliography

Student's Name

Instructor's Name

Course and Section

DD Month YYYY

Leaving Out the "Other": Le Ly Hayslip's *When Heaven and Earth Changed Places* as a Reiteration of Western Hegemony: Annotated Bibliography

Bow, Leslie. "Le Ly Hayslip's Bad (Girl) Karma: Sexuality, National Allegory, and the Politics of Neutrality." *Prose Studies* 17.1 (1994): 141–160. Print.

Bow argues that Hayslip's feminist pacifism serves to uphold American patriarchal standards. In Hayslip's texts, *When Heaven and Earth Changed Places* and *Child of War, Woman of Peace*, Le Ly submits her body to practice sexual favors, via prostitution and marrying for escape, in order to flee Vietnam. According to Bow, *When Heaven* makes use of Le Ly's family to represent Vietnam as a national allegory. Similarly, her various American boyfriends signify the United States and the affluence the U.S. has to offer. By relinquishing Buddhist values and adopting capitalistic ones, Le Ly refuses to be victimized. Bow maintains that Hayslip endorses neutrality, "rather than…an overt declaration of affiliation" (146). However, I claim that by leaving Vietnam for a better life in America, she does indeed affiliate herself with the West. Her decision to emigrate to the United States is a conscious and deliberate one.

Nguyen, Viet Thanh. "Representing Reconciliation: Le Ly Hayslip and the Victimized Body." *positions* 5.2 (1997): 605–42. Print.

According to Nguyen, Hayslip's text attempts to reconcile the U.S. with Vietnam and herself to the Vietnamese who view her as a "whore, traitor, and self-promoter" (610). Nguyen claims that Hayslip has become the "best-known Vietnamese person in the United States" (605) and along with that designation, is permitted the opportunity to speak on behalf of the Vietnamese, who prior to the publication of her texts had largely been "voiceless" among American Vietnam War discursive practices. Drawing

upon Elaine Scarry's notion of the function of the dead soldier in war,
Nguyen argues that the enemy's dead body, in this case the dead Vietnamese
body, serves to enable and substantiate the American cultural fiction that
capitalism and technology are superior to communism. Nguyen also contends
that by exhibiting Le Ly's unchaste body within her texts, she is able to use
her personal experience of rape as a metaphor for the multiple violations
enacted upon the nation of Vietnam. Nguyen is correct that Hayslip uses
her voice in order to relate atrocities that occurred during the Vietnam War.
However, since one cannot fully articulate pain, as Elaine Scarry explains,
I contend that there is still an essence of mutability within Le Ly. Often
she finds that words escape her when she speaks about reconciliation.
Furthermore, I think it is a bit dangerous to collapse the multiple voices of a
nation into one person, for that is essentializing in nature.

Scarry, Elaine. *The Body in Pain: The Making and Unmaking of the World.*
Oxford: Oxford UP, 1985. Print.

Scarry contends that when a body is subjected to intense pain, like one would
be under torture, one is rendered voiceless. Under such circumstances, people
revert to what she calls pre-language to express their distress, i.e.: moans,
groans, yelps, and so on. Pain can only be articulated when the experience
of such has receded into the past, and it is at this point that people can
describe their experiences to a doctor, Amnesty International, a court of law,
or a literary audience. In relation to this inability to express pain, I contest
Nguyen's argument that Le Ly is able to function as a metaphorical rhetor
for her native nation: Vietnam. If pain cannot be rendered into language,
then this negates Le Ly's ability to speak on the behalf of the citizens of her
native country. In fact, since the relation of pain is dependent upon it slinking
into the past, as Scarry argues, then Le Ly can only voice such pain once she
has moved to the United States and under such circumstances this pain is
ultimately colored by capitalist ideology.

» Sample Prospectus

Student's Name

Instructor's Name

Course and Section

DD Month YYYY

Leaving Out the "Other": Le Ly Hayslip's *When Heaven and Earth Changed Places* as a Reiteration of Western Hegemony: Prospectus

Leslie Bow argues that Le Ly in Le Ly Hayslip's autobiography *When Heaven and Earth Changed Places* endorses a position of neutrality. In a similar vein, Viet Thanh Nguyen reads this autobiography as one of reconciliation, one that tries to mend the broken and hurtful ties between the U.S. and Vietnam. Given this labelling of the text, Le Ly positions herself as *the* voice for the Vietnamese people, according to Nguyen. Maureen Denise Fielding, also reads Hayslip's text as one concerned with reconciling the American nation with Vietnam. However, she differentiates her argument from Nguyen's in that she also proposes that Hayslip's work is one that is also concerned with personal healing, one wherein Le Ly attempts to heal herself cathartically through writing.

In some disagreement with Nguyen, I propose that Le Ly expresses a voice that vacillates politically, rendering it unstable due to the fact that she is compelled to show allegiance to the National Liberation Front (also known pejoratively as the Viet Cong) by night and the South Vietnamese Government and Americans by day. Instead of dwelling on the past and re-experiencing the trauma she has undergone in hurtful ways, Le Ly decides to help Vietnam on a humanitarian level; thus, she turns her horrible experiences into productive, healthy behavior. Furthermore, this optimism allows her to personally cast off her label of victimhood. She locates the site for this ability to help her native nation in the West, the United States, for America provides the capitalistic and affluent means with which to help the impoverished. As such, she asserts that America can *afford* to take on this task, while suggesting that Vietnam cannot, thereby implying the inherent "superiority" of the West.

In order to prove the instability of Le Ly's voice, I will rely on Elaine Scarry's *The Body in Pain*, for Scarry contends that the experience of intense pain renders one voiceless. Given that Le Ly has experienced such pain throughout this autobiography, she cannot function as a "voice" for the Vietnamese people as Nguyen claims. Since a precondition of being able to express pain depends on the passage of time, time in which Le Ly emigrates to the United States, she can only articulate her past experiences while she resides within the American nation. Situating herself in the West, and eventually becoming affluent herself in Southern California, capitalistic influences eventually color her story. Under these ideological constraints, she ends up reaffirming American, Western values. At the same time, she casts her Vietnamese compatriots as caricatures, ones who are impoverished, ignorant, and in desperate need of American (monetary) aide.

Student's Last Name   3

Works Cited

Bow, Leslie. "Le Ly Hayslip's Bad (Girl) Karma: Sexuality, National Allegory, and the Politics of Neutrality." *Prose Studies* 17.1 (1994): 141–160. Print.

Fielding, Maureen Denise. "Karma and Trauma: Le Ly Hayslip's Healing Vision." *From Madwomen to Vietnam Veterans: Trauma, Testimony, and Recovery in Post-Colonial Women's Writing.* Diss. U of Massachusetts Amherst, 2000. 211–67. Print.

Hayslip, Le Ly. *When Heaven and Earth Changed Places: A Vietnamese Woman's Journey from War to Peace.* 1989. New York: Plume, 2003. Print.

Nguyen, Viet Thanh. "Representing Reconciliation: Le Ly Hayslip and the Victimized Body." *positions* 5.2 (1997): 605–42. Print.

Scarry, Elaine. *The Body in Pain: The Making and Unmaking of the World.* Oxford: Oxford UP, 1985. Print.

» Proofreaders' Marks

Correction	Mark in Text	Mark in Margin
insert text	insert text	⋏ the
replace text	replace to text	/the
delete text	delete the the text	ℰ
delete/close space	del͡lete text	℈
leave unchanged	please don't change the text	(stet)
make italic	make italic	(ital)
make boldface	make boldface	(bf)
make roman	make roman	(rom)
make lightface	make lightface	(lf)
make bold italic	make bold italic	(bf + ital)
capitalize	capitalize	(cap)
make lowercase	make Lowercase	(lc)
make lowercase	make LOWERCASE	(lc)
superscript	E=MC2	(su)
subscript	H2SO4	(sub)
run on (no new paragraph)	run on. Make sure you	no ¶
move to next line	word breaks in inappropriate places	(runover)
move up from next line	word breaks in inappropriate places	(move up)
transpose	switch letter word or order	(tr)
center text	]center text [	(center)
indent text	]indent text	(indent)
no indentation	[don't indent text	(flush)
wrong font	wrong font used	(wf)

254

Correction	Mark in Text	Mark in Margin
move text right	move text right ⌐	⌐
move text left	⌐ move text left	⌐
align text/column vertically	‖align text vertically. No indent here.	‖
align horizontally	align horizontally	align
add space	addspace	#
close up space	close up spa ce	⌒
equalize space	equalize ✓ space ✓ please	eq. #
spell out	15 min.	SP
abbreviate	15 minutes	abbrev
increase leading	increase leading	#
decrease leading	decrease leading	reduce
remove unwanted	remove unwanted	⊗
insert period	insert period Start the	⊙
insert comma	add commas periods and dashes	⌄
insert colon	two main groups the	⊙
insert semicolon	he said she said	⋮
insert em dash	em dash for everyday use	—⎯m
insert en dash	from 2002 2007	—⎯n
insert apostrophe	please dont forget apos- trophes	⌄
insert quotations	I said, Hey!	⟨⟨ / ⟩⟩
insert parentheses	I'm ready I think to go	⟨ / ⟩
insert ellipsis	And so it goes	⊙⊙⊙
insert hyphen	a three point shot	=/

255

» Index